Everard im Thurn

FOUR YEARS

IN THE

GOVERNMENT EXPLORING EXPEDITION;

COMMANDED BY

CAPTAIN CHARLES WILKES,

TO THE

ISLAND OF MADEIRA—CAPE VERD ISLAND—BRAZIL—COAST OF PATAGONIA—CHILI—PERU—PAUMATO GROUP—SOCIETY ISLANDS—NAVIGATOR GROUP—AUSTRALIA—ANTARCTIC CONTINENT—NEW ZEALAND—FRIENDLY ISLANDS — FEJEE GROUP — SANDWICH ISLANDS—NORTHWEST COAST OF AMERICA—OREGON—CALIFORNIA—EAST INDIES—ST. HELENA, ETC., ETC.

IN ONE VOLUME.

BY

LIEUT. GEO. M. COLVOCORESSES, U. S. NAVY,

AN OFFICER OF THE EXPEDITION.

FIFTH EDITION.

NEW YORK:

J. M. FAIRCHILD & CO.,

109 NASSAU-STREET.

1855.

Stereotyped by VINCENT DILL, Jr.,
No. 29 Beekman-st., N Y

PREFACE.

It may be proper to observe, as affording some guarantee for the correctness of the information contained in this Volume, that it has been compiled from a Journal, or a Diary, which the author kept in obedience to a "General Order" from the Navy Department, and that the Journal in question was frequently submitted to the Commander-in-Chief of the Expedition for his inspection and perusal.

The work will be found to embrace incidents occurring on board the ship, Descriptions of Natural Scenery, Manners and Customs, Government, Religion, and Commerce.

By adopting a more diffusive style, I might have exceeded my present limits; instead of one such volume I might have produced two or three, but the general reader would have gained nothing by this, his main object being to gather information, and the more succinctly it is conveyed to him the more rapidly he will acquire it, and more easily retain it. In short, I have endeavored to furnish a work which should have the merit of being instructive and entertaining, concise and cheap; and I hope that the present volume will be found to possess all these advantages.

G. M. C.

CONTENTS.

CHAPTER III.

CHAPTER IV.

CHAPTER V.

CHAPTER VI.

CHAPTER VII.

CHAPTER VIII.

CHAPTER IX.

CHAPTER X.

CHAPTER XI.

CHAPTER XII.

CHAPTER XIII.

CHAPTER XIV

CHAPTER XXV.

CHAPTER I.

FROM NORFOLK TO MADEIRA.

At 3 o'clock, P. M., August 18th, (1838,) the Vincennes made the signal to get under-weigh, and in obedience to the same we weighed anchor in company with the rest of the squadron, namely, " Vincennes," " Peacock," " Relief," and the two schooners " Sea Gull" and " Flying Fish." At 5 P. M. we came-to off Fort Monroe, on account of its falling calm, and of the tide making against us; but at 9.20 the breeze sprung up, and we again hove-up the anchor, and stood out to sea. At 4.15 P. M., on the 19th, we discharged the pilot, and took our departure. The day was beautiful, the sea smooth, the breeze favoring, and the vessels sailed finely. Indeed, we could not possibly have commenced our cruise under more auspicious circumstances.

The day following we received orders, in case of separation, to rendezvous at Funchal, the principal port of Madeira.

On the 24th, the " Relief" was ordered to proceed to Rio Janeiro, in consequence of not being able to keep up with the rest of the squadron.

At dawn on the 13th of September we descried the island of St. Michael, the first land we had seen since bidding adieu to our own shores. This island is of a volcanic origin; its conical-shaped mountains, and detached basaltic rocks, which line its shores, prove this most conclusively. The northern side, along which we sailed for some time, looked singularly beautiful and romantic. It is one of the Azores,* or Western Islands, and belongs to the crown of Portugal.

The next object which engrossed our attention was the immense fields of sea weed, so often met with to the west of the group of islands just mentioned. Two great banks of this singular stringy-looking weed are said to occur in the Atlantic ocean. One of them is to the west of the meridian of Fayal, one of the Azores; but the location of the other has not been correctly ascertained. According to Burnet, it vegetates within forty degrees of latitude on each side of the equator. It was known to the Phœnicians as the Weedy-Sea, and the Spaniards call it Mar de Zaragossa. It is related of Columbus, that the sailors who attended him on his first voyage of discovery to America, on passing through these fields of sea-weed, urged him to proceed no further on the voyage, but to return home again, as they superstitiously believed that this hindrance was designed by God to put a stop to his wild schemes. This floating fucus is supposed to be detached by storms from the submarine rocks on which it is said to grow; but that which we fished up presented all the appearance of belonging to a healthy growing plant, nor could I detect any roots which might have induced me to suppose that it had been once attached to the rocky bottom of the ocean.

On the morning of the 18th of September, we anchored off the city of Funchal, in twenty-five fathoms water. The

* The Azores, or Western Islands, a group of nine islands in the Atlantic, between 25° and 30° west longitude and 37° and 40° north latitude, were discovered in 1439, by Vanderberg, a merchant of Bruges, and received their name from the number of hawks found among them. The climate is favorable to human health, and the soil is in general fertile, abounding in corn, grapes, oranges, lemons, and other fruits, and feeding many cattle, hogs and sheep.

"Vincennes" and "Sea Gull" came in about sunset, and the "Flying Fish" an hour or two later. The "Peacock" did not arrive until about 10 A. M. next day.

Shortly after coming to anchor we were boarded by the health-officer, who, being assured that we had no sickness on board, granted us permission to communicate with the shore.

We had heard much about the beauties of Madeira, and now that we had it before our eyes, we were not disappointed; my own expectations were indeed more than realized. Valleys and hills, the former adorned with villas, groves, cottages, churches, and convents, the latter covered to their summits with verdure, presented themselves to our view in every direction. The climate is said to be among the finest in the world. Properly speaking, there is no winter, and the greatest heat in the summer is never so great as with us. The usual height of the mercury is 67°, and in the greatest extremes seldom sinks or rises 6° above the medium, and hence the excellent health so generally enjoyed by its inhabitants. Another remarkable fact about Madeira is, that it is free from the annoyances and inconveniences that so commonly infest warm climates. There are no snakes or reptiles of any sort. Flowers grow wild along the sides of the roads, and in the fields. Water is abundant, and of an excellent quality; even the streams at the bottom of the ravines, fed by the mountain dews, are never dry in the hottest season, and the height from which they descend enables the inhabitants to turn their course in any direction they please, which accounts for the cultivated parts of the island being so well irrigated.

The chief production of Madeira is the grape,* and that

*"The vine was introduced in 1425, from the island of Candia; but it was not actively cultivated till the early part of the sixteenth century. It is propagated from

which grows near the sea-shore is said to make the best wine. The quantity exported last year amounted to 8,450 pipes, of which about 4,000 pipes, valued at $793,000, went to the United States. There is a great difference in the spots where the vine grows, and some estates produced much better quality of wine than others, though the kind of grape cultivated is the same. After the juice is expressed it is put into casks, undergoes the process of fermentation, is clarified with isinglass or gypsum, and about three gallons of brandy to a pipe of wine is added. The common Madeira is obtained from a mixture of Verdelho, Bual, and Negro Molle grapes; the Malmsey and Sercial, from grapes of the same name.

The principal manufactures of Madeira are coarse linen, baskets, hats and bonnets, boots and shoes. The latter article is exported in considerable quantity to the East and West Indies; they are generally well made, but they do not stand wet weather as well as the American shoes, in consequence of the leather not being properly tanned.

The revenue of the island is stated to be about 210,000 dollars per annum. That portion which is derived from the customs is about one half, or about 110,000 dollars. The remainder is from taxes and tithes. The population is estimated at 115,000. The lower classes are industrious, sober,

cuttings, planted at a depth of from three to six feet and there is generally no produce for the first three years. During the second spring they are trained along a net-work of canes (which is extensively grown in low, moist situations, for that purpose), and supported by stakes, about three or four feet from the ground. The inferior descriptions of wine, after being clarified, are subjected, in stoves, to a temperature of 140° to 160° Fahr. for six months, by which process of forcing they assume an apparent age, but, at the same time, a dry and smoky flavor, which can never be entirely eradicated. This class of wines is shipped annually, in large quantities, to Hamburgh, where it undergoes a process which changes its character to that of Hock, under which name a large portion of it finds its way into the English and American markets. The wines of Madeira, with the exception of Tinta, should be kept in cellars of a moderate and equable temperature, and should be placed, for a short period, at a moderate distance from the fire before decanted, and the decanter heated in like manner. BY ONE WHO RESIDED FIFTEEN YEARS ON THE ISLAND.

Madeira Costumes.

and honest. They are supposed to be a mixture of Moors, Negroes, and Portuguese. Dark hair, eyes, and complexion are most common. The character of the features is usually a broad face, high cheek-bones, full lips, and good teeth. The men are very muscular, about the middle height, very erect, strongly built, and capable of enduring great fatigue. The women are not good looking, which is no doubt owing, in part, to the hard labor required of them.

The men wear loose trowsers, descending to the knee, made of coarse linen cloth manufactured on the island, a shirt, and a jacket of gaudy color. They sometimes wear boots or shoes made of white leather, but generally they go without either.

The women are dressed in bodices, with short petticoats of a variety of colors. Both sexes wear a blue cloth cap of very small dimensions, tied under the chin.

The houses of the peasantry are little better than huts; they are constructed of stone, one story high, with a roof rising on all sides to a central pole—are thatched with straw, and beneath the same roof are included the parlor, kitchen, and sleeping-room, without any intervening partitions. The only aperture for light or smoke is the door. Perhaps there is no need for chimneys, as fire is seldom required, and the cooking is usually done out in the open air.

Funchal is the capital of the island. It is built along the margin of a small bay, the houses in some parts rising one above the other on steep hills, and contains above 20,000 inhabitants, of which 500 are foreign residents. It is intersected by three rivers, which are kept in their course by strong thick walls, from ten to thirty feet in height. Most of these streams have pleasant walks along their raised banks, shaded with large overhanging plane-trees, whose branches almost meet over the centre of the channel. The cathedral has been recently repaired, and makes a fine display; its steeple is the most conspicuous of any in the town.

The other public buildings are hardly deserving of notice. The Governor's palace is situated near the water, and has a commanding view of the harbor, but its architecture is clumsy and tasteless. A few yards from the cathedral is the Praca Constituicas, a very pleasant promenade, shaded by three or four rows of trees, and provided with benches for the repose of the weary. The military band usually plays here during the afternoon of Sundays, and "festas." The native inhabitants then appear in all their finery, listening to the airs discoursed by the band. Beyond the Plaza is the market-place, which is very clean, and regularly laid out in streets and stalls.

Many of the convents are large and beautifully located, but in consequence of their being neglected by the present government, they have in a great measure become deserted, and their walls are crumbling down piecemeal. The monks are out of favor with the Queen's government; the zeal with which they supported the claims of Don Miguel to the throne of Portugal has not been forgotten, and consequently they are looked upon with a suspicious eye, both by the government and the people. During the short reign of the Constitutional Government in Madeira, the nuns were permitted to leave their convents, and a few availed themselves for a time of the privilege, but returned again to their cloisters, after a short enjoyment of the world's gayety. The celebrated Maria Clementina, to whose history Coleridge has imparted such interest, still lives in the convent of St. Clara, among some forty of her sisterhood. She is now somewhat advanced in life, and few, if any, traces remain of that beauty which the poet so warmly described. These nuns support themselves chiefly by the manufacture and sale of artificial flowers and fruits, with a few other ornamental productions. The former are made of dyed feathers and the fruit of wax, and are prized by many visitors as affording a pleasing remembrance of their sojourn in the island.

The dwellings are from one to two stories high, and the apartments are large and well lighted, but owing to the material of which they are constructed—stone, and the iron-grated windows of the ground-floor—they have a gloomy, cheerless aspect. Nearly every house has a kind of turret on the top, from which can be had a fine view of the harbor. The principal object of these is, for the inhabitants to look out for vessels; the first thing to be done in the morning being to mount the turret to see if any strange vessel had arrived in the course of the night.

The streets are narrow, and in some parts very steep, but they are kept clean. In the principal streets are some very good stores, kept by Englishmen, who are by far the most numerous of the foreigners that reside on the island.

The market is very good. Beef of good quality can be had for eight cents per lb.; fowls for thirty-seven cents; eggs for eight cents per dozen; vegetables and fruits of every description are also abundant. Clothing is as cheap as with us, and boots and shoes considerably cheaper; and I may here add, that this is the case with everything which is made on the island, and is to be attributed to the cheapness of labor, the highest wages commanded by mechanics not exceeding twelve dollars per month.

In passing through the streets of Funchal, you meet with many of the country people, who have come either to trade or to obtain employment. They are a hardy, athletic race, and to all appearance remarkably polite and kind-hearted. Whenever we met them, they invariably saluted us. They are extensively employed about the town as carriers, and a stranger is at times apt to be struck with the novel character of their load; when at a distance, he sees them bearing on their shoulders what he supposes to be a live sheep, but on nearer approach he discovers that they are only the skins of that animal filled with wine. These skins are preserved as entire as possible, even the legs being retained; they are kept steady by a band which passes over the forehead and supports a considerable part of the weight. Twenty gallons is considered an ordinary load, and they will carry it to any part of the city for a pistareen.

There are few public amusements to be found in Funchal, and strangers very soon complain of monotony. There is no theatre, no café, no resort, in fact, but the billiard-table. The members of the Portuguese Club have a ball, once a month during the season, and very agreeable and pleasing re-unions they are. According to Portuguese etiquette, previous to the commencement of dancing, the ladies sit formally at one end of the room, apart from the gentlemen, and it is customary at two or three o'clock in the morning, to hand round cups containing hot chicken broth. The ball seldom breaks up before daylight.

Visiting among the ladies of Funchal is performed in Palanquins, and a kind of vehicle lately introduced, resembling one of our New England sleighs. The latter is generally drawn by oxen, and seems to answer better than a wheel vehicle, on account of the steepness and narrowness of the streets.

The rides about Funchal are delightful; the roads are good, and lined on either hand with vineyards, mingled with groves of the orange and lemon tree. The most agreeable way of taking these rides is on horseback, horses being plentiful and generally well broken. Their owners invariably accompany them, and it is amusing to see how they manage to keep up when the animal is made by the rider to gallop or run; they seize the tail by both hands—thus making the horse drag them after him; and what seems singular is, the animal never gets frightened, and if not urged on by the rider, will soon come to a halt.

Every one who visits Madeira should certainly ride out to the Cural.* The road leading to it is one of the most interesting on the Island. It ascends gradually, and every now and then you are presented with a magnificent view of Funchal, and its bay. After riding some hours you reach a mount of considerable altitude; on ascending this you find yourself on the edge of the Cural, where the whole scene suddenly bursts upon your view, and its beauty and grandeur fill you with wonder and astonishment.

"Earth has nothing to show more grand;
Dull would be the soul who could pass by
A sight so touching in its majesty."

In the descent, the road winds along the sides of the precipice, and at every turn new and striking views are brought out, almost surpassing in grandeur the first. When about five hundred feet from the bottom, the path becomes less precipitous, and the country on either side is in a high state of cultivation and sprinkled with cottages, chapels, and convents.

Few places of sepulture can boast a more delightful prospect than the burying-ground of Funchal. Whilst the dark cypress groves give a saddening effect to the place itself, in harmony with its object, the surrounding scenery

* The Cural is supposed to have been a Crater.

presents some of the finest views in the neighborhood of the town. The most prominent object in the distance is the Peak Fort, the principal fortress in Madeira. Its commanding position renders it a picturesque object from many points of view.

The following story relating to the discovery of Madeira, and narrated by a historian may be interesting to the reader.

"Anna D'Arfet, the heroine of the tale, was a lady of high family and distinguished beauty. She was beloved by Robert Machim, an English gentleman of great merit, but her inferior in rank and wealth; the attachment, though mutual, was not countenanced by the proud family of D'Arfet, and finding her insensible to their admonitions, a warrant was procured from the King, Edward III., by which Machim was arrested and cast into prison, she being in the meantime compelled to ally herself with one more her equal in station. Machim on his release, determined to spare no means to become possessed of the object of his affections, and by the assistance of a friend, who introduced himself to his mistress in the character of a groom, succeeded in effecting her escape from a castle near Bristol, where her husband resided. Guided by their trusty friend, they embarked in a vessel bound for France; but in crossing the channel they were driven out of their course by a fearful storm. For thirteen days they were tossed about in the open ocean, where, being without a pilot, they knew not in what direction to steer. At length a faint haze in the horizon indicated their approach to land, and soon, to their infinite joy, they saw before them a beautiful and richly wooded island. Machim and his mistress, accompanied by some friends, landed under the shade of a venerable cedar, where they found a temporary shelter, there trusting to the genial climate and enchanting scenery, Machim hoped to succeed in administering consolation to the conscience-stricken Anna, but within a day or two of their arrival another storm arose, more terrible than the last, which drove their unfortunate vessel out to sea. Abandoned to despair, the beautiful Anna D'Arfet could not sustain this blow; she died in the arms of her lover three days after the disappearance of the vessel, and was buried by Machim under the tree which had afforded them shelter. The spirit of Machim now gave way. He survived his mistress but a short time, and was buried at her side by his companions. With his dying breath he entreated them to place an inscription upon their graves recording the fact, and requesting that, should the spot be ever visited by Christians, they would there erect a church. The survivors having punctually followed the last directions of their friend, embarked again in the boat which had brought them from their vessel, with the intention of returning to England. Borne to the coast of Morocco, they were captured by the Moors and cast into prison. They narrated their story to some fellow captives, amongst whom was the pilot Morales, who, returning from captivity, related the story to Zargo, and an expedition was soon after sent out by the Portuguese government to take formal possession of the island.

"The small church now standing near by the cedar tree is said to have been the one erected in compliance with this request. Bowles in his 'Spirit of Discovery,' gives the following poetical version of the inscription, supposed to have been written by Machim on the grave of Anna D'Arfet:

'O'er my poor Anna's lowly grave,
No dirge shall sound, no knell shall ring,
But angels, as the high pines wave,
Their half-sad Miserere sing.

'No flowers of transient bloom at eve
The maidens of the turf shall strew,
Nor sigh, as the sad spot they leave,
Sweets to the sweet, a long adieu.'"

CHAPTER II.

FROM MADERIA TO VALPARAISO, CHILI.

ON the 25th we took our departure and stood to the southward.

On the 6th at sunset, being near St. Jago, we hove-to, and continued so until next morning. The early part of the night was quite cloudy, a circumstance which greatly contributed to render the sea in the vicinity of the island appear much more phosphorescent than usual. Its brilliancy was so great that we cold almost see to read by it, and we all remained on deck for hours to enjoy the scene. By straining some of the water through a piece of muslin, it was found to contain myriads of animalculæ, which in the dark shone as brilliantly as the fire-fly.

At early daylight we filled away, and stood in for Porto Praya, where we arrived at 7 A. M. This harbor may be described as a semicircular bay, of several miles in circumference, with bold steep shores. The entrance is from the southwest, and is free from all danger. The usual landing is around the bluff, upon which the fort and town are built. Sometimes a heavy swell sets in the bay, which renders landing very difficult.

St. Jago is one of the largest of the Cape de Verde Islands. It extends from the 15th to the 16th degree of north latitude, and from the 24th to the 25th degree of west longitude. The population is estimated at 25,000. There are many fine pastures to be seen in the interior of the island, and here and there a valley of great fertility and beauty, but in general the island is barren and mountainous. The coast is high, especially at the southeast extremity. The hills, rocks, soil, and everything about the surface, bear unmistakable marks of volcanic origin.

The island is subject at intervals to droughts, and during their continuance the inhabitants suffer greatly from want of food and water. The exports are orchilla,* castor oil, beans, salt, hides, and goat-skins; the former article is a government monopoly, and forty thousand dollars are paid by the company for the yearly crop. The goat skins are sent to the United States and sold at a very profitable rate.

Porto Praya is the capital of the island; it is built on a piece of "table land," and looks much more inviting when viewed from the anchorage than when more closely examined. The houses are constructed of a rough stone, without any regard to symmetry, and very few are over one story in height. The streets are wide, but are not paved, nor kept clean.

A church, a barracks and a jail, constitute all the principal public buildings. The interior of the dwellings is in perfect keeping with their external appearance; a few chairs, a table, and a bedstead or two, are all the furniture which any of them can boast of.

The stores are very insignificant, for not only are the assortments small, but they are composed of the most common articles. The population is estimated at 3,000, of which number more than two-thirds are negroes. The women are the ugliest we have ever seen. They are fond of gay colors, and their most fashionable head-dress consists of a figured cotton handkerchief, tied round the head like a Turkish turban.

* A species of kelp, or Sea-weed, which, when burned, produces alkaline ashes, used in the manufacture of glass and soap.

The language spoken is a mixture of the Portuguese and the negro dialects. Many of the blacks are slaves, brought from the neighboring coast of Africa, and continue to speak in their mother tongue. They dress in a loose shirt, and seldom use a covering of any sort on their heads. Their children go entirely naked.

We have a Consul residing in the town. The climate is not considered healthy for strangers; it is subject to a fever, similar to that which prevails on the coast of Africa.

St. Jago, like the other Cape de Verde Islands, furnishes the Portuguese government with a place of honorable exile for distinguished subjects, whose political opinions may be adverse to the existing institutions. They are advanced a step or two in rank to repay them, and a poor compensation it is for six years residence in such a miserable place, for they are not allowed to return sooner.

During the short time we remained at the Island, our naturalists were actively employed, and many specimens were added to our collections in botany, ornithology, and shells.

On the 7th of October, we again spread our sails to the breeze, and stood to sea. During the 9th we experienced variable airs, with calms at intervals. At 10 A. M. on the same day, we found ourselves in the midst of a very strong tide-ripple. There can be no doubt that this agitation of the water was caused by a current, for the sea was perfectly smooth only a few minutes before. In the afternoon we were in the position given to Pattey's Overfalls, represented as being so alarming to navigators, but we could see nothing of them.

November 4th. The "Vincennes" saw ahead what she supposed to be breakers, but upon examining the place it proved to be an ocular deception, produced by the sun's rays throwing light upon the verge of the horizon, while it and the intermediate space between it and the ship, was rendered dark by the shadow of the clouds. Similar appearances caused by the moon, were seen during the night.

On the 5th, we crossed the equator, in longitude 17° west. The wind now blew from the southward and eastward. In the course of the afternoon we saw many shoals of flying-fish, and as they sprung unusually high into the air, we concluded that they were chased by other fish. The flying-fish has many enemies; the boneta, albacore, dolphin, &c., &c., are waging incessant war with them in the sea, and no sooner do they take to flight, than the prowling frigate-bird, or wide-a-wake, is ready to dash down among them, and drive them once more to seek shelter in their own native element. Very frequently, when they are trying to escape from their enemies, they strike against the ship's side, and are instantly killed. The largest of them are not over twelve inches in length, but their fins are much larger in proportion than those of other fish. Sailors sometimes eat them, but they are not considered a good article of diet.

An amusing circumstance occurred during the night of the 9th of November. In our course we passed very near a large sail, which, from the night being unusually dark, the officer of the deck mistook for the "Vincennes," although sailing on a different course. He immediately followed the vessel, and continued after her until morning, when, to his surprise, he discovered that it was a large Dutch ship. We considered it a capital joke, and during the rest of the passage had many a hearty laugh over it. When the mistake was discovered we resumed our former course, and soon after overtook the squadron again.

On the 10th, 11th, 13th and 14th, we kept watch for the periodical showers of stars. Forty were seen in the midwatch of the 13th, proceeding from the Pleiades, and shooting in a northerly direction. The weather was now delightful, and the southeast trades were wafting us along at the rate of nine or ten knots per hour. The nights recalled to our minds the beautiful description of the illustrious Humboldt: "One experiences an indescribable sensation when, as we approach the equator, and especially when passing from one hemisphere to the other, we see the stars, with which we have been familiar from infancy, gradually approach the horizon, and finally disappear. Nothing impresses more vividly on the mind of the traveler the vast distance which separates him from his native country, than the sight of a new firmament. The grouping of the large stars, the scattered nebulæ rivaling in lustre the milky-way, together with some spaces remarkable for their extreme darkness, give the southern heavens a peculiar aspect. The sight even strikes the imagination of those who, ignorant of astronomy, find pleasure in contemplating the celestial vault, as one admires a fine landscape or a majestic site. Without being a botanist, the traveler knows the torrid zone by the mere sight of its vegetation, and without the possession of astronomical knowledge perceives that he is not in Europe, when he sees rising in the horizon the great constellation of the ship, or the phosphorescent clouds of Magellan. In the equinoctial regions, the earth, the sky, and all their garniture, assume an exotic character."

About meridian on the 24th, we made the harbor of Rio Janeiro directly ahead. At 4.30 P. M., showed our number together with the rest of the squadron, which was answered by the United States frigate "Independence," the flag-ship of the Brazil station. At 5 we passed Fort St. Cruz, situated at the entrance of the harbor, and in the course of half an hour more arrived off "Rat Island," where we let-go the anchor.

We were much disappointed not to find the "Relief" here. The usual passage for vessels bound to Rio from our ports is fifty days, but she had already been out ninety days; we therefore began to feel anxious about her.

There were a great many foreign vessels in the harbor, and not less than fifty or sixty were American, belonging to Baltimore and New York. The trade with the United States has greatly increased. Within the last two or three years from two to three hundred American vessels take and bring cargoes to and from the United States. They bring out flour and cotton goods, and return loaded with sugar, coffee, India-rubber, medicines, and spices of every kind.

I visited the city as often as my duties would permit, but it is too well known to require much to be said of it. It is built on the west side of the bay formed by the débouché of the river of Janeiro, and has a very picturesque appearance from the water. It is the largest and one of the most flourishing cities in South America. At the last census Rio Janeiro had 250,000 inhabitants. It contains many rich churches, two hospitals, besides a miserecordia, a college, a museum open twice a week, two theatres, one opera, and several public gardens.

The population is perhaps more mixed than that of any other city in the world. It consists of Europeans, mulattoes, mamalucoes, or a mixed caste, between whites and aborigines, free negroes born in Brazil, manumitted Africans, mestizoes or zamboes, between the mamalucoes and negroes, &c.

The Imperial Palace fronts the Grand Plaza. It is a large three-story, stone edifice, with a handsome portico in front. The apartments occupied by the royal family are spacious and airy, and furnished with regal splendor. Rio is indebted for many of its public buildings to Don Pedro I. It was his ambition to make the capital of Brazil a second Lisbon.

The appearance of the city on Sundays is very much the same as on week days; the stores do business, and the workshops are kept open. A few of the inhabitants may be seen to attend divine service on that day, but the greater number spend their time at the billiard-rooms and theatres. Religion, which is Roman Catholic, according to the latest statistical accounts, is in a very depressed condition. The revenues of the church are so small that few respectable persons will undertake its duties; and those who do officiate are generally ill-instructed.

Another circumstance which struck me very forcibly was the immense number of slaves* employed about the streets as carriers of coffee and sugar. They go about almost naked, and bear upon their bodies the distinctive mark of their tribe. They appear to work with cheerfulness, and generally go about in gangs with a leader, who sings while they are carrying their loads. The song usually relates to their native country, and they all join in the chorus. They constitute a large proportion of the population of the city. In general, they are kindly treated by their masters, and may purchase their freedom. Their color operates less to their prejudice than with us. When free they vote, and are eligible to a seat in the national legislature, or to any situation in the army and navy.

The aqueduct which supplies Rio with water, is a splendid and substantial work. It extends from the city to a reservoir on the summit of Corcovada mountain, distant

* Previous to 1830, the number of slaves annually imported into Brazil amounted to 40,000. Since the prohibition of their importation the numbers have fallen off 11,000.

about twelve miles. This reservoir is supplied by the mountain-vapors which the night temperature converts into copious rains. The water is cool, delightful to the taste, and clear as crystal.

There is a navy-yard at Rio Janeiro. It presents, however, but little activity; for the Brazillian navy is now dwindled down to a few vessels; previous to the abdication of Don Pedro I.* it was large and efficient.

The currency is paper, the gold and silver being mere articles of commerce, and consequently subject to great fluctuation.

On the 26th, the "Relief" arrived. Her officers stated that the great length of the passage was owing more to calms, and variable winds than bad sailing. There were many days during which she did not make more than a mile on her course. On the 17th, she fell in with the hull of the brig "Nile," of Bath, both masts gone, within a few feet of the partners, and her hold was nearly filled with water. It was evident she had been in this situation for some time; clusters of shell-fish were fastened to her decks and bulwarks, and long sea-weeds flaunted at her sides. As her bowsprit was still standing in good condition, Captain Long caused it to be cut away, and taken on board the "Relief." Nothing more occurred during her passage worthy of notice.

On the morning of the 27th we hauled up to Enxadas; landed the provisions and stores, and then proceeded to "smoke ship." We performed this troublesome and disagreeable operation in the hope that we might destroy the roaches, which from the time of our leaving the United

* Don Pedro I. ascended the throne in 1822, under the title of Emperor of Brazil. After a reign of a few years, the violence of political parties rose to such a height, and became so unmanageable, that the Emperor thought it prudent to abdicate in favor of his son, the present Emperor.

States, had been a source of the greatest annoyance to us.

Enxadas is also the place where our observatory was erected. It is a small rocky island, situated opposite Rio, with a large dwelling-house standing at one end of it, and a number of other buildings which were formerly used by shipping as store-houses. It is at present the property of a wealthy French family, residing in Rio Janeiro, but formerly, we were told, it was owned by the church, and the dwelling-house above-mentioned was a nunnery.

December 1st was the anniversary of the Emperor's birthday, Don Pedro II. The occasion was celebrated with salutes, illuminations, and fireworks.

December 10th. I received orders to relieve Mr. C., on board the "Relief," he being obliged to return to the United States on account of ill health.

On the 17th, got under-way, and were towed out the harbor by boats from the "Independence" and "Porpoise," but the wind failing soon after the boats left, we let-go the anchor to prevent our being drifted on shore by the tide. At an early hour next morning the breeze sprang up from the southward and eastward, and we hove-up the anchor, and stood down the coast.

January 2d. The Barometer was observed to fall from 29, 84, to 29, 52; but the weather remained pleasant.

During the 4th many birds were seen; among others the albatross (diomedia exulans), giant petrel, cape pigeon, and a species of gull.

On the 10th we passed Cape St. Joseph. This cape is a rough, rocky headland, about 150 feet in height. A large number of guanacos were seen on a neighboring hill, and a great many birds on the beach.

At daylight on the 21st, made the land near the strait of

Le Maire. At 9 A. M., passed Staten Land. The aspect of this island is wild and savage beyond description, or even imagination. At 11 A. M., found ourselves in the Straits of Le Maire, and as the wind was unfavorable, we ran into the bay of Good Success, and anchored in thirteen fathoms water.

January 22d. Landed in a cove situated near the south-west end of the bay. Saw a stream of fresh water about 50 feet wide, which discharged itself into the bay; the water was of a dark brown color, but of excellent quality. Ascended the highest hill in the vicinity of the bay; found the ascent, in consequence of the density of vegetation and looseness of the soil, extremely fatiguing, but on reaching the summit, thought ourselves amply compensated for all our trouble, by the magnificent view afforded us of the surrounding country. Several of our number had taken their guns with them, expecting to find plenty of game, but were disappointed. We saw no living animals of any kind. At daylight we got under-way, and stood out of the bay with a light breeze, but it soon died away, and the ship was drifted back into the bay. About 6 o'clock, several natives were seen to come opposite the ship, and, in order to draw our attention, set up a shout. By 8 o'clock, having drifted back to our former berth, we again came to anchor. Soon after this we left the ship in three armed boats, to visit the natives. On our landing they came running toward us, and after welcoming us to their shores, which they did by first placing their hands upon their breasts, and then pointing to the ground, they commenced crying out, "cuchillo," "cuchillo." This being the Spanish for knife, and as Wadel in his book states, that they have many Spanish words in their language, we were all under the impression they were asking if we had any knives to sell. We were, however, soon convinced that we had not understood them, for on showing them our knives they still kept crying out "cuchillo." They also repeated the word when we showed them a string of beads, or a looking-glass. In short, although the word was kept up during the whole intercourse, it was impossible to learn its meaning. They were admirable mimics, and would repeat our own words with great accuracy, and even appeared to understand some of them. They seemed to attach great value to iron and steel, and would readily exchange their bows and arrows for a piece of an iron hoop, or a few rusty nails.

The party consisted of fourteen men, and, with the exception of the headman, or chief, were all young, well-formed, and good-looking. The two sons of the chief were particularly so; they were full six feet in height, and had very pleasing countenances. They all had their hair cut short on the crown of the head, leaving a narrow border of hair hanging down; over this they wear a kind of a cap, or a band, made from the skin of an albatross. The front teeth of all of them were very much worn, more apparent, however, in the old than in the young. Their faces were painted, or, more properly speaking, smeared with red and white clay. Their dress consisted of a single guanaco skin, which covered the body from the shoulders down to the knees. All had sore eyes, which we attributed to their long winters. None of their women or children were seen, but we thought they had them concealed in a piece of wood not far distant, as they objected to any of us going toward it, and showed much alarm when fire-arms were pointed in that direction. They appeared to have very little curiosity, and nothing seemed to excite their surprise; their principal characteristic seemed to be jealousy. It would seem that they have had intercourse with Europeans before. The report of our guns did not frighten them in the slightest degree. We also observed on one of them a string of glass beads.

Their food consists principally of shell-fish and fish. Their fishing-apparatus is made of the dorsal-fin of a fish, tied to a slip of whalebone in the form of a barb; this serves as a hook, and with it they obtain their food.

All our endeavors to entice them to come on board by friendly treatment, and the offer of presents, were useless. They shook their heads and pointed to the woods, and then ran some distance from the beach, as if they feared that we intended to carry them off by force.

On the 24th we quitted Good Success Bay. We experienced during this day a strong current, setting northerly. The coast here may be represented as a succession of peaks, some of which rise so high as to be covered with perpetual snows. The weather was mild and pleasant.

On the 25th the wind came out from the southwest, and blew very fresh at intervals. At 5 P. M., anchored off north-eastern side of New Island. After sunset the weather cleared, and we had a very pleasant night.

On the following morning, after breakfast, we visited the shore. We saw no human beings, but found near the beach a hut, which bore many traces of being inhabited. It contained a large number of muscle-shells which looked fresh, a part of a seal-skin, and a large heap of ashes. We also observed that the ground about the entrance was hard and destitute of vegetation. The hut was constructed of logs, the lower ends of which were spread round so as to form nearly a perfect circle, while the upper ends leaned against each other. The interstices were filled with earth and grass. In the centre was a hole, about two feet in circumference, for the smoke to pass through. The entrance was from the west, and was about three feet in height and two feet wide.

We had not time to examine much of the interior of the island, but that which did come under our observation presented a scene which we did not expect to witness in so high a latitude. There was an abundance of vegetation, and much more advanced than any which was seen at Good Success Bay.

On the 26th of January we left New Island, and stood to the westward. It was very provoking to find that our charts so entirely misrepresented this part of the coast and islands, as to destroy our confidence in them. At 11 A. M., saw what was supposed to be Saddle Island. At meridian it was so hazy that we were unable to obtain a meridian observation, which was greatly needed, in order to ascertain our true position.

On the 27th, at 2 P. M., we anchored in a small harbor. At first sight we were under the impression that this was Orange Bay, but upon further examination we found that we had been deceived; and at 7 A. M., Lieutenant Underwood was dispatched to reconnoitre the coast.

In the afternoon we took a stroll on shore. The land for some miles back from the beach was low, and the soil appeared less fertile than any we had yet seen. It bore in spots a small red berry, which had a pleasant flavor. Visited a hut, in which we found a knife and a piece of Guernsey frock; the knife was originally a part of an iron-hoop. The hut was not in such good preservation as that found on New Island.

The wild goose, the shag duck, and some others of the feathered tribe, were in great abundance here, and many were killed by the scientific gentlemen, and their skins preserved for the government. Found, by an excellent meridian observation, the latitude of our anchorage to be

55° 20′ 30″ south; longitude by chronometer 67° 37′ 00″ west. At sunset Mr. Underwood returned.

On the following day we quitted the harbor above referred to, and coasted along in search of Orange Bay. Passed a number of islands, which answered the description given of those in the vicinity of Orange Bay by Captain King. At 6 P. M., came-to in a large, beautiful bay; it was nearly circular in shape, and was bounded on all sides with undulating hills, covered with evergreen foliage, to their very summits.

We had scarcely let-go the anchor when a canoe, with five natives, three men, a woman and child, came alongside. Upon invitation two of the men came on board without manifesting the slightest hesitation or distrust, and we were not a little surprised to find them so entirely different from those we had seen at Good Success Bay. They spoke an entirely different language, were of a low, stature, ill-shaped, and wore their hair long. So great, indeed, was the difference that we could no longer doubt that those seen at Good Success were Patagonians, and had in all probability come there in quest of game; while these were the real Terra del Fuegians.

They were not more than five feet high, of light copper-color, which was much concealed by smut and dirt; indeed, it would be impossible to imagine anything in human nature more filthy and disgusting. They had short faces, narrow foreheads, and high cheek-bones. The hair was long, lank and black, hanging over the face, and was covered with ashes. Their bodies were remarkable, for the great development of the chest and shoulders; their arms were long and out of proportion; their legs were small and very much bowed. The woman was young, but no better-looking than the men. She was seated at one end of the canoe, and appeared to take an equal share with the men in the labors of the paddle. We invited her on board repeatedly, but she would not venture; doubtless she was afraid of offending the men, who are very jealous. The child had an interesting countenance, and was, I should judge, about three years of age, though it was still in arms. It was attired in the same manner as the rest; a piece of seal-skin, about a foot square, tied around its waist, being all the poor little thing had on to protect it against one of the coldest days that we had yet experienced.

Our two friends appeared to be much pleased with their visit; their countenances and manner plainly indicated the pleasure which they felt on seeing so many new objects. When about to leave, we made them some presents in the way of clothes, with which they all appeared to be greatly pleased, and insisted upon giving us in return some bows and arrows. It was very amusing to see them in their new dress; they moved about with strutting affectation of dignity, and gave themselves a thousand consequential airs.

Their imitation of sounds was truly astonishing; we tried them with the flute and guitar, and they followed the sounds correctly. They were also found to be great mimics in action; anything they saw, they would mimic, and with an extraordinary degree of accuracy. They were very talkative, and often burst out into a loud laughter when with each other; but whenever they discovered that we were watching them, they looked as grave as judges, and said but little. We also observed that they spoke to each other in a whisper.

Their arms consisted of bows, arrows, and spears. They use the latter for killing the seal, which is found in great abundance in all the bays, and which they esteem to be excellent food.

At an early hour next day another canoe, with seven natives, came alongside, and asked permission to come on board; but finding it could not be granted so early in the day, they paddled off again, and we saw no more of them.

In the afternoon we visited the shore, and very soon fell in with the natives, who came on board on the day of our arrival. They immediately commenced jumping up and down, which is their mode of expressing friendship. One of them, who had a pair of pantaloons given him, had them tied round his neck, and another had the skirts of his coat cut off; the reason he assigned for doing so was that they were in his way. Their hut was constructed after the manner of that we saw at New Island, and bore quite a neat and comfortable appearance. The ground was swept clean, and in the centre a large fire was burning, over which hung a string of fish. The other articles which it contained were some shells, which were carefully laid upon some clean leaves, and the blanket we had given to the woman on the previous day. They seldom cook their food much. The shell-fish are detached from their shell by heat, and the fish are partly roasted in their skins without being cleaned. It was evident that, notwithstanding our kind treatment to these people, we had not gained their confidence; for, on seeing us approach the hut, the woman fled with her child, nor could we prevail upon the men to cause her to return.

As this harbor was not put down on any of the charts in our possession, we believed it to be a discovery, and named it after our ship.

On the 30th, we once more got under-way, and after a further search of a few hours, we succeeded in finding Orange Bay. Our observations placed it in latitude 55° 31′ 00″ south, and longitude 68° 00′ 20″ west. It is capacious, easy of access, and better protected from the southwest winds than any place as yet known on the coast of Terra del Fuego. About a mile from the southern shore are two islands, the largest of which is two miles in length, of a moderate height, and called Burnt Island. The land to the southward is rocky and barren, but that to the northward abounds in wood and water. The trees grow nearly down to the water's edge, and some are from sixty to seventy feet in height, having all their tops bent to the northeast by the prevailing southwest winds. The beach was covered with rocks of trap formation; it also abounded in shells, especially in the muscle and petela.

On the morning after our arrival, a canoe with six natives, five men and one woman, came off to the ship, bringing with them spear-heads and necklaces made of shells, which they readily exchanged for cotton handkerchiefs and pieces of iron. They were invited to come on board, but at first only one would venture; this was a young man about nineteen years of age, and rather good-looking. They were evidently of the same race as those we had seen at Relief Harbor; they spoke the same language, and resembled them in their features and dress. The woman was old and extremely ugly, and as masculine in her appearance as any of the men. She declined coming on board. Her face was painted black and red in vertical lines, and she wore a necklace made of shells; her posture while she remained in the boat was that of a squat. Their canoe was made of strips of bark sewed together, and strengthened by ribs and gunwale pieces, and was about twenty-five feet long and three feet wide. The blades of the paddles were so narrow as to be of very little use in a sea way. The bottom of the canoe was covered with a layer of clay, upon which a fire was kept burning. It would seem from the great care they appear to take of their fire, that, when extinguished, it is no easy matter for them to rekindle it.

When this party left the ship, they employed themselves for several hours in fishing among the kelp, and then they pulled up towards the head of the bay where their hut was located, and which was found to be quite differently constructed from any we had previously seen. It was built of boughs, leaves, and earth; in shape it resembled a bee-hive, and was impervious to wind and snow. The entrance was low and oval-shaped. The floor was formed of clay, and in the centre was an excavation which contained the fire.

January 31st. Mr. C., with six seamen, took possession of Burnt Island, for the purpose of making observations on the tide. He met there several of the natives who had visited the ship; they were out gathering berries, of which one kind grows here in great abundance, and has a very pleasant flavor; its color is bright red.

February 1st, 2d, 3d, and 4th, we experienced strong southwest gales, accompanied with heavy rain. On the 5th the gale subsided, and the weather became mild and pleasant.

Mr. C. sent on board a great variety of birds which he shot on Burnt Island, and their skins were preserved for government.

February 12th. We experienced more very disagreeable weather.

On the 17th, the schooner "Sea Gull" arrived; she reported the rest of the squadron to be only a few miles off.

In the course of February 18th and 19th, the "Vincennes," "Peacock," "Porpoise," and "Flying Fish," arrived and anchored.

On the morning of the 25th, the "Peacock," "Porpoise," and the two schooners sailed on a cruise to the South Pole. Captain Wilkes took passage in the "Porpoise," and the report is that the "Vincennes" will remain here until his return.

At 8 A. M., on the 26th, we got under-way, and stood out through the southern passage. About 11 passed False Cape Horn, and 00.20′ P. M., descried the islands of Ildefonsas.

March 3d. We had fresh breezes from the westward, accompanied with rain and a heavy head sea. The barometer was referred to frequently, but was found very fluctuating, and gave no indications of the weather.

During the night of the 6th, the wind increased to such a degree as to oblige us to reduce sail to a close-reefed main-topsail and fore-storm staysail.

About noon on the 8th, the gale moderated, and we flattered ourselves we should have fine weather once more; but a little before sunset it began to increase again.

During the 10th and 11th, the wind was moderate, but very variable, and accompanied with rain at intervals. In the afternoon of the last mentioned day an albatross was shot, which measured nine feet from the tip of one wing to the tip of the other. We caught several smaller ones with hook and line. To kill these, the region of the brain was pierced with a large sewing needle, which produced instant death. At sunset the coast of Terra del Fuego was reported in sight from aloft.

On the morning of the 13th an alarm of fire was given; but it proved to be the igniting of the alcohol of the lamp belonging to the dispensary, and was soon extinguished without doing any damage.

March 18th. Finding the wind was increasing, wore ship and reduced sail. At 1.30 P. M., descried Noir Island under our lee ; and soon after the Tower Rocks, a short distance ahead, and on our lee bow. The wind continued to increase; the waves rose in mountains, and the ship was rapidly drifting towards the coast of Terra del Fuego. To avoid, therefore, being wrecked, after passing Tower Rocks, we hauled up for the southeast point of Noir Island, and at 4.45 P. M., came-to in seventeen fathoms water with both bower-anchors, veering on one cable to 105 fathoms, and on the other to 120 fathoms.

The following morning, the gale moderating, we began to hope for a favorable change of weather; but towards sunset the wind shifting to the southward, all hope of such change vanished. The wind now freshened again, and by midnight blew with such force that we let-go our last anchor, in the hope of keeping the ship off shore till daylight, when perhaps we might make sail and stand out to sea. It was so uncommonly dark, that there was quite as much, and perhaps more danger in attempting to get to sea, than in holding on.

At daylight we found that the larboard bower-chain had parted, and the larboard sheet become unshackled at forty-five fathoms; we also found the ship had dragged so as to be much nearer the reef off Penguin Point.

The sky grew more angry as the day declined;—

" The setting orb in crimson 'seemed to mourn,'
Denouncing greater woes at his return;
And adds new horrors to the present doom,
By certain fears of evils yet to come."

After the sun went down the storm raged with greater violence than at any previous time. Never had we seen it blow so hard before, nor ever beheld such billows. A little after 8 o'clock the ship commenced dragging, and a tremendous wave came over the bows, which dashed a number of the crew against the masts and guns, and completely inundated the berth-deck. Though, about 9 o'clock, the wind changed its direction, so that the ship tailed clear of the above-mentioned reef, yet we were not rescued from the danger of being shipwrecked. At every moment the water was becoming more and more shoal. In less than half an hour it shoaled six fathoms, and the storm still raged with unabated fury; however, to our great delight, about midnight it began perceptibly to moderate.

We hailed with joy the ray of comfort this afforded us. It was like the arrival of an old friend, whose presence in the hour of misfortune affords consolation. It was believed that we passed within twenty yards of the reef; and had the storm continued a few moments longer we would inevitably have been lost.

At 3.30 A. M., the ship fell-off before the wind, upon which we slipped the remaining cables, made sail, hauled on a wind on the larboard-tack, and stood out to sea. By 7 A. M. the ship was under whole topsails and main-top-gallant sail, and was rapidly increasing her distance from the spot, which, only a few hours before, filled every bosom with so many death-like apprehensions.

On the 27th, we fell in with the "Montezuma," a whale-ship, from Talcauanaha, bound to Nantucket. Her captain informed us of the taking of Lima by the Chilian army. He also presented us with a quantity of vegetables, for which he received our warmest thanks. We had not tasted anything of the kind since we left Rio Janeiro. During the night, the breeze became very light.

April 4th. We captured with the hook seven albatrosses; the plumage of two of which was extremely beautiful. This is the best mode of taking them when the ship has but little head-way. Two were prepared for dinner, but they were far from being good eating, the flesh being very tough and fishy.

At daylight on the 13th, we made the coast of Chili on our lee-bow, and at 7 Mount Quillota bore per compass north 60° east. In the afternoon sent Lieutenant Underwood into Valparaiso to procure an anchor. At an early hour on the following morning he returned, and reported there was a chain-cable in the government stores, but no anchors; the only one to be obtained belonged to H. B. M. ship "President," which Captain Lock kindly offered us the loan of. Received the anchor on board, and got it ready for letting go.

On the 15th, we came-to in the roads of Valparaiso;—

"Where Valparaiso's cliffs and flowers,
In mirror'd wildness, sweep
Their shadows round the mermaid's bower,
Our steadfast anchors sleep."

On the same day the American ship "Meriposa," from New York, with stores for the squadron, arrived. Her master was kind enough to send us a large file of newspapers, all of which we read with infinite satisfaction.

CHAPTER III.

CHILI AND VALPARAISO.

Chili is washed on the west by the Pacific Ocean; on the east bounded by the Cordilleras; on the south by Patagonia; and on the north by Bolivia. Like all other parts of South America, it is subject to earthquakes; deep ravines may be seen intersecting the surface in all directions. The appearance of the coast is far from being inviting, especially in the vicinity of Valparaiso; but there are in the interior many extensive and fertile valleys. The southern part is admirably adapted to the growth of wheat, of which large quantities are now raised. Chili is also rich in mineral productions; copper ore is found in the mountains in the greatest abundance.

The climate is variable—the southern part being, on account of its higher southern latitude, considerably colder. At Valparaiso the mean temperature at midday is 65°, in the evening and morning 60°. During the winter, which commences the first of May and ends in September, the rains sometimes last for two or three days, and during their continuance the rivers swell to three and four times their usual size.

Earthquakes are sometimes very violent—that of 1835 nearly destroyed the towns of Talcahuana, Aranco, Talca, and Conception. At Valparaiso the sea receded two feet, and the ground was much rent. In order to lessen the destruction of human life, the houses are usually built low and of light material.

The population of the republic is estimated at one million and a half.

The capital is St. Jago, which is situated at the foot of the Cordilleras, and distant about sixty miles from Valparaiso. All of our officers who visited it were delighted with it. A long line of turrets, domes, and spires, occasionally screened by intervening trees, planted along its numerous avenues, indicated the city. The population is 60,000. It has a national college, a military academy, various private seminaries for both sexes, an extensive hospital, and several handsome churches.

Valparaiso is the next largest town in the republic, and is one of the most flourishing places in the Pacific. In 1820 it consisted of fifteen or twenty huts, and now it contains eight or nine thousand buildings, and individual houses fetch an annual rent of more than three thousand dollars. Its principal street runs parallel with the beach—is tolerably wide, and contains many large and commodious shops, well supplied with English goods and various other kinds of merchandise. The remaining streets are paved, but are narrow and winding. The public buildings consist of the churches, the Governor's palace, and the custom-house. The dwellings are slightly built, and never more than two stories high, on account of the earthquakes, and in general have a wooden balcony in front. There are many Americans and English living in the city, who carry on a lucrative business, the export trade being mostly monopolized by them. They reside on the hill in the rear of the business part of the town, in neat white cottages, surrounded by flower-gardens. This is the most pleasant part of the city, and commands a fine view of the harbor. From here may be seen the vessels of the United States, England, France, Holland, Denmark and Sweden, displaying their gay flags and mingling their bright streamers in the brilliant effulgence of a cloudless sky.

The police of Valparaiso is celebrated for its efficiency. Good order and decorum prevail everywhere. Crime is rarely heard of, and never suffered to go unpunished. The credit of forming this institution is given to Portales, a man of rare talents and great energy of character. It consists of two distinct bodies, one mounted, and the other on foot; the former patrol the streets on horseback, while the latter watch over a particular ward or district, for which they are held responsible. They wear a uniform and a sword, to distinguish them from the other citizens.

The market is well supplied. Fruits and vegetables are abundant and cheap; the grapes, peaches and pears are of the best kinds. Beef is as good as we have at home. There is also a great variety of fish.

The population is estimated at 34,000, and is rapidly increasing.

The principal seaports of Chili are Valdavia, Talcahuano, Copiapo, Coquimbo, Chiloe, and Guasco. Talcahuano and Valdavia we have in particular heard represented as most eligible places for vessels which visit these seas, to touch at. As for Valparaiso, it is not a good seaport; it is entirely exposed to the ocean from the north, so that, when the wind blows with violence from that quarter, which is the case during the winter season, a heavy sea sets into it, and renders the anchorage highly dangerous. It is, however, more frequented than any other harbor. Vessels make it a point to stop here, whatever may be their destination.

The common people of Chili are a mixed race, sprung from the union of the Spaniards with the native Indian women. They are generally well made, of a dark brown complexion, and have a healthy look. They bear the best character of any of the South Americans. They are honest, industrious, and brave. The men are good riders, and very skillful in the use of the lasso. The women have very pretty feet and hands.

Their habitations are built of reeds, plastered with mud and thatched with straw. The poncho is universally worn by the men; it is a piece of cloth of a home manufacture, of the shape of an oblong square, with a hole in the middle, through which the head is passed, the longer ends hanging down to the knees before and behind—the shorter at each side falling over the shoulders.

Their favorite amusements are the two dances, Fandango, and Sama Cueca. The latter is performed in cities and large towns at the Chingano; the performers are usually a young man and woman, gaudily attired; they stand on a kind of stage, and begin the dance by facing each other, and flirting handkerchiefs over each other's heads—then they approach and retreat alternately—occasionally they dart off on each side. The whole is well calculated to display the graces of a fine figure to the best advantage. Its moral tendency may be questioned. Some of the gestures are quite lascivious, and may be esily understood by every one who witnesses the scene. The music is executed altogether by females, and consists of the harp, the castanets, and the guitar. They also add to this a national love-song, sung in Spanish, which the audience seem to enjoy more than any other part of the performance.

The higher classes are of a pure Spanish blood, and are intelligent and courteous; they pass their evenings in small social assemblies, called Tertulias. The women cannot be said to be beautiful, but they are virtuous and amiable. They are fond of dancing and music, in both of which they excel. Nearly every house is furnished with a piano; they dress with much taste, and in the Parisian style.

The men have been accused by travelers of being indolent; no doubt such was the case when they were under the Spanish rule, and had no inducement to be otherwise, but I have been assured by foreign gentlemen, who have resided in the country for the last fifteen years, that such is not their character at the present day; on the contrary, they are industrious and enterprising.

The religion of Chili is the Catholic; but the government has repudiated the interference of the Pope in the appointment of bishops and arch-bishops. The clergy have great influence over the people, and much political power in the state; but they are liberal in their notions of government, and encourage the diffusion of knowledge amongst the lower classes.

Commerce has more than doubled within the last ten years. According to the statistical accounts of the past year, Valparaiso alone exports thirty thousand hides. Grain is sent to Peru and Equador in large quantities. Six hundred quintals of wool are shipped annually from Conception. Copper, hemp and platina are largely exported. The iron mines are also sources of great wealth, and the miners annually extract vast quantities of the ore; indeed, there is no doubt that Chili is blest with all the elements necessary to make her a powerful commercial nation.

The army which was sent to invade Peru in the war just concluded, is said to have consisted of 8,000 men, and to have been well appointed. The navy is larger, and by far more efficient, than that of any of the other South American States.

The prospects of education are bright. There are several good colleges in the republic, and common schools are being established in all the towns for the instruction of the lower classes; and the system of education introduced into the schools and colleges is said to be superior.

The administration of public affairs is better conducted than in any other country in South America. Generally speaking, the magistrates are men of ability and integrity, and nowhere else are life and property better protected. Universal suffrage is granted by the laws of the constitution to every one above twenty-five years of age, and no public measure can be carried which is adverse to the welfare of the masses.

On the 28th of April, General Joaquim Prieto, President of Chili, arrived from St. Jago. He was received by the inhabitants with all due respect. The civil authorities and the military went several miles out of the city to receive him; the batteries saluted, and the streets through which he passed were decorated with flags and evergreens.

On the evening of the 30th, we attended a ball given by the citizens of Valparaiso, in honor of the recent victory of Yungai over the Peruvians. It was a brilliant affair, equaling anything of the kind we ever witnessed in the United States, or any other part of the world. The place selected for it was a space between two large buildings; temporary arches were erected over head, and the whole was covered with an awning, lined with blue and studded with stars. The room was brilliantly lighted by handsome chandeliers suspended from the arches over head; the floor was carpeted, and the pillars which supported the roof were decorated with emblems of the victory and nation. At the upper end there was a transparency of General Bulnes, the hero of Yungai, surrounded with scrolls of his deeds. On the sides were hung paintings and rich mirrors, in which hundreds of lights were reflected, while the national flags, formed into festoons, intermixed with wreaths of flowers and evergreens, encircling emblematic designs of the nation's glory, produced an effect that was truly beautiful. The president's reception-room and the card-rooms were also very handsomely decorated. The company amounted to five hundred, of whom about one-fourth were ladies; many native and foreign officers were present, dressed in their uniforms. At 10 o'clock the ball was opened by the president in person. He was dressed in a richly-embroidered coat, gold epaulettes, and a field-marshal's sash. He is a fine-looking man, about fifty years of age. He danced a minuet with a lady of Valparaiso, after which the dancing became general, consisting of waltzes, contra dances, quadrilles, and the sama cueca. The music was very fine, and many marches and national airs were played during the intervals between the dances. The ball did not break up until 8 o'clock, at which hour the president was escorted home by a procession of the dancers. His unblemished private character, together with the success of his policy toward the Peruvian government, have rendered him extremely popular with all classes of society.

CHAPTER IV.

CALLAO AND LIMA.

On the 1st of May we sailed for Callao, where we arrived after a passage of twelve days. Nothing of interest occurred during this period. The wind most of the time was favorable, and the weather warm and pleasant.

We found in port the United States ship "Lexington," belonging to the Pacific squadron; also the Chilian fleet, amounting to ten sail, commanded by Admiral Blanco, an English and a French frigate, and about fifty merchant vessels, six of which were American.

Callao, the seaport of Lima, is celebrated for its safety and convenience. The island of St. Lorenzo shelters it from the swell of the ocean to the west, and there is no danger from any other direction. The Mole affords every facility for landing goods from the boats. Water is conducted to the Mole by an aqueduct, and a railway conveys the goods to the far-famed fortress,* which is now converted into a depôt. There are a number of sentries stationed on the Mole night and day, for the double purpose of preserving order among the boatmen, and to aid the custom-house in preventing smuggling, which, notwithstanding, is carried on to an extent that is hardly credible. This is effected by the owner of the goods bribing the custom-house officials.

* It was here that the last stand of the royalist was made in New Spain; and it was in the same castle that the brave Rodil, with a handful of devoted followers defended themselves with heroic courage against the insurgents in 1826. Surrounded, but not dismayed, they still kept their assailants at bay, until famine stalked before them, and they were forced to yield. History tells us that horse-meat sold among the besieged for a gold ounce the pound, and a chicken for its weight in the same precious metal

The town is situated several miles from the site of old Callao,* and numbers about five thousand inhabitants. It has not much to commend it. The only well-built houses are those on the main street. The churches and other public buildings are too insignificant to deserve description. The market is held in a large open square. Oranges, apples, figs, grapes, granadillas, and chirimoyas, are abundant in their season. Vegetables of every sort are also to be had. Beef is cut into small pieces to suit the purchasers, and poultry is cut up in a similar manner; the former is killed in the outskirts of the town, and the hide, head and entrails are left for the buzzards, which are very numerous and protected by law; the rest of the carcase is brought to market on the backs of donkeys.

The inhabitants are addicted to gambling, and pass most of their time at the billiard-rooms and monte-tables.

The old castle claimed our attention; it covers a large extent of ground, and its walls are high and very massive. One of the officers told us that it was capable of quartering ten thousand troops. It was once looked upon as the key of the country. Whichever party had it in possession, were considered masters of Peru. As I have already remarked, it is now used as a depot for goods, and is nearly dismantled—only five of the guns remain out of the 140 which it mounted; the metal of these is brass, and their proportions are beautiful. The garrison consisted of eight hundred men. I cannot say much for their personal appearance; they were quite short, had an awkward gait, and dull, stupid countenances. If they are a fair specimen of the soldiers of the country, it is no wonder that the Chilians have been able to conquer it so easily.

*Old Callao was destroyed by the memorable earthquake of 1746. In the same earthquake a first-class frigate, lying in the harbor, was lifted several hundred feet and carried inland a considerable distance, where a monument was erected to commemorate the event.

The distance from Callao to Lima is about eight miles, and stages run between the two places almost every hour in the day; the fare is one dollar. The road leads over a plain, but it is not kept in good repair, and is, besides, very dusty, on account of the extreme dryness of the climate. In this part of Peru, there are heavy dews, but no rain.

We had an opportunity of visiting the "City of the Kings"* several times. We went up in the coaches, and always set out at an early hour, that we might avoid the heat of the sun and the dust. During the first ten or fifteen minutes of the ride, we saw nothing to interest us, for we were passing through the filthy streets of Callao, and its still more filthy outskirts. Of all the places we have as yet visited, civilized or uncivilized, Callao has been the most filthy and disgusting. When about two miles out, we passed Bella Vista, which, ever since the revolution, has been in ruins.

We next came to the so-called half-way house, where the drivers invariably stop to rest the horses, and to regale themselves with a glass of pisco from its dirty pulperia. This part of the road was formerly infested by banditti, and no one thought of appearing on it without being well armed; but now this is not necessary, as the police has taken steps to disperse the robbers.

Resuming our course, we soon reached a section of country laid out in gardens, filled with all kinds of fruit-trees, shaded walks, lined on either hand with stone seats, and intersected with running streams of water. It is the usual evening-drive of the Limineans, and a delightful one it is.

* The name bestowed on the infant capital was Cuidad de los Reges, or City of Kings, in honor of the day, being the 6th of January, 1535, the Festival of Epiphany, when it was said to have been founded by Pizarro. But the Castilian name ceased to be used even within the first generation, and was supplanted by that of Lima, into which the original Indian name was corrupted by the Spaniards.—*Prescott's Conquest of Peru*, vol. ii.

In a few minutes more we found ourselves passing under the great gate of the city. Its aspect is that of rapid decline; there is no stir or life among the inhabitants; many of the shops are closed, and hundreds of houses are untenanted, and in a state of decay. The streets are broad and paved, and many of them have a stream of water running through their centre. It is not, however, a clean-looking city, for these streams are used for very disgusting purposes, and buzzards are seen feeding all over the city.

The style of building is well adapted to the climate and nature of the country. Most of the dwellings are of two stories, with a spacious court in front; the main object of these courts, is to afford the inhabitants a place of refuge when the city is threatened with earthquakes, which is a very frequent occurrence. The material employed in the construction of the walls, is sun-burnt brick. The roofs are perfectly flat, and the ground-floor is used as store-rooms and stables.

The population is estimated at 40,000. In the time of the Viceroys, it is said to have been 70,000.

The Grand Plaza contains several acres, and should be visited by the stranger, if he wishes to form a correct idea of a life in Lima. From sunrise to sunset it is filled with people. On two sides of the Plaza stand the portales, or arcades, where all kinds of dry-goods and fancy articles are sold. The cathedral and the arch-bishop's palace occupy the east side of the plaza, and that of the viceroy's the south side; this last has now become the residence of the presidents, and, although it covers a great extent of ground, there is nothing very attractive in its architecture. The fountain in the centre of the plaza is a splendid piece of work, and was erected, according to the inscription, in

1600, by Don Garcia Sarmiento Sotomayer, the then Vice-roy, and Captain-General of Peru.

In this plaza, the Saya y Manta, or the peculiar dress of the Lima ladies, is seen to the best advantage. It is certainly a very bewitching attire, for it betrays the whole outline of the female figure; neither does it conceal the foot and ankle, which, when prettily shaped, (and those of the Liminean ladies are rarely otherwise,) are a charming sight, especially to bachelors; but, on the other hand, the Saya y Manta offers strong inducements to carry on a love-intrigue, and for that reason was once put under the ban of a legislative statute. It still survives, however, and is worn by the ladies of the best families. It consists of a kind of hood and a petticoat, both usually made of black satin, with numerous vertical folds. The manta, or upper garment, is fastened at the waist, and is so gathered over the head and shoulders as to conceal every thing but the right eye and the right hand. The disguise is so complete that a husband may meet his wife in the streets, or any of the public places, without being able to recognize her; and it is, no doubt, too true, that it has been the means of destroying the peace and happiness of many a Liminean family. It is asserted that the original intention of this singular costume, was to enable a lady to go out in the morning to mass, or shopping, before she made her toilet.

The Almeda is extensive and handsomely laid out. The walks are lined with rows of willows on each side; its centre is ornamented with fountains, and artificial streams of water run parallel with the walks. Towards evening it is very much resorted to by the ladies and gentlemen, and I have seen there some of the former, who were really beautiful. The women of Lima are usually handsome, but

Pizarro.

Lima Costumes.

their minds are neglected, nor are their morals what they should be.

There are other sights in Lima well worth seeing; among the rest, the Convent of St. Francisco, which covers about eight acres of ground. In former times it must have been equal to anything of the kind in the world. Its cloisters are ornamented with fountains and flower-gardens, and the chapels are rich in gilding and carved work. Part of the convent is now occupied as barracks, and the soldier's muskets are stacked on the altars of several of the chapels. We observed in the church a shrine and an image of St. Benedict, with a jet-black infant Saviour in his arms! There are but few Friars here at present, but in the days of its prosperity there were four hundred connected with it, and had an income suited to the easy and luxurious style in which they lived. Its collections of paintings have been highly spoken of by connoisseurs.

I attended the theatre several times; it is a spacious, handsome edifice, and seemed to be well supported, although the performances were of a very ordinary character. The acting president, Lafuente, was present each time, dressed in his uniform; bnt he did not appear to receive much attention from the audience, and I was subsequently told that he was not generally popular with the people, as he was in favor of the Chilians, and, in fact, owed his present position to them. He has the Spanish features, and appears to be about fifty years of age. The ladies in the galleries wore the saya and manto, and made great display in ornaments.

During our stay in Lima there were no bull-baits, although it is a common and a favorite amusement with all classes of society.

The present state of Peru is far from being promising, if we may be allowed to judge from what we saw and heard during our stay in the country. The Chilian army was still quartered in Lima, at the expense of its devoted inhabitants. Public confidence was destroyed, commerce at a stand, the mines were neglected, the people looked discouraged, and war with Bolivia was inevitable, unless Gamara, the present incumbent and usurper, placed by force in the presidential chair by the Chilians, was removed. The most uncompromising hostility is evinced by the Bolivian government towards the administration of this president; and we were assured, both by intelligent natives and foreigners, that until he shall be banished from the country, no reconciliation of affairs can take place between the two governments. The English, also were very clamorous, and threatening to sieze upon the revenue of the country, if their claims were not speedily attended to. Indeed, it seemed to have every trouble before it. The people are as yet in infancy as regards self-government. Instead of taking matters in their own hands, they allow themselves to be governed by a faction of military men, whose only desire is their own self-aggrandizement. A few months since they met to make some new elections, but they allowed Gamara to overthrow them, and by force of arms destroy their ballot-boxes; and nothing is more common than to hear of officers being exiled, and rich citizens stripped of their wealth, merely for their political opinions. Nor is this all:—The depraved morals of the church are proverbial in Peru; and there is scarcely a crime perpetrated of which its members are not guilty. Even on the Sabbath the priests may be seen resorting to the theatres, billiard-rooms, and gambling-houses. The public revenue of this fine country is imposed in the mest oppressive manner, and impoverishes the people from whom it is collected. The hordes of robbers it nourished during the revolutionary war, still continue to annoy its peace; and there is, perhaps, no country in the world where murder and robbery are so prevalent. Until a better state of things be brought about, its improvement is hopeless.

On the 11th of June the "Porpoise" arrived from Valparaiso. She reported that the "Vincennes," "Peacock," and "Flying-Fish," were to have followed her in a few days. As for the "Sea-Gull," she had not been seen or heard from since the time she was separated from the "Flying-Fish" in a storm off Cape Horn.

On the 19th the "Peacock" arrived, and the United States ship "Lexington" sailed for the coast of California. The following report was now very current, namely, that as soon as the "Vincennes" arrived, this ship would be detached from the squadron, and ordered to return home.

June 20th the "Vincennes" made her appearance, and anchored near us. We understood she left Lieut. Thomas Craven at Valparaiso, with orders that if the "Sea-Gull"* did not arrive there by a certain time, to charter a vessel and go in search of her. It was the opinion of many of the officers that she was lost.

On the 21st I received orders to report for duty on board the "Peacock," it having been decided that the "Relief" should return to the United States, after taking a cargo of stores for the expedition, to Sydney, New South Wales.

* She did not arrive at Valparaiso at the appointed time, and Lieutenant Craven acted agreeably to his orders; but he could neither find or hear anything of her.

CHAPTER V.

FROM CALLAO TO SOCIETY ISLANDS.

At 5.30 P. M., July 13th, we quitted Callao, with a light breeze from the southward and westward, "Vincennes," "Porpoise," and "Flying-Fish," in company.

The day following, it being Sunday, Mr. Elliot, the chaplain of the "Vincennes," came on board and performed divine service.

August 5th. During this day the heat was exceedingly oppressive, although the thermometer did not at any time stand higher than 80°. In the evening zodiacal lights were visible until half-past eight. In the course of the night many meteors were observed, some of which were remarkable for their brilliancy. At meridian, the latitude was 18° 08′ 30″ south, and longitude 122° 25′ 45″ west.

August 13th. At 1.30 P. M., made the Island of Calermont de Tonnerre, bearing west-by-south half-south, distant about six miles.

At first sight the island appeared like a forest growing in the middle of the ocean, so low is the land. It is of coral*

The collected labors of united lithophytes raise their cellular dwellings on the crust of submarine mountains, until after thousands of years the structure reaches the level of the ocean, when the animals which have formed it die, leaving a low, flat coral island. How are the seeds of plants brought so immediately to these new shores?—by wandering birds, or by the winds and waves of the ocean? The distance from other coasts makes it difficult to determine this question; but no sooner is the newly raised islands in direct contact with the atmosphere, than there is formed on its surface, in our northern countries, a soft, silky net-work, appearing to the naked eye as colored spots and patches. Some of these patches are bordered by single or double raised lines running round the margins; other patches are crossed by similar lines traversing them in various directions. Gradually the light color of the patches becomes formation, with an extensive lagoon in the centre, and is encircled by reefs and rocks, against which the surf beats with great violence. At 5 A. M., tried the current, and found it setting north-west-by-west half-west, one fathom per hour. Wishing to survey the island, we "lay-to" during the night.

August 14th and 15th. At early daylight made all sail and stood for the island we discovered yesterday, and by 10 A. M. were so near it that we could distinguish with the naked eye the natives standing on the beach. These savages walked about in groups, and appeared to be armed. At 11 A. M., we proceeded with the rest of the squadron to take our station for surveying. In the afternoon several of the "Vincennes" boats effected a landing, but were not very courteously received by the natives. They assembled in considerable numbers on the beach, and commanded our people to return to the ships. Finding the order was not heeded, they commenced throwing stones at the boats and brandishing their spears, nor could they be induced to desist, until a musket or two, loaded with

darker, the bright yellow which was visible at a distance changes to brown, the bluish gray of the lepraides becomes a dusty black. The edges of neighboring patches approach and run into each other; and on the dark ground thus formed there appear other lichens of circular shape, and dazzling whiteness. Thus, an organic film or covering, establishes itself by successive layers, and, as mankind in forming settled communities, pass through different stages of civilization, so is the gradual propagation and extension of plants connected with determinate physical laws—HUMBOLDT.

According to another high authority, (Charles Darwin,) the process of formation is the following:—He supposes a mountainous island, surrounded by a coral reef. (a fringing reef attached to the shore,) to undergo subsidence; the fringing reef which subsides with the island is continually restored to its level by the tendency of the coral-animals to regain the surface of the sea, and becomes thus, as the island gradually sinks and is reduced in size, first, an "encircling reef," at some distance from the included islet, and subsequently when the latter has entirely disappeared, an atoll. According to this view, in which islands are regarded as the culminating points of a submerged land, the relative positions of the different coral-islands would disclose to us that which we could hardly learn by the sounding-line, concerning the configuration of the land, which was above the surface of the sea at an earlier epoch.

* Lagoon, is the Spanish word for Lake.

blank cartridge, had been discharged at them. It was remarked that these islanders were in general tall and exceedingly well-formed. Their complexion was dark-brown, and their hair black and straight. The chiefs had their hair drawn back and tied in a knot behind; the others had theirs hanging loose. Their bodies were perfectly naked, except around the waist, to which was fastened a small maro made of leaves. No tattooing was observed upon either the men or women. The dress of the latter consisted of a piece of tapa, large enough to cover nearly the whole body.

The spear appeared to be the only weapon which they possessed; these were from ten to fifteen feet long, and pointed at both ends. They understood and spoke the Tahitian dialect.

Throughout the night we observed a large number of fires burning on the beach, which we concluded were alarm-fires.

August 16th. At 9 A. M., filled away, and steered for Serle Island, and by noon came up with it, and commenced surveying operations. This ship had no communication with the island, but the other vessels had, and from them we learn that it has a few inhabitants, and that they are of a more friendly disposition than those found on Calermont de Tonnerre.

The island, according to our survey, is seven miles long and one and a quarter in width. It is situated about twenty-five miles to the northward and westward of Calermont de Tonnerre, and both its formation and vegetation are similar to that island.

August 19th. This afternoon made Homden, or Dog Island; landed, and found it covered with trees and shrubbery, and abounding in turtles and birds—the latter being so tame that they allowed themselves to be caught by the hand; the most conspicuous among them was the frigate-bird. They were seen as they flew off inflating their huge pouches, and looking as if they had a large bladder attached to their necks. Immense quantities of fish were also found in the lagoon; but human beings there were none, or even the traces of any; neither the remains of huts, nor canoes, nor marks of fire, were anywhere visible. There were a great many sharks both in the lagoon and outside, and they were so ravenous as to bite at the oars of the boats.

Large and valuable collections were made in all the scientific departments. Some beautiful specimens of coral were procured here.

Our observations placed the island in latitude 14° 56′ 00″ south, and longitude 138° 48′ 00″ west.

August 23d. In the morning the barometer began to fall rapidly, the horizon lowered to the southward and eastward, and soon after the wind blew with such violence as to compel us to close-reef the topsails. Towards noon we discovered Disappointment Islands on the lee bow, and in the course of the day frequently observed the natives standing on the beach and cautiously watching our movements.

These islands are two in number, called Wytohee and Otoohoo, and were discovered in 1765. They trended nearly east and west, and are bounded by reefs and rocks. They are well covered with trees of the cocoa-nut and pandanus kinds.

About sunset, saw a canoe pulling along the shore.

Lay-to during the night, in order to survey the islands the next day.

August 24th and 25th. At early daylight made all sail, and stood in for the land. At 10 A. M., nine canoes, from two to three natives in each, came off to the ship. They approached near enough to seize the ropes we threw them to hold on by, but declined coming on board. They were very gay and talkative, and every few minutes would entertain us with a song which we supposed to have been made up for the occasion, and to have an allusion to our coming among them.

They were a good-sized people, with dark-brown complexions, and lively, interesting countenances. Their hair was black and a little curly. Some had beards and a moustache. Their dress consisted of a piece of matting fastened to the waist.

We very much admired their canoes; they were beautifully shaped, and so ingeniously put together that it was some time before we were able to determine whether they were formed of several pieces or one entire piece. They were made of a number of pieces of cocoa-nut wood sewed together with bark, and each was furnished with an outrigger. The paddles were from three to four feet long, and the blade on one side was a little curved.

These natives knew the use of iron, and coveted its possession so much, that even when we had our eyes upon them they tried to steal all that came within their reach; two men were seen twisting and pulling away at the main-chain plates, while others tried to draw the bolts out of the ship's side.

Their weapons were spears and clubs, several of which were purchased for the government. In the bows of several of the canoes were some species of shell-fish, which were intended as food.

Towards noon the canoes returned to the shore, and we proceeded to ply to windward, in order to take our station for surveying.

When this was finished several of the scientific gentlemen visited the largest of the islands—Wytoohee. They had not been landed long when they encountered seven of the inhabitants. These at first received them with an air of respect blended with fear; but when they were made to understand that they had nothing to apprehend, they smiled, rubbed noses* with the gentlemen, and then invited them to their huts. There they spread mats for them to sit on, and treated them with the milk of the fresh cocoanut, which they found to be delicious.

No women or children were seen, and the gentlemen supposed they had been sent off by the men.

They were highly pleased with a chisel and some pieces of iron that were given them. Their huts were inferior to those seen about Cape Horn, and their baskets and other articles were suspended on the trees.

The scientific gentlemen having returned, we resumed our course.

Aug. 29th. This morning we made an island ahead which is not marked on any of the charts; considered it a new discovery, and named it after the man who first reported it in sight—King.

In the afternoon, Captains Wilkes and Hudson, and Lieutenant Emmons and myself, effected a landing on the western side of the island. Near the beach we found the remains of two huts and a canoe. Further on we saw some fish-bones and a large heap of cocoa-nut shells, and also a piece of a fishing-net. Proceeding then in a southeast direction, we soon came to a lagoon, upon the shores of which we found a raft and a large quantity of cocoa-nuts—some of which, as might be supposed, we eagerly enough took possession of. The lagoon was several miles in cir-

* This is the usual mode of salutation.

cumference, and, like all those we had seen before, abounded in curious fish.

As it was already late in the day, and the ships "laying-to" a considerable distance from our boats, we did not deem it prudent to continue the examination. We were, however, perfectly satisfied the island was uninhabited, except by birds, turtles, and rats, and that the huts we found near the beach had been erected by the men of some vessel engaged in the pearl fishery.*

Though the soil was light, there was no want of vegetation. The cocoa-nut, pandanus, and other subjects of the vegetable kingdom, grew in the greatest abundance in all parts of the island. Fresh water, however, we saw none, except here and there in pools. The shells found on the beach were the turbo, volutis, venus, and the pearl oyster.

At the distance of two hundred yards from the shore we could find no bottom with the hand-lead; boats may approach very near the beach. Harbors there are none. The whole island is of coral formation, and our observations placed it in latitude 15° 44′ 00″ south, and longitude 14° 45′ 15″ west.

August 30th. During this day we had frequent showers of rain. At 6 A. M., when King's Island bore northeast, descried land bearing southwest—steered for it; it proved to be the island of Raraka. This island is very narrow, and higher than any we have yet seen. There are a few transient inhabitants on it, left by an English schooner in quest of pearls—one of them is a white man, the others are natives, of Tahati. In other respects it so much resem-

* The vessels engaged in this fishery belong to foreigners who reside at Tahiti. The mode of taking the oysters is by natives, who are employed as divers for a small compensation.

bles the island we discovered yesterday as to render any further description unnecessary.

We made the Tahitians several presents, and they in return gave us some hooks made of mother-of-pearl.

We observed on the beach two double canoes. Found the position of the island to be, latitude 16° 03′ 00″ south, longitude 145° 03′ 00″.

August 31st. We had scarcely quitted Raraka when another island was descried to the northward and westward, which was not laid down on the charts. It is very long and narrow. In some places it is well clothed with trees and other subjects of the vegetable kingdom; in others it is entirely naked. This is particularly the case towards the northwest and westward, where it is so low that the sea washes over it and forms large pools. Here and there on the beach we observed large detached pieces of coral, some of square shape, others round, and of a color nearly black.

This island is destitute of harbors. The lagoon was very extensive and apparently deep, and as far as the eye could reach appeared entirely free from banks and rocks.

Noodies and Curlews were the only kind of inhabitants we found on the island. Not a human being was seen anywhere, or even the traces of any.

We named the island Vincennes. It is situated in latitude 16° 08′ 04″ south, and longitude 144° 59′ 45″ west.

September 3d. Having finished the survey of Vincennes Island, we stood for Karlshoff's Island, discovered by the Russians. As we approached we perceived the natives making signals to us to land, which invitation we accepted. They received us kindly, inviting us to their huts, and doing all in their power to render our stay agreeable. They informed us that they emigrated from the

Chain Islands.* Their houses are little better than sheds, but kept very clean; the furniture consisted of some mats, which were spread over the floor, some half-dozen glass bottles, and a calabash or two, in which they keep their water.

We obtained from them several pigs, some cocoa-nuts, and a few shells. Of all the articles we offered them, they gave a decided preference to calico, tobacco and knives. Looking-glasses, beads, and such like trinkets, they would scarcely receive. On taking leave of our friends, we took a short walk into the interior of the island. It is well covered with trees, among which the cocoa-nut makes a conspicuous appearance. The lagoon is several miles in circumference, and is well-stored with fish, which constitutes the principal food of the inhabitants.

September 6th. At an early hour commenced surveying Waterland. This island was discovered by the Dutch, and is situated in latitude 14° 26′ 55″ south, and longitude 145° 12′ 00″ west. It is covered with luxuriant vegetation, and has an extensive lagoon.

In the afternoon we landed on the western side, and took a series of observations on the dipping-needle. Four men were the only natives we saw here; they very much resembled those we found at Raraka.

One of the boats remained ashore a long time after the signal for her return was made. The officer in charge gave as the cause for this, that he discovered that one of the crew was missing, and he was waiting for him to return. Some supposed that the man strayed from the boat, but I am of the opinion that he deserted. His name is Penny—

* These islands are under the government of Tahita. The inhabitants were formerly cannibals; but now missionaries are established among them, and they have made many advances in civilization.

has been much among the islands engaged in the pearl-fishery, and speaks the Tahitian language well.

September 7th. During this day we surveyed and examined another island, not down on the charts. We found it pretty much the same as the rest, with no inhabitants, but bearing evident marks of its being recently visited by pearl-fishermen. The lagoon terminates within a few yards of the sea-shore, and is so shallow that it can be forded. Numbers of cocoanut-trees were found growing on the margin.

Captain Wilkes, with several of the Vincennes officers, landed here to observe the eclipse of the sun, just as we got into our boat to return to the ship. We named the island after our ship—Peacock. It is situated in latitude 14° 32′ 00″ south, and longitude 146° 20′ 45″ west.

September 8th. At 7 A. M. made Rurick Island, discovered by Captain Kotzbue, of the Russian service. Soon after sent two boats to examine it, but only one succeeded in effecting a landing, on account of the violence of the surf. The place was a small cove, round the shores of which were a number of houses, and hard by a fine cocoanut grove. No people were to be found in any of these houses, but the other boat saw plenty along the beach; they appeared to be a mild, inoffensive people. No arms were seen about them.

September 9th. During these twenty-four hours we made a flying survey of Dean's Island. Judging from appearances (for the weather would not permit our leaving the ship), the character of this island is similar to those which have been already described.

We are now clear of the Coral Islands, and really we are glad of it. They soon ceased to interest us; nay, towards the last we almost sickened at the very sight of them; they all seemed to us alike. In vain did we look for a change or variety; they invariably presented the same uniform appearance, the same uniform flatness, the same scenery.

September 10th. This morning we found ourselves in sight of the island of Aurora. In many places the coast of this island rises abruptly and precipitately from the sea to the height of six or seven hundred feet; the interior is diversified with hill and dale, thus forming a pleasing contrast to the dull and monotonous scenes we had been accustomed to for some time past. The soil in the valleys is fertile, and produces abundance of sweet potatoes, yams, and tarro, as also several kinds of fruit.

The inhabitants are of a Tahitian extraction, and like them have embraced Christianity, and established schools. All the men we saw, and most of the women, were tattooed. In trading with them, we found that they preferred old clothes and cotton-stuffs to anything else. They took us for missionaries at first, and I believe that many of them are of that opinion still, a circumstance which shows that their intercourse with the whites has been confined to that class of men. Indeed, this can never be very extensive, as the island affords no harbors.

When the boats which had been sent ashore to take some observation returned, we made all sail again, and stood for Tahiti.

> "Huzza for Otaheite! was the cry,
> As stately swept the gallant vessel by;
> The breeze springs up, the lately flapping sail
> Extends its arch before the growing gale."

CHAPTER VI.

FROM ARRIVAL AT TAHITI TO DEPARTURE FOR TUTUILLA.

At 5 P. M., September 12th, we at length reached Tahiti, and anchored in Matavai Bay, in fourteen fathoms water. The shores of this island, as far as we could see, were well clothed with the tropical trees peculiar to Polynesia, but the interior appeared very uneven, and was almost destitute of other vegetation than that of grasses. Many of these hills are very curiously shaped—some are conical, some pyramidal, others castellated.

A coral-reef, with occasional openings, surrounds the island. Between this and the shore there is a continuous channel for boat-navigation, and on the northern side there are many safe and commodious harbors for large vessels.

The fertile portion of the island lies in the valleys, and in the plain which extends from the sea-shore to the base of the mountains. These produce tropical plants in great abundance and luxuriance, and are well watered.

The cottages of the natives are to be found in retired and beautiful spots. They are indolent, but are mild and amiable people.

We had no sooner let-go the anchor than we were environed with canoes, laden with poultry, pigs, tarro, yams, bananas, cocoa-nuts, via apples and oranges. Yet, notwithstanding this profusion, we found everything very dear. There were from two to three men in each canoe, few only had any women in them, and these, if we may be allowed to judge from their behavior, were not the most chaste. They wore a loose dress resembling a night-gown, and had their hair decorated with a profusion of flowers. The Tahitian women are very fond of flowers, but the use of them in dress has been discouraged by the resident missionaries, who have declared that such vanities are unbecoming Christians. Consequently, when they are to appear before their teachers, they dispense with this simple and harmless ornament.

The governor of the district of Matavai, Taua, called on us at an early moment. He came alongside in a whale-boat, and it was soon found that his visit was not one of mere ceremony, but was intended to engage our washing, a business which is monopolized by the chiefs. He is a large, fine-looking man, about 45 years of age. He was dressed in a striped cotton-shirt, nankeen pantaloons, and a round jacket of blue cloth. He has a large establishment near Point Venus, and he invited the officers to come there whenever they visited the shore.

About dusk some dozen women, of a character similar to those above alluded to, came alongside, and applied for permission to come on board, but finding their request could not be granted they returned to the shore again. Several of these females were certainly not more than twelve or thirteen years of age. Were all visitors to act in like manner, these depraved females would not be so numerous as they are at present; but, I regret to say, that the opposite course is usually pursued. It is due to the missionaries to state such facts, for they certainly add very much to their other difficulties, in trying to improve the moral and religious condition of the natives. Who will deny that bad example may not prove even more potent than the most wholesome teachings?

September 13th. This morning the sick were sent on shore, where they will have more comforts than it is possible for them to receive on board the ship. The climate here is said to be uncommonly salubrious, and invalids coming from other parts rapidly recover their health.

After quarters we gave the natives permission to come on board with their merchandise. Some supposed this would have a tendency to make them reduce somewhat their exorbitant prices, as it would give rise to competition; it however produced no such effect. Among other articles they brought on board were several kinds of shells, which we had not seen before. Some of them had also pearls for sale. They procure these when they are employed by European vessels that are engaged in that trade.

In the afternoon I took a walk on the road leading to Papeite, the capital of the island, situated about seven miles to the westward of Matavai. I found the traveling exceedingly bad, until I reached what is called "One-tree Hill." The road, or rather path, difficult thus far from its steepness and ruggedness, was rendered infinitely more so by the recent rains. In some places it was so slippery that I was forced to make use of my hands as well as feet. With the remainder of the walk I was highly delighted. I sauntered along over a broad, level road, lined on either side with groves of the orange and bread-fruit trees, sprinkled with the habitations of the natives, and intersected by numerous streamlets. Indeed, the scene was one of the most beautiful I ever beheld.

The houses were all constructed in the primitive style, which consists of an oval-shaped roof, supported by round sticks, from two to three inches in diameter, placed some distance apart, so as to allow a free admission of air. Neat grass paths, fringed with flowers, from the pure white to the bright red and yellow, and filling the air with their sweet odors, lead from one house to the other through the groves, while the surrounding trees were literally alive with songsters of every plumage imaginable.

I entered several of the dwellings, and was received by the inmates in the kindest manner. They treated me with the milk of the fresh cocoa-nut and several varieties of fruits. I did not see any cultivated land besides the little patches attached to each house; these were planted with sweet potatoes, yams, and tarro.

On returning I called in at our observatory, erected on Point Venus.* There were great numbers of men and women assembled around it—the latter dressed in their best, and evidently come to see and to be seen. Though many of them were young, I observed none whose looks were deserving of the high encomiums passed on them by the generality of former voyagers. There is a kind of languor about their eyes that may be pleasing to some, and their feet and hands are also small, but their figures are short, and the features are too gross to be called handsome. A large number had their heads decorated with wreaths composed of Cape jasmine and orange flowers.

September 15th. It being Sunday to-day, the crew were sent to the native chapel to attend divine service. Our chaplain performed the service, with the aid of Mr. Pratt, one of the resident missionaries. This chapel is oval in shape and spacious, and plastered, and white-washed on the outside; the roof is made of plaited reeds, and covered with the leaves of the pandanus. The windows are furnished with blinds, but

* It was here that Captain Cook erected his Observatory. It is a low, narrow tongue of land running out northward from the island, and is thickly covered with cocoa-nut trees.

remain unglazed, as free circulation of air is here desirable at all times. The interior is well supplied with benches, arranged in rows, so as to face the pulpit at the side. There is no steeple to it.

Near by the chapel is the residence of the Rev. Mr. Wilson, the only survivor of the missionaries who first came to the island. Notwithstanding his great age, he continues to enjoy good health, and to watch over the spiritual welfare of his flock, which I understand is large.

It is worthy of remark, that although the day has been Sunday with us, it has been Monday with the people a-shore, a circumstance to be attributed to the first missionaries (who arrived here by the way of the Cape of Good Hope) not having made a proper allowance for the gain of time.

September 20th. This morning the "Vincennes" got under-way, and ran up to Papeite. The females here have certainly a very great passion for singing. Every evening they assemble in great numbers down by the water-side, and sing away for hours. Last night it was 2 A. M., ere they ceased. This would be a great annoyance to us were their voices unmusical, but they are not. More soft, rich and clear voices we have never heard in any part of the world. Besides, they do not confine themselves to their national songs, but occasionally, as if they wished that we should share with them in their innocent amusement, strike up some one of our own which they have learned from the whalers, and which seemed to be as familiar to them as to any of us.

Papiete, September 24th. We arrived here a little after meridian. When about two miles from the anchorage of Matavai, we passed two white-plastered buildings, shaded with a variety of trees, one of them, we were informed by the pilot, was the house of the queen; the other, the building in which the remains of the Kings Pomare II. and III. were deposited.

The next object that attracted our attention was the ruins of the great chapel erected by Pomare II., after his conversion to Christianity. The original size of this building is said to have been immense.

The anchorage of Papiete is much superior to that of Matavai. There, when the wind blows fresh from the seaward, vessels are exposed to a very heavy and dangerous swell; here they lay perfectly protected from both sea and wind. Indeed, there is but one objection to Papiete harbor—its entrance is so very narrow, that unless there be a fair breeze it is not accessible.

The town stretches around the curvature of the shore forming the harbor, and presents many evidences of civilization. Many of the houses are built in the European style, and the native church is really a fine building. Several of these houses are owned by natives, but they rarely occupy them themselves, as they prefer those constructed in the primitive style, which, indeed, are better adapted to the climate of the island. They keep them to rent out to foreigners.

The adjacent country does not differ materially from that about Matavai.

In the centre of the harbor there is a charming little island, upon which the Tahitian national standard was waving to the breeze as we entered. This flag displays a white star on a red field, and owes its origin to the missionaries. The people here promise to be less troublesome than those were about Matavai. We have seen but few of them alongside, and none on board.

Soon after we came to anchor, we received a present from the queen, consisting of pigs, cocoa-nuts, bananas, and other products of the islands.

I understand that yesterday Captain Wilkes had an interview with the principal chiefs, and succeeded in forming a commercial treaty with them, which promised to be highly advantageous to both nations.

October 3d. During these past four or five days nothing remarkable has transpired. This evening some dozen natives came on board, and gave us one of their old dances. After they had seated themselves round in a ring, they commenced making a kind of grunt, or noise, made by the throat and nostrils, accompanied with motions of the arms and fingers, by throwing them about in all directions. This they continued for some minutes, when the noise gradually became louder and louder, and the gestures more violent, until at last they wrought themselves to the highest pitch of excitement, and looked as if it was the greatest effort to keep it up; every blood-vessel was much swollen, and the perspiration ran in streams down their faces. At this time two of the party sprung up into the middle of the ring and began dancing, and making all sorts of grimaces and most violent licentious motions of the body; the noise still increasing, all the others rose up in the same manner. It now appeared to have attained its highest pitch; it became by degrees less and less, until it almost died away, when they kicked up their heels and fell on deck, which was the signal that they had finished.

October 6th. This afternoon Pomare Taire, or the king consort, arrived from Eimeo, where he has been residing for some time past. He came in a small fore-and-aft schooner.

When Pomare III., only surviving son of Pomare II., died, he was succeeded, in the supreme authority of the islands of Tahiti, Eimeo, &c., &c., by the present queen, under the style of Pomare Vahina IV. of Tahiti.* She is about 28 years of

* The Crown is hereditary—descending either to males or females.

age, and has been twice married—the first time to a young chief of Taha, from whom she was divorced. She was married to her present husband about two years since, and thus far the union has proved a happy one. She has several children, one of whom is a son. I have been informed that she possesses many excellent qualities, and is much beloved by her people.

October 7th. This morning the king-consort and Mr. Pritchard, H. B. M. consul, came on board, and breakfasted with Captain Hudson. The king is probably 23 years of age, well formed, and rather good-looking. His dress showed no evidence of his rank; it consisted of a calico shirt, brown drilling pantaloons, a black bombazine jacket, and straw hat. He wore no stockings, and his shoes were old and patched, which induced our good purser to make him a present of a new pair. When breakfast was over, he went round to look at the ship, with which he appeared much pleased.

Mr. Pritchard was formerly connected with the mission. His house is decidedly the best I have seen on the island; he owns large tracts of land, and he is said to exercise much influence over the queen and the government.*

At 10 o'clock the king left the ship, accompanied by Captain Hudson.

* The Government is a Constitutional Monarchy. Tahiti now belongs to the French.

CHAPTER VII.

FROM TUTUILLA TO AUSTRALIA, OR NEW SOUTH WALES.

At 9 P. M., October 10th, we bade adieu to Tahiti, and steered to the westward.

On the 18th we descried land, bearing northwest, which proved to be Tutuilla, one of the Samoan, or Navigator Islands. At meridian kept away for it, and shortly afterward anchored in the harbor of Pango-Pango. We had no difficulty in entering this port. The principal danger is a large rock, which is situated near the middle of the passage; but is easily seen, as the surf breaks upon it at all times.

It is a beautiful harbor; the land all around rises abruptly, some places perpendicularly from the water to the height of a thousand feet or more, and everywhere it is covered with the most luxuriant vegetation; even the rocks are covered with festoons of creeping-plants. It likewise abounds in fresh water; several fine streams are visible from our decks.

The shores are thickly studded with houses, and they differ materially in shape and construction from any we have before seen. They are circular in form, with a high conical roof coming down to about five feet from the ground—the space between the eves and the ground being shut in by mats, which, when the weather is pleasant, are rolled back, and thus the fresh breeze circulates through every part of the dwelling.

There are many runaway sailors, and some Botany Bay convicts, living on this island.

October 19th. This day we visited the village, situated at the head of the bay. It contains about forty houses, all constructed after the manner before described, save that of Mr. Murray, the resident missionary. This is built after the English cottage-style, painted white, and surrounded by a wooden paling. The interior aspect of the native buildings varies according to the circumstances of the owner. If he be rich, the floor is covered with the finest quality of mats, and presents an air of great neatness throughout. If poor, the floor remains uncovered, and but little attention is paid to cleanliness or order.

We saw in the Council-House a war-canoe, which was capable of carrying fifty warriors. It is said that every village on the island has one of these council-houses. They are the places where the chiefs and other principal men meet to discuss all matters concerning the state. The one here stands near the landing, has a circular shape, and is capable of containing several thousand people.

Curiosity brought crowds of men, women, and children around us. They are not in general as well-formed people as the Tahitians, and we observed that very many of them were afflicted with ophthalmia and elephantiasis. Their dress consisted of long, narrow leaves, thickly strung on a piece of bark, long enough to tie round the loins. All of them were tattooed, more or less, about the legs and arms, but ornaments they had none. Both men and women are fond of bathing, and they spend much of their time in the water. They seemed to have no idea of money, but set great value on everything in the way of clothing and iron tools. They eagerly exchanged their largest and finest-wrought mats for a hatchet, or a plain iron; ink and paper were also sought after by some.

On the afternoon of the 20th we sailed for the neighboring island, Upolu. A few days after the "Peacock's" arrival here, an American, named Terry, gave information against a native, who had murdered an American seaman that was living on the island some twenty months before. Mr. Baldwin and the master-at-arms, with several marines, were immediately sent to secure him. After looking for him for some time, he was pointed out to Mr. B., who arrested him and brought him on board the ship, where he was confined and ironed. Some days afterward Captain Hudson demanded an investigation of the matter. On the 26th the chiefs assembled from the different parts of the island in the Council-House. The missionaries, Messrs. Williams and Mills, and Mr. Cunningham, H. B. M. Vice-Consul for the Samoan Islands, were present, and offered to act as interpreters during the investigation between Captain Hudson and the chiefs. The prisoner was sent for on board the ship, and brought before the assembly in charge of an officer, and a file of marines. He owned that he committed the murder, and assigned his reason for doing it. He wanted, he said, to get possession of the white man's property. This admission established the guilt of the prisoner, and Captain Hudson decided that he must die; but the chiefs expressed great repugnance to this punishment, and proposed buying him off with mats, tappa, &c., according to the Samoan custom. Captain H. told them the Christian custom was to take life for life; therefore they must punish him with death. After much deliberation the chiefs approved of the sentence, but objected to its being carried into execution on shore. They again asserted that they knew no such laws, and strenuously urged that the criminal should be carried on board the ship and executed there. To this it was replied that the execution must take place on shore, in order that the people might see what they had to expect when they killed an American citizen.

It was believed by the officers of this ship that the chiefs would have finally complied with all of Captain Hudson's demands, had the "Vincennes" kept out of the way, but she now made her appearance, and upon its being reported to Captain Wilkes what was going on, he repaired to the Council-House, and after holding a private interview with Captain Hudson, ordered the prisoner to be returned to the "Peacock," at the same time requesting Mr. Mills to state to the assembly that the criminal would be taken away from Upolu, and left on some uninhabited island.

Upolu is one of those islands which, together with Savi, Tutuilla and Manono, constitute that group of islands which go under the cognomen of "Navigator's Group." The soil is, generally speaking, very fertile, being in most parts composed of a dark, rich mould, from which spring spontaneously a strong luxuriant vegetation of perpetual verdure. This manifests itself in various species of grass, shrubbery, fruit trees, and forest timber.

From the location of the island, almost in the centre of the tropics, it might be inferred that an atmosphere of very high temperature must be the necessary consequence. Such, however, is not the fact. Experience has shown that it is more temperate than many regions beyond the torrid zones. The hour of greatest heat is about 3 o'clock P. M., when the thermometer averages 78° of Fahrenheit. Earthquakes are frequent, though not violent.

By far the largest portion of the inhabitants live on the sea-coast, because they have there great facilities for fishing. They construct their houses after the manner of those we saw at Tutuilla. The men only are tattooed, and the part of the body thus ornamented is from the waist to the knee. It is very tastefully done, and one would imagine it to have been adopted in imitation of breeches. It does, in fact, somewhat abate the appearance of nakedness, and thus give an air of decency. It is the ceremony of initiation into manhood. Fish is an almost daily article of food with those who live on the coast. They have various ways of catching these; they use the hook, net, and spear, and for lobsters, &c., a kind of a trap-basket. They construct also a sort of pond, or inclosure of mats and cocoa-nut branches, leaving one end open. A party then spread about, and drive the fish in, and thus often inclose a large number at once.

Their manufactures consist of mats, cloth, and baskets. This is the work of women; they make various sorts of mats—some of the strong leaf of the pandanus, in nearly its full breadth, for spreading on the floor—some of the same leaf split into small shreds for sleeping upon. A much finer mat, the weaving of which will occupy a woman twelve or eighteen months, is woven with the same leaf into very narrow pieces, which are made tough and durable by being baked in an oven, and then soaked in sea-water. The mat is so fine as to be almost as pliable as linen. These are the dresses on special occasions—the common one being like that we saw worn by the people of Tutuilla. They look very rich and elegant, especially when trimmed with red or yellow feathers.

The Tapa is made as elsewhere from the Chinese paper-mulberry. This is also in extensive use for clothing and bed-covering. They print some of it in neat patterns, and dye some pieces all black, or brown. It wears better than the cloth made at Tahiti.

Nets are made from the bark of the hibiscus, a tree which is very common. Their construction is very much the same as the ordinary fishing-net in use among us, with stones instead of bits of lead, and pieces of light wood instead of cork. The making of these is a distinct trade. They also make from the above materials some very neat and useful baskets.

Their food is prepared in the way practised in Tahiti, and they have many dishes which are rich and agreeable to the palate.

The women are treated with as much consideration as in any part of the world, and are not suffered to do any out-door work. They are cleanly in their habits, and bathe daily, after which they anoint themselves with oil and turmeric. The girls are pretty, and quite modest. Their complexion is a lighter brown than that of the Tahitian women. It is the practice of mothers here to suckle their children until they are five or six years of age, and I myself saw a woman who gave nourishment to two children of different ages at once.

The mariage-vow is observed with strict fidelity. The usual mode of courtship is for the man to take a basket of fruit and offer it to the object of his choice. If the young woman partakes of it, his addresses are favorably received, and he applies to his chief for permission to marry. When this is granted, he calls on the parents of the girl, and pays them a stipulated price for her, which varies with the respectability and circumstances of her family. The ceremony is concluded with a grand feast, to which the relatives and acquaintances of the parties are invited.

Children are brought up without severity. As soon as the boy can make use of his hands and feet, his father furnishes him with a little bow and arrow, and exercises him in shooting at a target, or throwing stones at a mark by the sea-side.

Their burials are conducted as follows:—The body is enveloped in several thicknesses of tapa, and placed in a grave about three feet deep, with flowers and shrubbery planted around. No arms, or food is deposited with the bodies; for, according to their belief, they have all these things provided for them in the world of spirits. After the body has lain in the grave a year or two, they take up the skull and place it in a box in their houses. The object of this practice, I am told, is to prevent their enemies obtaining possession of them in times of war, when it is a common custom to violate the sanctity of the grave. The relatives of the deceased show their grief by burning themselves and scratching their faces.

Their amusements consist of dances, wrestling-matches, sham club-fights, and a variety of games. All the dances I saw were very indecorous, so much so as to make it improper to attempt a description of them here. Young women had a share in them, and it seemed to me that their attitudes were of a character still more disgusting than those of the men. The music accompanying the dances consisted of drums,* flutes,† and singing. It is said that the sham-fights sometimes last a whole day, and usually end in bloody noses and broken heads and limbs. Their arms consist of spears, clubs, bows and arrows. The spear is pointed with bone, and is considered a very formidable weapon.

The government resembles the early state of the European nations under the feudal system. Their orders of dignity answers to barons, vassals, and villeins. Great respect is paid to the chiefs, and particularly to the highest class. The "Tuper," or barons, are lords of the several districts into which the island is divided. The vassals superintend the cultivation of the ground, and the villeins, or the common people, perform all the laborious work. The whole power lies in the

* The Samoan drum is made of a piece of wood hallowed out.

† This flute is made of bamboo.

chiefs of the first class. Their meetings are called "Fonos," which signifies in English, a General Assembly. The eldest chief present presides, and they are conducted with much ceremony. The person who wishes to speak must first obtain the permission to do so from the presiding chief. The common people are required to stand at a respectful distance from the chiefs, nor can an inferior chief stand or lie down before a superior one. It is the custom, before the Fono proceeds to business, to compliment the presiding chief, and to invoke blessings on him that his life may be prolonged and prosperous.

The most usual forms of punishment for crimes, are cutting off the nose and ears of the offender, flogging, exposure of the naked body to the sun, confiscation of property and banishment. Adultery is punishable with death. The punishment for murder is not specified by law, but is left for the relatives of the person slain to demand the atonement. Most generally, however, pardon is purchased for the murderer by his friends, who, like himself, are liable to be revenged on by the aggrieved party, so long as the affair remains unsettled.

There are several missionary stations* on Upolu, and many of the inhabitants have embraced Christianity. Those who still adhere to their ancient religion† are called Devils. They may be distinguished from the Christians by their hair,‡ which they allow to grow luxuriantly all over the head; they

* The first missionaries to these islands belonged to the Wesleyan denomination, but they were soon after succeeded by those of the English Board, the Wesleyans abandoning the field for that of the Fejee Group. They are much respected by the natives, and their labors have been attended with beneficial results.

† It very much resembles the religion of most heathen nations. Its divinities are the offprings of fear. The Priesthood is hereditary. The priests are the men of science, and to their care are intrusted all the sick, whom they attempt to cure by ridiculous ceremonies and enchantments.

‡ The Christians cut their hair short, and have abandoned their old dances.

are also more indolent and less intelligent than those of their brethren who have been converted.

During our stay at Upolu the trading-master was stationed on shore daily, for the purpose of purchasing provisions for the squadron. Here all sorts of articles were displayed; but those which took best with the natives were hatchets, knives, blue nankeen, and chisels. Though the weather was generally unfavorable, we obtained very good rates for our chronometers. The scientific gentlemen were constantly employed in making excursions into the interior of the island, to collect specimens and information in their respective departments. Officers were also stationed on shore day and night for the purpose of making observations on the tides. In short, every exertion was made to promote the interests of the Expedition.

On the afternoon of November 10th we proceeded to sea, in company with the rest of the squadron.

On the 11th, I received orders to join the "Vincennes." During the early part of this day we experienced a very heavy shower of rain, accompanied with much thunder.

At 11.30 P. M., we arrived off Wallis Island. While we were making a survey of this island, a canoe, paddled by two men, came alongside, a circumstance which Captain Wilkes availed himself of to land the native prisoner who killed our countryman.

The island is well inhabited, but the two natives who came off to the ship assured us that there was no communication between it and the Samoan group. Tuvi—for that was the prisoner's name—was kindly treated during his confinement on board the "Peacock," and seemed much distressed in parting with her officers and crew. He was about thirty years of age, and had a wife and several children. His stature was that of an ordinary-sized man, and there was nothing of the sinister expression in his countenance.

Wallis Island is situated in latitude 13° 24′ 00″ south, and longitude 176° 09′ 00″ east. From the name one would naturally suppose it was a single island. Such, however, is not the case. It is a group of small islands encircled by one extensive reef, against which the swell of the ocean may be seen breaking at all times. The native name of the principal island is Wea, and it is tolerably high, but the others are low, resembling the Coral Island of the Paumato Group. All are thickly covered with trees, and well inhabited. The two natives who came on board informed us that there was a good anchorage inside of the reef, and plenty of provisions to be had from the inhabitants. It is said that the Catholic missionaries who were expelled from Tahiti, were landed here, and that they have made many converts among the natives.

When the survey was finished we again made all sail, and stood to the southward.

On the following morning we passed Horn Island, discovered about the year 1616, by Le Maire. It is high and well wooded. As for the inhabitants, I am unable to speak of them.

At early daylight on the 18th, Matthew's Rock was reported in sight. We bore away for it, and when within half a mile of its northernmost point, measured base by sound with the "Peacock," and angled on it in order to fix its position. A boat, with Drs. P. and F., was also sent to make an examination of the rock. It is about half a mile in circumference, and very steep and rugged; our boat, therefore, found great difficulty in effecting a landing. Here and there in spots may be seen some soil bearing bushes. In general a nakedness of rock characterize the prospect. Immense numbers of birds were perched upon it. The boat having returned we resumed our course.

On the 24th of November we experienced a severe thunder storm. The ship was struck by lightning several times, and the forward conductor was broken into many pieces, but neither the rigging nor hull were damaged. The wind blew violently from the southwest, and during the continuance of the storm the thermometer was observed to fall from 85° to 69°. After sunset, as the wind increased in strength, "all hands were called," the topsails were close-reefed, and a signal made for the rest of the squadron to adopt the same precaution. Our position at meridian was, according to dead reckoning, in latitude 32° 56′ 00″ south, and longitude 160° 20′ 48″ east.

Two days after this storm we passed Lord Howe's Island and Ball's Pyramid, and several other small islands, called Admiralty Rocks. The two first mentioned are high, bleak, rugged rocks.

On the 27th we saw several fin-back whales, also a great number of birds, among which were four or five very large albatrosses.

At 10 A. M. on the 27th, we made the coast of New Holland, or New South Wales, on the weather-beam. At 7.40 P. M. descried Sydney light-house, and at 9 called all hands to work ship into port. We then stood for the harbor, and by 10.37 anchored in seven fathoms water off the town of Sydney, abreast of Fort M'Quarie, without any of her citizens, or the garrison's being aware of our character. The "Peacock" followed in our track, and anchored within a cable's length of us. The remaining vessels came in the following day.

The fact of our coming in here in the night, and that too

without the aid of a pilot, appeared to have excited no little sensation among the people on shore. Several of the newspapers spoke of it next morning as something very remarkable, and jocularly declared it to be a "Yankee trick," done for the purpose of saving the pilotage, and in perfect keeping with our usual keenness in money matters. It would have been rather a serious joke though, had the object of our visit been hostile, for we might have possessed ourselves of the fort, and then bombarded the town with the greatest ease.

Of this, however, they were as sensible as ourselves, and the necessity of fortifying the harbor more effectually, and of being more vigilant, became fully impressed upon their minds. There are many excellent sites for fortresses, so that the harbor might be rendered perfectly inaccessible to an enemy's vessels.

CHAPTER VIII.

AUSTRALIA, OR NEW HOLLAND, OR THE LAND OF ANOMALIES.

WHILE the Portuguese and the Spaniards, early in the sixteenth century, were extending their enterprise through the seas of the further east, rumors reached Europe of a new continent on the south. The navigator, driven by contrary winds and currents beyond the bounds of his ordinary enterprise, discovered different points of land, which, for a long period, none endeavored to examine. The Spaniards had been navigating the Indian Archipelago for more than eighty, and the Portuguese for nearly a hundred years, before the name of any mariner became connected with the discovery of Australia. The unknown southern land, (Terra Australis incognito,) and the southern land of the Holy Spirit, (Australia del Spiritu Santo,) were indefinitely mentioned in their records, yet no explorer ventured to approach the mysterious coast, dimly seen by the chance-voyager in those remote seas.

In 1605, however, the Dutch, eager to obtain a maratime superiority in thoso distant regions, equipped the yatch "Duyfen," which sailed from the port of Bantam, in Java, to explore the coast of New Guinea. Returning from this expedition, the little vessel entered the waters of the shores of Australia, and sailed into the great Gulf of Carpentaria. To these early voyagers all seemed desolate and barren, for, since the discovery of America, the voyage of Vasco di Gama, and the exploration of the Indian Archipelago, the navigator continually thirsted for some new Chersonese, where gold was to be found in every stream, where amber was washed up on the beach, where spices perfumed the forests, and pearls were plentiful in the shallow waters near the shore. The wild aspect of the Australian coasts consequently offered little temptation to them. Nevertheless, Spanish, Dutch, and English mariners continued to visit those seas, Dampier, between 1684 and 1700, exploring a portion of the north-western coast, and surveying it in the rude manner of his time. Half a century of further research added little to the world's knowledge of this great region; but 1770 brought the advent of Captain Cook, whose immortal memory is associated with so many seas and shores. He discovered the eastern coast of Australia from Cape Howe to Cape York, naming the region New South Wales. Many successive voyagers followed, each of whom contributed some tracing to the sea-board of this vast territory, until Captain Stokes, about eight years ago, made the entire circuit of the island, and first enabled the geographer accurately to lay down the leading features of its mighty outline.*

The daring navigators of Europe explored the shores of Australia, marking its outlaying islands, endeavoring to discover the mouths of rivers, fixing the position of harbors, and laying down the general outline of the island; while inland discovery commenced much later, and made a slower progress. In the south, ridges of hills were known to exist, and believed to be impassable. Not lofty, but precipitous and rugged, they were intersected by deep chasms and broad, barren valleys, sprinkled with half-blasted trees, and piled with masses of sandstone rock—landscapes sublime in their melancholy desolation. The blue mountains, so named from their habitual

* To those familiar with the history of maratime discovery, the mention of such names as New Holland, New South Wales, Tasmania, Van Dieman's Land, De Witts, &c., will at once recall the numerous voyages and voyagers connected with the gradual exploration of Australia.

aspect, were long considered impassable; but when English colonists in New South Wales were straitened for room, they looked for wider pastures for their flocks, and more extensive lands for the cultivation of corn and vegetables. Necessity then opened a passage through the hills—the Bathurst plains were discovered, and a stage-coach rattled along a well-made road winding among the mountain-passes. In other directions adventurous men, starting from different points, attempted to explore the interior of Australia; but as yet all have been unsuccessful in their endeavors to reach the centre, and he who traveled farthest, at the utmost point of his journey, has only cast his eyes over a monotonous desert, apparently of interminable extent.

Australia is situated in the immense ocean stretching to the southeast of Asia, and lies in nearly the same latitude as the Cape of Good Hope and Brazil. Equal in surface to four-fifths of the European continent, it extends from 113° 05′ 00″ to 153° 16′ 00″ east longitude, and from 10° 39′ 00′ to 39° 11′ 00″ south latitude. The area is calculated at 3,000,000 square miles, and the coast line at 7,750. The whole of this immense mass of land is solid and compact, broken by few indentations of the ocean.

The mariner, for the first time approaching Australia on its western coast, perceives few of those natural charms painted by so many writers. Along these shores, even now very rarely visited, there is little to allure the eye. A monotonous plain, bounded in the distance by a chain of bleak hills, stretches from the sea, and over the surface of this vast level are scattered sweeps of ground blackened by the passage of flames. The few wandering tribes leading a nomade life in this part of the island, frequently, by accident, or intentionally, kindle the tall, dry grasses or the low bush. The fire, seizing greedily on the parched vegetation, travels with great rapidity, and driven by the wind spreads to the base of the hills, where the conflagration spends its fury. As we proceed further northward, the shores become strewn with enormous masses of rock, extending to some distance from the beach. It is supposed that formerly the land here was considerably more elevated than at present, and that the action of water has levelled it, leaving the more durable masses unremoved. Some eminences, covered with a vegetation richer than that of Brazil or Borneo, with occasional fertile plains, present themselves in marked contrast with the general aridity of the coast.

On the northern shores the same level prevails. Flinders sailed 175 leagues without seeing any hill higher than the mast of a sloop.

Along the Gulf of Carpentaria few elevations occur; but reaching the eastern coast, the view is no longer monotonous or dreary. New scenes continually unfold themselves—forests and open plains, and valleys running up between the hills, and a more numerous population enlivening the country. Passing between the shore and that great barrier-reef which outlies the eastern coast of New Holland for more than six hundred miles, we enter the principal field of British enterprise, where the coast is marked by a thousand fantastic irregularities. A line of precipitous cliffs extends far towards the south, a huge breach in this natural wall becomes apparent; and while the eye is resting on the grim magnificence of these granite barriers, the vessel glides between the rocks, and reposes in the superb harbor of Port Jackson. The shore, sweeping in gentle slopes toward the hills, is covered with a natural growth of verdure. The sea, blue and brilliant, flows into beautiful bays, where vessels lie safe after their long voyage from Europe. White stone-built villas, with graceful gardens and groves, lend artificial charms to a landscape naturally picturesque; and Sydney, the capital of New South Wales, with its forts and light-houses, its churches, hospitals, and custom-house, full of traffic, and smoking in the heat of industry, appears like the creation of enchantment. The industry of Europe, planted in Australia, now ploughs the sea between Port Jackson and Moreton Bay with steamers, which prepare the mind for the scene presented within; but with this exception, the change from the outer view to the panorama of Sydney, is as that from a lifeless desert to an English seaport.

Towards the west the surface again becomes level—irregularities are few—tall, sloping cliffs commence, and the country sinks into a plain covered with scrub, and extending as far as the south-western point of the island. There, rises a range of low hills, continuing as far as Gautheaume Bay, where we reach again the desolate level from whence our circuit commenced.

The streams in South Australia and Western Australia are, in comparison, insignificant; but it is a received opinion among many geographers that great water-springs exist in the island, which will ultimately burst from the earth, flow together, form themselves channels, and find outlets at various places along the coast. At present, in the river-system of Australia, as well as in its mountains,* valleys, and geological formation, its botany and its zoology, we discover a strong support of the theory that this region is of recent emergence from the ocean. Formerly, Captain Sturt believes it consisted of an archipelago of islands. The bed of the ocean, upheaved by the agency of subterranean fires, raised

* In the countries of the old world, every range, however tortuous, agrees in general direction with the length of the continent. In Australia the case is reversed—the hills run transversely from north to south.

the whole to a level, and the action of the great sea sweeping over it has produced these strange appearances, which have earned for Australia its curious title—the Land of Anomalies. The researches of travelers in the interior will at no distant day, lay it open to examination; and when the great doubt is removed, science will explain with accuracy phenomena at the present day so perplexing.

Eighty years ago the adventurous voyager, Captain Cook, sailed along the eastern coast of Australia, and there, in latitude 33° south, discovered a commodious inlet. Near the water's edge he saw many curious flowers blooming wild, and from them named the place Botany Bay. The account of his visit was circulated in England, and, sixteen years later, it was resolved to establish a colony in some part of the unknown southern land. Botany Bay was thought of. In 1787, the "Sirius" and the "Supply," with six transports and three store-ships, sailed with the germs of a new colony on board. Besides the crews and 166 marines, there were 757 convicts —565 men and 192 women. Stores and provisions for two years were taken, besides agricultural implements and tools, with all the necessaries for the foundation of a permanent settlement. Captain Philip, the appointed governor, took command of the squadron, and sailed first to the Cape of Good Hope, then belonging to the Dutch, where live stock and seeds were procured. At Rio Janeiro more stores were taken in, and the expedition steered direct for the new land. Continuing their course, they reached Australia after a voyage of eight months and one week. Botany Bay appeared to promise little; water seemed scarce, and an aspect of aridity on the surrounding land decided them to go elsewhere in search of a place of rest. The fleet, therefore, weighed anchor; and, as they left the bay, two French ships, under La

Perouse, entered it. That adventurous discoverer stayed two months in this haven, and then set sail for the Pacific, disappearing forever from the sight of civilized man.

Drawing near an opening in the cliffs, a few miles further north, the governor went to examine it in person. The natives collected on the rocks, shouting to the strangers to go away; but they persevered. Captain Cook had reported the existence in this neighborhood of a creek, where boats could be sheltered. A sailor, named Jackson, however, declared that a great haven lay within the mighty rocks that frowned above them; and entering between these, the explorers were delighted to find a harbor of many miles in extent. A fine anchoring-ground was at once chosen, and the name of the sailor bestowed on the harbor.

The spot chosen for debarkation was near a stream of fresh water, over-shadowed by trees. Every man literally stepped from the boats into a forest. They detached themselves into parties, and the primeval silence of the shore was immediately broken by sounds which have never since died away. Some shouldered the axe and commenced clearing ground for the different encampments; some pitched the tents; some brought from the ships the necessary stores, and others examined the capabilities of the neighboring soil. Every one wandered freely over the country, and wholesale disposals were made of land which, fifty years later, was worth more than a thousand guineas an acre.

The people were then collected together, and the governor's commission was read, with letters patent for establishing courts of justice. The ground was gradually cleared, a rude farm was prepared to receive the live stock, and gardens were laid out for the planting of seeds and roots. Thus was planted the colony of New South Wales.

CHAPTER IX.

AUSTRALIA OR NEW HOLLAND.

The colony of New South Wales is exceeding precocious, approaching fast to commercial and political greatness. It promises fair to occupy a commanding position with respect to the quarter of the globe in which it is situated. There is very little doubt that when sufficiently powerful, the colonists will shake off the yoke of the mother country, and erect themselves into a separate sovereignty, such a spirit being abundantly evident, even at present. They have not as yet the strength necessary for an undertaking of so great a magnitude; but none of the inclination is wanting, particularly since the home government has threatened to subject them to what they consider unjust taxation. Already the storm-cloud has began to show itself above the horizon, and we will venture to predict, the time is not far distant when it will overspread the heavens, and shower upon them all the horrors of family strife. A population composed, as this chiefly is, of the most turbulent and refractory, and of the self-exiled, who have been driven from their native land by misery and persecution, are not likely to remain long in patient subjection to a country which has been the source of their former misfortunes and disgraces, and with the recollections of which so much is mingled to awaken the bad feelings of the heart. They are constantly looking forward for the severance of the tie which binds their new home to the parent land. The vicious, because such characters hate and fear the power that has chastised them; and the unfortunate, because they anticipate from a longer connection a recurrence of their past adversity by an introduction of the same causes which had led to them in a country where the unassisted poor man, if he would not die of starvation, must plunge himself in crime. They know well that when the majority is nearly on a footing with regard to wealth, chances are great, that each will secure to himself a competency. In a community so circumstanced, the struggle is not with the overwhelming advantages of the rich, but with more surmountable obstacles. The road to affluence is denied to none, and success is dependent on a man's own exertions. He will soonest reach the goal who is most industrious and enterprising.

The town of Sydney* is in the most flourishing condition, trade is extending and becoming more and more profitable, and emigration flowing into the colony with an enlarging current, and composed of individuals of that most useful class to a young colony—artizans, agriculturists, and such like.

The principal article of export is wool. Wheat ranks next in importance; but the crops are uncertain, owing to the long and severe droughts to which the country is liable some years. These, by the way, are most serious evils to the country, and one of the greatest checks to its advancement, and, unfortunately, irrigation cannot be resorted to as a substitute in consequence of the scarcity of fresh-water streams. The dry periods are sometimes so constant and protracted that every-

* Sydney is the capital of New South Wales, and contains about 25,000 inhabitants. The streets are well laid out, and are rapidly filling up with good houses constructed of brick. In the eastern part of the town is a large square, upon which are situated the Catholic Cathedral, the Church of St. James', and the offices of the Colonial Government; on the western quarter are extensive public grounds, and many handsome buildings.

thing becomes parched; all nature withers under their fiery influence; vegetables, plants, herbs, are destroyed, and the fields literally take fire. The ground becomes intensely heated, and the fine dust is whirled into the air in such vast clouds that the wayfarer is threatened with the same fate that sometimes befalls the unlucky traveler in the deserts of Africa. These are times which distress not only the grain-merchant, but the market generally. Agriculture becomes almost neglected, flocks and herds suffer for the want of sustenance, and are no longer driven, and inland traveling is rendered difficult; hence the supply of wool, provisions, and indeed of every marketable commodity, is most sadly diminished.

In the course of time, when the wool-trade ceases to be as attractive as now, no longer holding out such allurements to the seekers after wealth, many articles will enter into exportation which are as yet but little attended to by agriculturists and manufacturers. Wine will probably be one of the number, the soil and climate being admirably adapted to the cultivation of the grape, of which a great abundance is annually raised.

With respect to mineral resources, this country is not without them. Lead and iron have been found in considerable quantities. Coal is plentiful, and used most extensively, as well for comfort in cold weather as for manufacturing and other purposes. It is inflammable, but emits an exceedingly disagreeable smell, and before the appearance of flame throws out an immense deal of smoke. As the country becomes explored other minerals* will be discovered, which may be expected to form materials for future prosperity.

* I see by the last accounts from Sydney that both copper and gold have been discovered, and the former is said to be of a very superior quality. At Mount Alexander a piece of gold was found, weighing 58 oz. 18 dwts

At present but little is known of the internal parts of the island of New Holland. Exploration has been carried but to a small extent, owing principally to the difficulties attendant upon traveling. Water and food cannot always be procured, and the natives are hostile. The trifling knowledge that has been obtained of this region, shows it to be one of the most peculiar in the world—distinct from others, not only in its general character, but many individual features, producing trees, plants, &c., and several kinds of animated creatures which are totally unlike those found elsewhere; for instance, we have cherries growing with their stones outside; trees which shed their bark instead of their leaves; black swans, white eagles, quadrupeds with birds' bills, and crabs of an ultra-marine color.*

The human occupants† of the land even are not without their singularities. There is, perhaps, no race of people

* Of the 70,000 or 80,000 species of plants described by botanists, 5,710 are already known to exist in Australia; of these only 270 are common to it and to other countries, while 5,440 are altogether peculiar to its extrordinary soil. Thus, this island contributes to botany nearly a twelfth of the plants known; but they are generally of a very low order. Ferns, nettles, flowers, and grasses, having the form, bulk and habits of trees, are abuudant. No dense woods have been found, and the groves, from a peculiar arrangement of their foliage, present a strange appearance, many of the trees having their leaves hanging with the edge downwards. Flowering plants of excessive beauty are found; and the lily, tulip and honeysuckle grow to the size of a large standard tree. In the interior immense numbers of prickly plants cover the ground, binding down the loose soil, and preventing the drift which distiuguishes the deserts of Arabia and Africa from the Australian wastes. The zoology of this region also presents extraordinary features. The number of known species of mamalia is about one thousand; fifty-eight are found in Australia, of which forty-six are peculiar to it, leaving twelve only which it contains in common with other regions. Even of these, five are whales and four seals; another is the strong-winged bat of Madagascar; another, like the jerboa of America; and the last, the dog—the animal found always where man exists, and rarely, if ever, where he does not. Kangaroos, however, are almost the only important animal. In the birds and reptiles similar peculiarities exist.

† The people who inhabit this extraordinary region belong to the Ethiopic, which is the lowest family of the human race. Many writers with great ingenuity have

known to whom they can be compared; all would suffer by the comparison. A resemblance may be traced between them and certain tribes of negroes in Africa; the complexion is the same—if anything, blacker—the shape of the head and some of the features similar, but the countenance far more hideous; in fact, imagination cannot conceive the extent of their ugliness. Perfectly satanic in appearance, one fancies himself in the midst of a horde of sooty imps just escaped from the dominions of his cloven-footed majesty. They are generally tall and shapeless, with exceedingly slender limbs that have scarce even the ordinary enlargements occasioned by the muscles. Their manner of living, habits and customs, are those of a people plunged in the lowest depths of barbarism, and showing but a slight superiority over the beasts of the field. They do not settle in communities for mutual protection and benefit, but roam at large over the country, supporting themselves as they best can upon what chance throws in their way—sometimes upon fruits and berries, and even roots, and sometimes upon snakes and whatever animals they succeed in ensnaring. They do not even build huts, but

attempted to trace the original colonization of Australia to a horde of Malays passing over in canoes from the Indian Archipelago, across Torres's Straits to the unknown southern land. The color of the skin, however, the formation of the skull and the limbs, with the genius, the habits, and the general character of the Australians identify them with the negro race of New Guinea. The weapons they employ are similar, and their progress in the industrial arts, as well as their mental qualities and condition of existence, being infinitely lower than those of the Malay, and closely similar to those of the Papuan, destroy the theory of their Malan origin. Traditions they have few, and those but faint and incoherent. It is probable, however, that the wild savages of the Indian Archipelago, driven from their original homes by the superior civilization of the Malays, put to sea in rude canoes, and reaching the mysterious southern land, debarked, and gradually peopled the wilderness. They left their own rich islands to the conquering Malays, deserting a contested heritage for one where security and peace made up for the loss of a soil spontaneously productive. That infusion of other blood has taken place is probable, but not to such an extent as to have influenced the character of the population.

shelter themselves from the inclemencies of the weather under decayed trees. In truth, they are a strange race; and the greatest wonder is that there should be so great a dissimilarity between them and the natives of the surrounding islands—not only are they altogether unlike in personal appearance, but in every other respect. Most of the other islanders have light brown complexions, strait hair, and are handsome and active—live together in villages, under the government of something like bands, and in the internal arrangement of their huts, manner of living, &c., exhibit quite a correct idea of domestic comfort; but these, on the contrary, lead a life literally that of wild animals.

Both sexes have the disgusting practice of rubbing fish oil into their skins; but they are compelled to do this as a protection against mosquitoes, which are very large and bite with much severity. Some of them have been seen with the entrails of fish frying in the burning sun upon their heads until the oil ran down over their foreheads. On particular occasions they besmear themselves with red and white clay, using the former when preparing to fight—the latter, when going to have their dances. The women are subjected to mutilation of the two first joints of the little finger of the left hand. This operation is performed when they are very young, and is done, it is said, under the idea that these joints of the little finger are in the way when they wind their fishing lines over the hand. While fishing the women sing. Those who occupy the sea-coast live chiefly on fish, which they roast, for they are ignorant of the effect of fire upon water. A story is told of a shipwrecked sailor, who obtained among them the reputation of a sorcerer, by boiling a potfull of water.

The men do not confine themselves to one wife, but live with two or three; though it has been observed that the first wife claims a superiority of attachment, and an exclusive right to the conjugal embraces, while the second, or the one last chosen, was compelled to be the drudge and slave of both.

Between the ages of ten and twelve, both males and females undergo the operation which they call *Inaonoong*, viz., that of having the nose perforated to receive a reed or bone, which by them is considered a great ornament. It is a common practice, also, to gash their bodies and to knock out one or two of their front teeth. An English trader once made a large profit by selling in London a quantity of these teeth for the use of the dentists.

Their habits are unsociable; they talk very little even among themselves, and never permit any one to joke or laugh with them. Nor is their character more alluring in other respects; to lie, cheat, and steal are practices almost universal, and owners of sheep, and isolated settlers often suffer from their depredations. This is not because they do not know any better, for their ideas of property are very distinct, and they never steal from one another. They are proud and insolent, and nothing will induce them to acknowledge any human being as their superior, or to show any marks of respect. They address the settlers without the Mr. prefixed to their names; and on entering a room, they never salute or remain standing, but immediately seat themselves. Jealousy is a prominent feature in the character of the men. The husband who suspects another of seducing his wife, either kills one or both. The affair is taken up by the tribe, if the party belongs to another, and the manner in which it is settled is as follows:—the guilty person is furnished with a shield,* and the

* The native name for this shield is *Nicklemara*. It is made of the bark of the gum-tree, and has an oval shape.

whole tribe which he has insulted, cast their spears at him—the first throw being made by the member most injured.

Their mode of making war is peculiar. The aggrieved tribe assemble and consult relative to the course to be pursued. This having been decided on, a messenger is dispatched to announce their intention to commence hostilities to the opposite party, and fix upon a day for the combat. The latter immediately proceed to make all the necessary preparations for the approaching contest; and on the day assigned, both parties take the field, accompanied by the women. The first onset is made by the oldest woman abusing and taunting the opposite side. Then a warrior or two advance, and commence throwing spears at each other. This exchange of missiles continues sometimes for a whole day, and generally ends without any fatal consequences, for the warriors are picked men, and are celebrated for their skill in avoiding missiles with their shields. When a warrior of either party is killed, the fight ceases, explanations are made, and the parties meet amicably to bury the dead; after which they all join in the performance of a dance called *Corrobory*.

They make use of two weapons which we have not seen elsewhere—the *Dundernel* and the *Boomereng*. The former has a flat curved handle, about two feet in length, and in its general appearance resembles a hatchet. It is thrown from the hand before coming to close quarters. The Boomereng is a flat stick, three feet long and two inches wide, crooked in the centre, forming an angle of fifty degrees. It is an implement used both for war and in the chase, and can be thrown by the natives with great precision.

As might be expected, a people so ignorant as the Australians, must also be very superstitious. When the wind groans over the hills, they imagine it to be the voice of an evil spirit, and build fires about their habitations to drive the evil one away. A grave placed before the door of a house is a safeguard against thieves. When beneath a rock they will not whistle, because they say this will cause the rock to fall upon them; of thunder and lightning, they are likewise much afraid, and believe that by chanting certain words and breathing hard they can dispel it.

Of their opinions with respect to a future state we had very defective information. They spoke of some place which they believed to be the abode of the dead, but we could not learn that they had any idea of rewards and punishments. Their ideas of a deity are distinct—they believe in a being who is all powerful, who created themselves and their country, and delights in giving them all the good things of this world which they enjoy.

There are other English settlements in New Holland besides that of New South Wales, but as our ships did not visit them, I am unable to give any detailed description of them.

CHAPTER X.

> " Uptorn, reluctant, from its oozy cave,
> The ponderous anchor rises o'er the wave."

ANTARCTIC CRUISE.

DECEMBER 26th. At an early hour this morning the squadron sailed from Sydney, on an exploring cruise in the Antarctic Ocean.

We have not visited a place since we left the United States with which we have been so well pleased, as the capital of New South Wales. We received the most marked attention while on shore, and had daily invitations from the inhabitants to partake of their hospitalities. His Excellency the Governor sought an early opportunity to invite Captain Wilkes and a number of the other officers, to come and spend several days with him at his residence in Paramatta. The officers of the 50th Regiment gave us a splendid dinner, and the Australian Club another. In short, everything was done, both by the authorities and citizens, to render our visit a pleasant one.

December 27th and 28th. During these two days nothing of much interest occurred. In the afternoon of the 27th we saw several albatrosses, and during the night the sea appeared uncommonly phosphorescent. Our observations place us in latitude 36° 48′ 00″ south, and 151° 00′ 00″ east. The wind is from the eastward, and the weather is pleasant.

December 29th. The mechanics have been engaged this day in securing the ship from the cold, boisterous weather which we may very soon expect to encounter. The hatches have had casings built around them, furnished with doors, the seams of the ports are caulked and covered with tarred canvas and sheet-lead, and a stove has been put up on the gun-deck, which is to answer the double purpose of warming the ship and drying the wet clothing. The temperature of the ship is, I understand, to be regulated by a thermometer, and is never to be higher than 50°, in order that the crew may be compelled to take exercise, which is very necessary in cold latitudes. The weather continues pleasant, and the nights are beautifully clear and starlight. We are now in latitude 38° 35′ 00″ south, and longitude 150° 55′ 00″ east.

January 2d. There has been a great change in the appearance and feeling of the weather within the last twenty-four hours. The horizon looks threatening, and it is cold enough to make one feel the want of an overcoat. Owing to the heavy mist which prevailed during the night, we lost sight of the schooner "Flying Fish," and we have spent a large portion of this day in looking for her, but without success. This has compelled us to steer for Macquarie Island, the first appointed place for the squadron to meet in the event of a separation.

January 3d. The fog continues very thick, and we have reason to believe that we have separated from the "Peacock," as we have not seen her since this morning. Two guns were fired about noon, in hopes that she might hear us. According to our observations, we are in latitude of 49° 25′ 00″ south, and 159° 18′ 00″ east. The weather grows cold, and the wind blows fresh from the northward and eastward.

January 4th and 5th. During these two days we have had much rain, accompanied with thunder and lightning. A vast number of Port Egmont hens, petrils, and albatrosses, and one or two seals have been seen. The fog has prevented our obtaining any astronomical observations for ascertaining our position. The wind is still blowing fresh from the northeast.

January 7th. We have been trying all this day to reach Macquarie Island, supposed to be about thirty miles to windward of us. But the wind, weather and current being against us, we have been obliged to give it up, and are now steering for Emerald Island, our second rendezvous. During the greater part of the forenoon the mist was so dense that we were unable to see the "Porpoise," although she was not more than six hundred yards from us. The temperature now is below 40°. Our observations make the latitude to be 54° 17′ 38″ south, and longitude 160° 58′ 00″ east. Since sunset the wind has moderated, and the sky appears much more promising than it has done for some days past.

January 9th. This morning we passed the locality given on the chart to Emerald Island, but saw nothing of it. We therefore concluded that the chart is incorrect. A great number of gray petrils have been seen, and we have also passed several patches of kelp. The barometer stands at 30.00 inches, but the thermometer has fallen to 32°, and the atmosphere is very raw.

January 10th. We encountered to-day, for the first time, several icebergs and some drift-ice; the former were several miles in circumference, but there was nothing very striking in their shape. The sea beat against their sides, and produced a noise similar to that made by breakers. A dense fog has succeeded to the clear weather we had yesterday. Our latitude is 61° 07′ 00″ south, longitude 162° 32′ 00″ east.

January 11th. There has been a great number of icebergs in sight this day. We estimate several to be five miles long and three hundred feet in height. They all had flat tops, with sides full of cavities, caused by the waves dashing against them.

About 9 P. M., we passed to the eastward of a point of field-ice,* which proved to be the edge of a "barrier;" stood in to the southward until 10.35 P. M., when we found ourselves completely embayed, having solid ice as far as could be seen from the mast-heads, except to the northward. We are now "hove-to" to wait for daylight. The barometer continues to stand at 30.00 inches, though the wind has hauled around to the westward, and the temperature is two degrees colder than yesterday. According to our observations the latitude is 64° 10′ 00″ south, and longitude 164° 31′ 00″ east.

January 13th. At early dawn we made sail, and commenced to work along the "barrier" to the westward. About 9 P. M., it being very foggy, we lost sight of the "Porpoise," and have not seen her since. The temperature is now 30°, and our decks and rigging are covered with ice. A great number of icebergs have been seen, and owing to the thickness of the weather, we came very near running into several. The latitude by "dead reckoning" at meridian was 64° 08′ 00″ south, longitude 165° 27′ 00″ east.

January 14th. The weather continues thick and disagreeable, but the wind has shifted to the northward and westward. About noon the fog lifted for a short time, and we counted sixty icebergs in sight. They excited much curiosity, as they presented a magnificent spectacle. Every fantastic form and variety of tint was there. Masses, assuming the shape of a Gothic church, with arched windows and doors, and all the rich drapery of that style, composed, apparently, of crystal, showing all the shades of opal, or of emerald green; pillars and inverted cones, pyramids and mounds of every shape,

* A piece of ice so large that its extent cannot be seen.

valleys and lakes, domes supported by round transparent columns of cerulian hue, and cities and palaces as white as the purest alabaster. The liveliest imagination could not paint to itself a scene more rich and grand, and we stood gazing at it with astonishment and admiration until it was again enveloped in the fog.

January 16th. Towards noon the wind shifted to the northward, and at 8 P. M., to the southward and eastward, when it also became very light. Weather, during the first part, thick; during the latter part, mild and pleasant. In the afternoon sounded with 250 fathoms line—no bottom. Temperature at that depth 31°, the same as at the surface. During the day passed through great quantities of drift ice; saw several whales, a seal, and a great number of snow-birds. Latitude at noon 66° 00′ 02″ south, longitude 156° 02′ 00″ east.

January 17th. Commenced with light airs from the southward, and thick weather. Lay-to from 1 to 3.30 A. M., when it cleared off. At 4 P. M. the wind shifted again to the westward. At 6.15 P. M. we descried two sail—one to windward and the other to leeward—proved to be the "Peacock" and "Porpoise;" passed several icebergs of a pinnacle-shape. We have now reached the latitude of 66° 26′ 00″ south, and our nights are only four hours long. The weather has become more mild since the fog has disappeared, and being able to see our way among the ice-islands, we are making a fine progress.

January 19th. Yesterday nothing worthy of notice transpired. This morning we found ourselves in a large bay; the "Peacock" was in sight, and appeared to be standing to the westward. The water has a green appearance, but we have not been able to obtain bottom. It is believed by many of us that we are in the vicinity of land; saw, in the course of the afternoon, several whales, and a flock of petrels of a species different from any heretofore observed by us. For the past three hours appearances have been visible both to the southeast and southwest which very much resemble mountains.*

January 20th. Last night we witnessed a magnificent Aurora Australis. It rose in the south—a sort of semi-arch of light—and then across the heavens in almost every direction, darted columns of a luminous character. The light was so bright that we could see to read the finest print with ease. In half an hour it had all disappeared. The weather is still mild. Saw several sperm-whales, and a flock of ice-pigeons, of which we were fortunate enough to obtain specimens.

January 22d. At 3 P. M. the wind came out from the southward. Towards noon we stood along a line of icebergs, the surface of which was of a yellowish color. We also remarked about the same time, that the water had become very much discolored. A flock of ducks were also seen. Latitude in at noon 66° 12′ 26″ south, longitude 149° 44′ 00″ east. Temperature of air 25°, water 31°. After sunset the wind shifted again to the southward and westward.

January 23d. The weather continues mild and pleasant. At 12.30 P. M. tacked ship to the southward and eastward to clear the "barrier" of ice, which bore east-by-south. At 2 P. M. a large, deep bay showed itself to the southward, which we entered, and soon after observed appearances of land, both to the eastward and westward. By midnight we again reached the "barrier," and therefore were compelled to stand back. Numerous birds were seen about the ship.

* The same appearances were observed by the "Peacock" and the "Porpoise," and it is now fully established that they were high land, and formed a part of the Antarctic continent discovered by the Expedition.

January 25th. To-day the crew has been employed in filling up the tanks with ice, obtained from an iceberg which was towed alongside. Those who have used the water procured by this method, represent it as being of an excellent quality. Each piece was allowed to remain on deck some time for the salt water to drain off. In the afternoon we landed on the solid ice, and took some magnetic observations. We are once more steering to the southward. Latitude in at noon 67° 04′ 37″ south, longitude 147° 42′ 00″ east. Temperature of air 26°, water 29°.

January 28th. During these twenty-four hours we fell in with the "Porpoise," and communicated with her. We found both officers and crew well and in good spirits. We received from her some specimens—among others the skins of two sea-elephants. The wind is now blowing fresh from the southward and eastward, and the weather has again become very thick. The cold is intense, and coffee has been served to the crew at the commencement of each watch, which is found very warming and refreshing.

January 29th. The weather continues unfavorable. At 9.45 A. M., the fog lifted, and we again discovered high land a-head. We steered for it by the most open route, but after a run of about forty miles, we were obliged to retrace our course. We found ourselves beset by ice-islands and floe-ice,* while at times the fog was so dense that the largest objects could not be seen through it. At 10 P. M., the wind blew very fresh, and we had many narrow escapes. We passed so near several of the bergs, that we could distinctly hear the waves dashing against their sides. Latitude in by "dead reckoning" 65° 28′ 00″ south; longitude 140° 45′ 00″ east. Temperature of air 28°. We are now hove-to, it being too dark to run.

* A piece of ice of considerable size, but the extent of which can be distinguished.

January 30th. Early this morning we discovered more land to the southward and westward. It was several thousand feet high, and extended to the east and west as far as the eye could reach. We steered for it under all sail, intending, if possible, to effect a landing upon some part of its coast; but by 8 o'clock we reached the icy barrier, and thus were the third time compelled to turn back. How very provoking! We found our latitude to be, when nearest to the barrier, 66° 38′ 00″ south; longitude 140° 00′ 00″ east. Depth of water was twenty-five fathoms—the color, a yellowish cast, or dirty green. Two ledges, composed of volcanic rock, were distinctly seen; we also observed some columns bearing south, which had the appearance of volcanic smoke. To the westward of our position were numerous icebergs, which appeared to be aground. In the course of the afternoon, the wind, which in the morning had been moderate, freshened to a gale; and, by 6 o'clock, we called all hands, and reduced sail to a close-reefed main-topsail and fore-storm staysail. The cold is very severe, and a number of the "look outs" have been badly frozen.

January 31st. There is no improvement in the weather.

February 1st. Last night the gale abated, and we are now favored with mild, pleasant weather. How grateful this feels after the stormy scenes we have passed through within the last forty-eight hours! Our sick-list the last week has been very large. The fleet-surgeon attributes it to the climate, and has recommended to Captain Wilkes to return north.* Many of the men are affected with boils, which renders them almost useless. Rheumatic affections are also exceedingly prevalent.

February 3d. On this day we experienced another severe storm.

* This recommendation was not listened to.

During the 4th, 5th, and 6th, the weather continued unfavorable.

On the 7th, we had clear weather and made very good progress. The Antarctic Continent was several times in sight in the course of the day, and a point of it, situated in latitude 65° 48′ 00″ south, and longitude 131° 40′ 00″ east, was named Cape Carr, after the first-lieutenant of this ship. The health of the crew is improving.

February 11th. We had moderate breezes from the southward and westward, accompanied with snow at intervals. Great numbers of penguins and petrels seen about the ship; also a flock of birds, about the size of a gray plover, having black heads and bills, a white ring round the neck, and a small white spot on the tail—the rest of the body of a pale ash color; their flight and whistle were also similar to the plover. The continent was in sight to the westward, and the sea quite smooth and studded with icebergs of every variety of shape. During the night we hove-to, it being very dark.

February 12th. At 8 A. M., we made sail. At 1 P. M., observed a range of mountains covered with snow, for which we steered until we came to the barrier of ice. From 2 to 4.30 P. M., we "lay-to," in hopes of discovering an opening by which we could get near the land; but none appeared. As usual, the barrier was formed of solid ice, and its line was nearly straight. Our latitude was 64° 56′ 00″ south; longitude 112° 17′ 00″ east. At 4.45 sounded with 150 fathoms line—thermometer attached—temperature at that depth 29°, at the surface 30°. The color of the water was dirty green. Current there was none. At sunset land was still in sight, bearing from southwest-by-south to west half-north.

February 14th. The weather continues pleasant. At daylight worked up for the clearest passage, and stood in for the continent among large brash-ice,* until 11.30 A. M., when the masses of ice became so thick as to render all further approach impossible. We were compelled to put the helm up and wear ship, picking our way out through passages not more than thirty feet in width. We saw distinctly from sixty to seventy miles of coast, and a mountain in the interior, which we estimated to be 2,500 feet in height. At 1 P. M., we effected a landing on an iceberg, and found imbedded in it sand, gravel, and rocks. These last were several feet in circumference, and composed of basalt and red sandstone. Many of the smaller stones were brought on board, and they very soon disappeared, for every one was anxious to possess themselves of a piece of the *new continent.* There is no doubt in my mind, but that this mass of ice had once been a part of the icy barrier, and that the surface now exposed to view had rested on the bottom of the sea. Many species of zoophytes were seen about the berg. At 5 P. M., the boat returned, leaving on the ice a flag flying, with a bottle containing orders for the "Peacock" and "Porpoise," which vessels we have not seen for the past three weeks. When the boat was secured, we again filled away, and stood to the westward. We have now reached the longitude of 105° 30′ 00′ east. Temperature of air 26°, water 30°.

February 15th. This morning the wind hauled to the southward and westward, and ever since the weather has been cloudy and snowy. All the ice seen to-day has been discolored, more or less, by what appeared to be mud and gravel. Numerous whales, seals and penguins have been about the ship.

January 17th. Last night another display of the Aurora

* Ice in a broken state, and in such small pieces that the ship can easily force through.

Australis was observed to the northward and westward. It reached to the zenith, the light shooting across the heavens in columns 40° or 50° broad, of a light-yellow color, slightly tinged with red, and moving very rapidly from east towards west. So brilliant and remarkable was the phenomenon, that almost every person in the ship came on deck to witness it. The star Canopus was in the zenith at the time, and its brightness appeared much diminished.

At 2 P. M. we landed on an iceberg, upon which were found more stones. Upon it were also found a vast number of penguins, and several were captured and their skins preserved for the government. They made a stout resistance, biting and striking those who seized them with their powerful flippers. One of them was a king penguin, and he could only be taken by knocking him down with a boat-hook. His height was 22 inches, and the circumference of the body 45 inches. He was a showy-looking bird, his head being adorned with bright yellow feathers, resembling a graceful plume. We also saw in the afternoon a sea-elephant, and we tried our best to kill him, by firing into him no less than sixteen musket balls, but he seemed not to mind them, and finally disappeared. Appearances of land have also been seen this day. The health of the crew continues to improve.

February 20th. We have now light breezes from the westward. At 3.30 A. M. made the barrier a-head, and on the weather-bow kept off and set all sail. At 4 one hundred icebergs were counted in sight from aloft. At 6 made the barrier again, bearing southwest-by-west; shortened sail, and hauled on a wind. At 11.30 lowered a boat to try the current, but found none; at the same time sounded with 850 fathoms line—no bottom ; temperature at that depth 35°, at the surface 31°. Our longitude at noon was 101° 46′ 00″

east, latitude 62° 08′ 05″ south. The sea is quite smooth, and the surface is covered with shrimps.

February 21st. This morning Captain Wilkes announced to the officers and crew his intention to bear-up and return north. The intelligence was received with much rejoicing, for we all felt worn out with fatigue and exposure. He also called aft all hands, and thanked them for the assistance they afforded him, and in addition he promised the sailors that he would use his utmost exertions to obtain extra pay for them.

On the 11th of March, at 1.30 P. M., we again dropped our anchor at Fort Macquarie, Sydney. Here we found the "Peacock." She arrived a few days before, and was now undergoing repairs, having sustained heavy damages during her late cruise by coming in contact with large masses of ice. We also heard here of the arrival at Hobart Town, Van Dieman's Land, of the French Expedition,* commanded by Admiral D'Urville.

We remained at Sydney until the 19th of March. We then took our departure for New Zealand, where we arrived after a pleasant passage of eleven days. The "Peacock" received orders to follow as soon as her repairs were completed.

* In 1837 the French Government sent out an Expedition under Rear-Admiral D'Urville, an eminent explorer, who had already made three voyages round the world. Two corvettes, the "Astrolabe" and "Zeleé," sailed from Toulon, and by the end of the year had followed Waddell's track in the Antarctic Seas until they were stopped by the ice between the 63d and 64th parallels. On three occasions an entrance was forced into it, but they were driven back each time, and forced to return. After a protracted cruise in Polynesia and the Indian Archipelago, D'Urville resolved to make another attempt to get to the south, and touched at Hobart Town in a distressed condition, having lost three officers and thirteen men by dysentery. He sailed January 1st, 1840, his special aim being to approach or reach the magnetic or terrestial pole. On the 21st he was surrounded by numerous ice-islands, and saw a lofty line of coast covered with snow, stretching from southwest to northwest, apparently without limit. With some difficulty a landing was effected, and not being aware of our discovery two days before, possession was taken in the name of France, and the land was called La Terra Adélie, after the wife of the discoverer.

CHAPTER XI.

NEW ZEALAND.*

On the morning of the 30th of March, having made New Zealand, we tacked ship and by 10.30 P. M., "came to" in the Bay of Islands in five fathoms water. Both the "Porpoise" and the "Flying Fish" were found at anchor here. The former reported that, after parting from us, she coasted along the solid barrier of ice several hundred miles, seeking in vain for an opening by which to approach the land beyond the barrier; that she passed many icebergs in which were imbedded gravel and boulders; also, that she fell in with the French exploring squadron, and attempted to speak with the admiral's ship ("Astrolabe"), but when they had almost reached her, she tacked ship and stood away—thereby declining any communication.

The "Flying Fish" experienced very severe weather, by which her safety was much endangered, but she did not discover any land. The Bay of Islands is very capacious, and affords excellent anchorage to vessels of all classes. It is studded with many islands, and hence the name. These islands are of a very irregular figure, and destitute of vegetation. The bay has been surveyed several times by the French, and we believe very thoroughly. It is ten miles from head to

* The two islands that go by the name of New Zealand are situated between the latitude 34° 22′ 00″ and 47° 25′ 00″ south, and between the longitude 166° 00′ 00″ and 180° 00′ 00″ east.

head. The shores are divided into steep cliffs and heads, with intermediate beaches. Its anchorages are numerous, but those which are now more generally used are the River Rawa Kawa and the Bay of Kororakia; they are preferred on account of the convenience they afford for watering, repairing, and communicating with the shore.

The adjacent country is hilly, and much more barren than productive, the soil containing too great a quantity of clay to be good. The vegetation consists of fern, a few stunted trees and patches of brush, close-set, and almost impenetrable. The soil in the interior of the island is richer, and produces various natural productions,* some of which are extremely valuable. The flax-plant, which is indigenous, meets the eye in every direction. It is converted by the natives to a variety of purposes. It supplies them with excellent materials for clothing, cordage, and fishing-nets, and the preparation being simple, requires very little trouble.

There are many English and some French who have settled in this part of New Zealand. They are mostly ship-carpenters and farmers. They live in houses built in the European style, and cultivate corn, potatoes,† onions, &c., &c., for which they always find a ready market among the shipping.

Pahia, the Episcopal mission establishment, is situated on the west side of the Bay, and commands a beautiful water-prospect, and is the residence of all those connected with the mission. About five miles further toward the north is the site chosen by the British government‡ for the future City of

* Pines are here to be met with soaring to a height which leaves no similarity between them and the tallest that ever grow on the pine-lands of the United States. Here are also several kinds of trees admirably well adapted for ornamental work.

† The potato was introduced by Captain Cook. It has been cultivated ever since his visit, and is now very abundant.

‡ A few weeks previous to our arrival at the Bay of Islands, Captain Hobson, of the Royal Navy, called a meeting of all the principal chiefs, and effected a treaty

Victoria. It is not a pleasant location, nor is the anchorage as good as some others in the bay.

The Aborigines of New Zealand are of good size, well formed, and have fine eyes, but their noses are inclined to be flat, the nostrils large and thin, and their mouths wide. Both men and women have their faces elaborately tattooed, which gives them a striking appearance. Their hair is straight, coarse, and black. The complexion varies from dark olive to copper-color. Their dress formerly consisted of mats made of flax and skins, but now they generally wear trowsers and jackets; some wear hats, but we saw none who made use of shoes. The females wear a loose petticoat made of blue nankeen or calico. They all have their ears bored, and wear ear-rings made of sharks' teeth, tipped with small bright-colored feathers. The chiefs and their wives wear round their necks what is termed "heitiki,"* an ornament which the common people are not permitted to use, and which is handed down from father to son. Fish, potatoes and shells constitute the chief articles of their diet. Meat they seldom or never use, except on important occasions. Their fishing-tackle does not differ materially from that which is used by the Tahitians and Samoa people. When a party has fixed upon a place where they intend to haul the seine, they taboo† it—that is, they prohibit others from fishing upon the same place. When they take a greater number of fish than they can consume at once, they

with them, which made a cession of their lands, authority and persons to Queen Victoria. We were told by the French and American residents that at first a large number of chiefs were opposed to the treaty, but had been gained over by presents of powder and rum.

Since the above was writen, the whole island has passed into the hands of England, and Lord Derby's administration conferred upon the colonists a free constitution.

* The Heitiki is made of a stone of a green color found on the borders of a small lake, called Terrai Pounamu.

† The Taboo laws are strictly observed, even among those who have become Christians, and are always resorted to, to protect their property.

dry them on hot stones, by which means they keep a long time. That they may better protect themselves against their enemies, they build their villages on the tops of the highest hills, and surround them with palisades and trenches. They are said to have improved in the construction of their houses, but there is still great room for improvement; they are yet small, low, and very filthy. Their furniture consists of a few mats and baskets, an old sea-chest and an iron pot or two, in which they cook their food.

The New Zealanders are industrious, compared with most of the South Sea Islanders. They cultivate a surplus of provisions for sale, cut timber, clean flax, raise pigs, poultry, &c., &c. They also ship as sailors on board of whalers* and other vessels, which may stand in need of their services. They are apt in learning the names of the rigging, and are very active aloft.

In disposition they are zealous, revengeful, and cunning; but, on the other hand, they are hospitable and generous to strangers. Their courage is not to be questioned. Their wars often last till one or the other of the parties are exterminated, and it is said that the horrible custom of feasting on the flesh of their prisoners is still practised by the tribes who occupy the interior of the island. These wars are oftentimes occasioned by the bad conduct of single individuals, their crimes being charged to the whole tribe to which they may belong. The tribes who live about the Bay of Islands are well acquainted with the use of money. They are also well acquainted with fire-arms, and in their conflicts prefer them to the weapons of their own manufacture, which consist of spears

* Whales are very numerous about New Zealand, and a great number of vessels resort there to engage in the whaling business. The American vessels alone amount to seventy or eighty a year

and clubs. Both sexes are addicted to rum-drinking and tobacco-chewing—bad practices—which, no doubt, they have acquired from the convicts and other low whites who have settled among them. Suicide is very common among all the tribes. A woman who is badly treated by her husband will immediately go and hang herself. This is also frequently done at the death of a near relative.

Their laws are simple, clear, and few in number. The most important ones are those which concern the division of land. The lower classes are perfectly subordinate to their superiors, whom they style Etakatika and Epoda. Here is a mode of government entirely analogous to that which prevails in the islands of the Indian Seas, where the chief authority is vested in the Rajah, whose rank resembles that of the Areekee of New Zealand, and who commands the services of the pangeran or heads of the dusums, or villages. These latter correspond exactly with the subordinate chiefs above mentioned, and like them they acknowledge a superior, though, with respect to their possessions, they are independent of his control.

The religious belief of those who have not embraced Christianity is as follows:—That they are surrounded by invisible spirits, who must be conciliated by prayers and ceremonies, as they have power over the elements, and can at any time raise the wind and waves against them. They also believe their priests to be prophets, who can foretell future events, which they (the priests themselves) pretend have been communicated to them directly from some genii, or spirits, which supposed to have taken them under their especial care.

A few days after our arrival, Pomare, the chief of the town of Para, paid us a visit. He came off in a war-canoe, and was attended by forty of his people, men and women. He was a tall, well-formed man, and I should judge about

35 years of age. His dress consisted of a blue naval cap, with a gold-lace band, a blanket tied around his neck, leaving his right arm free, a shirt, and a pair of trowsers; his feet were bare. In his hand he carried a short cloak, made of dog-skins, dressed with the hair on—it is his state-dress. His face is handsomely tattooed, though its expression is not a pleasing one. He is a great beggar, and as great a drunkard, and is said to openly carry on the infamous traffic in women. The females who accompanied him to the ship were, I was informed, his wives, and one or two of them were quite good-looking. When about to leave the ship, Captain Wilkes made him a present of a cutlass, with which he appeared much pleased, and which he handed over to his favorite wife for safe keeping.

During our stay at the Bay of Islands, the mean temperature was 65°. The prevailing winds were from the southeast and west. From what I could learn by conversing with the foreign residents, the climate of New Zealand is best suited to a European constitution of any in the south seas. The aboriginal inhabitants are liable to rheumatism and consumption. The venereal disease is also very common among them, and from want of proper medical treatment, it but too fr quently

CHAPTER XII.

ISLAND OF TONGA.

On the 6th of April, at 10 A. M., the squadron sailed from New Zealand for the Friendly Islands.* It was a delightful day, and every one appeared in fine spirits. At 2.30 we discharged the pilot, and by sunset land was out of sight.

On the 13th the wind shifted to the southward and westward, and was accompanied with a rough sea, which caused the ship to roll heavily. We passed over the position assigned to Roseta Shoal, but could not find anything of it.

At daylight, April 14th, we made Sunday Island, but owing to the unfavorable state of the weather we did not attempt to land upon it. It is high and rugged, and showed no evidence of being inhabited by human beings.

During the 15th we communicated with the American whaler, named Tobacco Plant. She had been out two years, and during that time had captured only seven whales. The following night was a very clear one, and many meteors were observed, some of which left broad, luminous tracks, that were visible for thirty seconds after the disappearance of the bodies.

On the 19th we saw a water-spout. It commenced forming about a third of a mile to the windward of the ship, and the water, for many yards in circumference, appeared in great agitation, flying up in jets to the height of forty or fifty feet.

* This cognomen was given to the Tonga Islands by Captain Cook, who experienced great kindness from the natives.

It had considerable motion, and crossed the ship's bows, but did not proceed more than two or three miles before it broke.

During the 21st we passed through large "fields of sperm-whale-feed," a scummy-looking substance, floating on the surface of the water, and of a color nearly red. It seems almost impossible that so immense an animal could subsist on food apparently containing so little nutriment. We were now in latitude 22° 45′ 00″ south, and longitude 174° 50′ 00″ east.

At 2 P. M. on the 24th we came-to off Nookualofa, the principal town of Tonga Island, and the station of the Wesleyan Mission. We found here the "Flying Fish," which had separated from us some days previous. The missionary gentlemen, Messrs. Tucker and Rabone, paid us a visit on the same afternoon, and from them we learned that the Christian and heathen parties were at war* with each other.

About sunset a large double canoe, filled with warriors, arrived. They belonged to the neighboring islands, Hapai and Vavao, and came to assist the Christian party. This was the first double canoe we had seen. It consisted of two canoes joined together by a deck thrown across them both. On the deck a small house was erected, which answered as a cabin; above the house was a square platform, with a rail around it. The mast was from forty to fifty feet in height, and carried a long yard, upon which was spread a triangular sail made of matting. It was steered by an oar. These canoes tack and wear in all weathers, are good sea-boats, and sail from eight to ten miles per hour.

April 25th. It is reported that eight heathen, or "Devils," and two Christians were killed last night in a skirmish, which

* During our stay at Nookualofa, Captain Wilkes did all in his power to restore peace between the parties, but without success, and I am sorry to add that the Christians were the authors of the principal difficulties thrown in his way.

took place between five hundred of the latter, who had gone out to work upon their yam-patches, and about an equal number of the heathen. These last out-numbered the Christians, but the latter are assisted by Yaufahau, or King George of Hapai and Vavao, who can bring in the field 800 fighting men.

About 10 A. M., Captain Wilkes, accompanied by several of the officers, left the ship to pay a visit to King Josiah, or Tubau, who resides at Nookualofa, and is the king of the Christian party. In the course of the afternoon another double-canoe arrived, having one hundred of King George's warriors on board. They were tall, fine-looking men, and all ready for meeting the enemy; some being armed with clubs, some with spears, and others with muskets. They had their faces painted in the most grotesque manner with yellow, red, black and white stripes. I saw several with a red nose, black cheeks, yellow chin, and green eyebrows.

April 28th. To-day several of the chiefs of the heathen party visited the ship. According to their statement the Christians are entirely in the fault. They assert that they did not commence the present war, but that they were forced into it by the Christians, who seemed determined to exterminate them unless they exchanged the belief of their fathers for that of the new religion. They also complained that the Christians endeavored to deprive them of their national amusements, by prohibiting dancing and singing.

In the afternoon I visited Nookualofa. It is pleasantly situated, and contains from five to six hundred houses. It is surrounded by an embankment composed of logs and earth, on the top of which is a wicker-fence; on the outside of the intrenchment is a ditch about twelve feet wide by six feet deep. There are three principal entrances, which are very narrow and low, and have loop-holes on either side, through which muskets may be fired in case of an attack. The buildings are of elliptical or circular form; they are divided into two or three apartments by matting or tapa screens, and those of the better class look clean and comfortable. The furniture consists of the ava-bowl,* a box containing all the valuables of the family, a pile or two of mats, serving both as beds and settees, and a few rolls of thin tapa, which the inmates use as a covering at night, and to protect them from the mosquitoes, which are not only very abundant, but extremely troublesome. The house of King Josiah is no larger nor better constructed than those of his subjects. All the women and children whom I saw were nearly white, and had pleasing features. It is the custom here for children of both sexes to go about in a state of nature. In the outskirts of the town I fell in with several young girls, who were employed in making tapa cloth. The mode of proceeding was as follows:—Each piece of bark was taken singly, and laid on a piece of wood fifteen or twenty feet long, six inches square, and smooth on the upper side. It was then beaten with a mallet of hard, heavy wood, about twenty inches in length by three inches wide, till the required extent and texture were produced. Three sides of this piece of wood are carved in ribs or grooves, in order that one mallet may answer for the different kinds of cloth that are made. Sometimes four or five pieces of bark are necessary to make one piece of cloth. When the cloth is made it is laid out in the sun, where it soon dries, and is ready for use. Two of these girls had European features, with jet-black locks, which almost

* The Ava is a root of a pungent and an intoxicating nature, with which the men are fond of indulging themselves. They employ young girls to chew it for them, and spit it into a wooden bowl used for no other purpose; after which a small quantity of water is added to it, when the juice is strained into cups made of cocoa nut-shells, and passed round among them. It has the effect of making the skin fall off in white scales, affects the nerves and appetite, and brings on a premature old age.

reached the ground. They were also very sociable, and gave me to understand by means of signs, that the tapa I saw them making, was intended as a bridal present to a near relative.

April 29th. At 2 P. M., the two kings, Josiah and George, came to the Observatory to pay a visit to Captain Wilkes. The latter is about forty years of age, and is a remarkably fine-looking man, being six feet and upwards in height, with regular features, a dignified mien, and a very intelligent face. His attire consisted simply of a large piece of white tapa wound round his waist in loose folds, hanging down to the feet, and leaving his arms and breast entirely bare. He is, as has already been observed, master of Hapai and Vavoa,* and no doubt he will ere long possess himself of Tonga, as King Josiah is represented as a very weak-minded old man, and caring little about the affairs of government. Their majesties were attended by about a hundred of their warriors, who were armed and painted after the manner of war. Previous to returning to Nookualofa, Captain Wilkes brought them on board the ship, and, after treating them to a lunch, he made them some presents in the name of the government. Josiah, or Tubou, is a son of Mumuz, who was king in the time of the celebrated Captain Cook. He is about sixty years of age, but he appears much older.

The two kings had scarcely left the ship, when one of the heathen who had been alongside for the purpose of trade, came running up to Lieutenant Case and begged him to get his canoe, which, he said, two of George's warriors had taken from him by force. The circumstance was reported by Captain Wilkes to King George, who immediately gave orders for the canoe to be returned to the owner.

* These islands are situated about thirty miles from Tonga, and are represented as being high, and subject to severe storms. The inhabitants are of the same extraction as the Tongese.

May 1st. At 11 this morning, the "Porpoise" arrived. In the afternoon we sent for the pilot. He came on board, but stated that he could not take us to sea, because he had been ordered by King George not to do so. Captain Wilkes told him that if such was the case he might leave the ship. He then gave orders for the vessels to get under-way, and anchor as near the town as possible. This being done, Lieutenant Case was sent to call on his majesty, and demand an explanation for his unfriendly behavior. In a few minutes, Mr. C. returned, and reported that King George was out fighting, but that he had seen King Josiah, who assured him that George had no desire to prevent our going to sea; that the pilot had told us a falsehood, and if Captain Wilkes wished it, he would have him punished. We are now convinced that King George knew nothing of the matter, and that the pilot's story was the result of fear, he having heard another pilot say that if the ship went ashore he would be hung. He therefore did not wish to have anything to do with us, and supposed by pretending to act under the orders of the king, we would not force him to take the vessel to sea.

May 2d. To-day King Josiah sent on board both his pilots, one of whom is a native of Tahiti and speaks very good English. Towards noon, a fine breeze sprung up from the northward and eastward. At 2 got under-way; shortly after the "Peacock" hove in sight—beat to windward until we joined company with her, when we stood for the western passage, and at 5.15 we anchored again.

May 3d. This being Sunday, at 10.30 divine service was performed as usual. At meridian, compared chronometers with the other vessels of the squadron. It is reported that we leave here to-morrow.

May 4th. During these twenty-four hours the wind has

been blowing from the southward and eastward, accompanied with rain at intervals. At an early hour the squadron got under-way and proceeded to sea.

I propose before I conclude this chapter, to make a few general remarks.

Tonga Island, or Tangataboo, was discovered by the Dutch about the middle of the seventeenth century, and was by them named Amsterdam. It is of coral formation, and has a lagoon, which extends about twelve miles into the interior.

The climate is not considered salubrious. The temperature is frequently 96° in the shade, and the transitions from heat to cold are sudden. Hurricanes prevail during the months of January, February and March; they vary in duration from twelve to twenty-four hours; and after a severe one, a famine generally follows, in which great numbers of the inhabitants die; they blow down trees and destroy all kinds of crops. The native name for them is "Afa hagi fagii," which signifies in English, the storm that throws down the trees and houses. The soil is very fertile, being composed of several feet in depth of vegetable mould, and is overgrown with a dense forest of cocoa-nut trees. The productions are yams, taro, bread-fruit, bananas, sugar-cane, shaddocks, oranges, and a species of nutmeg.

The inhabitants are probably of the same extraction as the natives of the Society Islands, Marquesas Islands, and the Navigator Group, since there is an evident resemblance in their manners, customs and language. The women are handsome and graceful in their manners. Those who have children show a remarkable tenderness for them, and pay the greatest attention to their wants.

They generally rise with the sun, and after having enjoyed the cool of the evening, retire to their repose a short time after sunset. The chiefs are occupied in making canoes and implements of war; the common people are chiefly employed in the cultivation of the soil and in fishing; and the women are engaged in the manufacture of cloths and mats. It is a common practice for parents to make a present of their children to chiefs, or others, who adopt them as their own. This custom gives the chiefs many adopted children, and tends to increase their influence and power. After the child is grown up, one-half of its earnings goes to its adopted parent. Rank descends altogether by the female line—hence, if a woman is noble, the children are also noble. No people respect old age more than the Tongese. Every aged man and woman employ the attention and services of the younger classes of people.

At Nookualofa, schools have been established; houses for stated religious worship erected; a printing-press put into operation, and books published in the native dialect; and the children are taught, both by the missionaries and native teachers, reading, writing, and the elementary principles of refined education.

They barter their commodities chiefly for whale's teeth, blue nankeen, tortoise-shell, glass beads, looking-glasses, cutlery and small axes. With the whales' teeth they decorate their spears and clubs, and make neck and ear ornaments. They are acquainted with the use of most of our tools, and prefer them in the construction of their houses and canoes to their own. For some years past considerable intercourse has been maintained with the natives of the Fejee Islands, which are situated about 350 miles from Nookualofa. The trade with American and European vessels is, I understand, very limited and precarious.

CHAPTER XIII.

FEJEE ISLANDS.

On the 6th of May, the second day out from Nookualofa, we made several of the southern islands of the Fejee Group, and sent the brig "Porpoise" to survey them. All these islands appeared high, woody, and picturesque. The weather during the night was very misty and disagreeable.

On the morning of the 8th, we reached the harbor of Levuka, the principal port of the Island of Ovolau. Great numbers of the natives had collected on the beach to witness our coming to anchor, and the sensation which the manœuvre created among them can be better imagined than described; it is no exaggeration to say, that for the next fifteen minutes it was impossible to hear our own voices, so loud and deafening were their shouts of admiration.

Levuka is a fine harbor, being capacious, easy of access, and perfectly safe. Soon after we came-to, a small cutter, belonging to the ship "Leonidas," of Salem, Mass., arrived and anchored. She had come to purchase provisions for the use of the ship, which was at anchor at one of the neighboring islands.

In the afternoon, the principal chief of Ovolau, accompanied by an American, named David Whippy, came on board to welcome us. Our countryman told us the chief had a great number of names, but he was best known by that of Levuka. He is a middle-aged man, of a good height, strong and well-proportioned. The color of his skin was nearly black, and he was entirely naked, except about the loins and head. The latter was enveloped in rolls of very thin white tapa, which, I was told, none but the chiefs were allowed to wear. He has a good-natured face, and offered to procure provisions for us, or do anything else in his power. He remained on board upwards of an hour, and received a number of presents from the officers; among others, a whale's tooth, than which nothing can be more valuable in the estimation of a Fejeean. Two of these will buy a boat-load of yams and a dozen pigs, or a thousand cocoa-nuts.

We learned from Whippy that there were altogether five white men residing in Levuka Town, and that they were much feared and respected by the natives, on account of their superior knowledge. He also mentioned their being married to Fejee women, and having large families of children.

At an early hour on the 9th, Captain Wilkes, with a number of the officers from this ship and the "Peacock," set out on an excursion to the heights in the interior of the island. On this day we also sent on shore all the scientific instruments. About sunset Captain Wilkes and party returned. They succeeded in reaching the summit of Andulong, the highest mountain in the island, and made many interesting discoveries in the botany of the country.

The following day Mr. B. and myself visited the shore. We landed on the beach abreast of the town, where we found great numbers of men, women and children assembled. A walk of but a few yards brought us to the Spirit-house, or "Booree," which we were invited to enter by the Chief Levuka, and his attendants, who were sitting in it at the time.

Each town or village has one of these buildings. This one stands on the top of a mount, which has been raised by the hands of man eight or ten feet above the common buildings. It has a square shape, with a roof running up to a point in the centre, and is profusely ornamented with the white cowry. The sides are made of reeds of a uniform size, bound together, side by side, with senet. In the front, there are two stone-steps, each of which leads to a doorway. The floor is raised about six inches above the ground, and is covered with mats, two and three thick. At one side there is a fire place, over which is suspended a platform made of reeds There were also some spears and clubs standing up in one of the corners; but no images, nor anything that gave the slightest indication of its being a place of worship were to be seen. While we remained here several of the people who inhabit the mountainous parts of the island, came to make presents to Levuka, in proof of their good faith. It was a novel and singular ceremony. Each one, as he entered the Spirit-house, paused, and in a loud and solemn tone pronounced the word "Booree;" he then advanced to the centre of the building, where he deposited his present, consisting of yams, taro, bananas, ava, pigs, &c., &c. This over, he threw himself on his knees, and bowed to the chief three times; after which he arose and took his leave. These dissentions between the natives occupying the shores and those who live in the interior, are common to all the islands, and are carried on in the most cowardly and brutal manner. Often in the dead hour of night a band of these savages will pounce upon some unsuspecting family, or hamlet, and make an indiscriminate slaughter of men, women and children. A man and his wife, going to cultivate their yam-patch, may be surprised by 50 or 100 warriors, carried off, cooked and eaten. A brave, fearless meeting of hostile parties in the open field to decide their disputes by deeds of noble daring never takes place.

From the Spirit-house we went to visit some of the common houses. These had very steep roofs, low sides, and only one door, and that made low and narrow, as a protection against the entrance of enemies, or that they may club them while creeping in, should they attempt it. Cocoa-nut or pandanus-wood and bamboos, with leaves of sugar-cane, are the materials employed in their construction. The interior is without partition or separate apartments; the floor is made of earth, sand, or gravel, strewed over with cocoa-nut leaves, and covered with mats. One side of the floor is raised about eight inches higher than the rest, which is called the bed-place, where they sleep. It is generally covered with a double layer of mats. Their pillows are made of a round stick, about the diameter of a spade-handle, with pins about four inches long stuck in it for the feet. Some of these are sufficiently long to accommodate three or four persons. Towards one corner of the building, a space, about five feet square, is inclosed by four large square logs of hard wood. This inclosure is the general cooking-place. The principal cooking-utensil is a large clay-jar, with a spherical bottom; it is permanently fixed on its side, near the bottom, at an angle of about forty-five degrees from perpendicular, with a space under it to admit fire. Over the cooking-place is a platform, upon which they dry and smoke much of their provisions. As these houses have no chimneys, they are, as might be supposed, filled with smoke and soot. I was surprised to find the houses belonging to the white residents no better furnished than those of the natives. They eat, sleep, and sit on the floor like the savages with whom they associate. I also observed that their children are brought up like those of the natives, in ignorance and nakedness.

Having seen all that was new or strange about the town, we set out to take a walk into the interior of the island.

Though mountainous, it is very fertile and picturesque. Change of place changed not the scene. Everywhere it presented the richest soil and most luxuriant vegetation—the verdure running even into the sea. Vines and trees sprung from the very rocks, while the neatly-thatched cottages of the natives, seemingly dropped, perchance, over the landscape, and peeping through cocoa-nut and bread-fruit tree groves, gave a lively appearance to the *coup-d'oeil*. In this delightful walk we met numbers of people, some traveling down to the ships with their burdens of fruit, others returning empty. They all gave us the road, turning to the right and left, and standing still till we passed.

We got back to the town just in time to witness another interesting sight. During our walk several of the "Peacock's" officers came on shore, and they prevailed on Levuka to give them a native dance and song. The performers were all young unmarried women, and the dance consisted of a kind of a hopping-step, accompanied with clapping of the hands. The subject of the song was the return of the king, Tanoa, to Ambou, after a war which obliged him to fly to a neighboring island. When the performance was over, most of these damsels came to the place where we were standing, and desired us to give them some paint. We each happened to have some about us, and shared it out among them, and in a few minutes after we saw them with their faces besmeared with it. They, like all the other women we had seen, were almost naked. In color they were a shade lighter than the men, and several had delicate, pleasing features.

On the morning of the 11th, several of the boats left the ship on surveying duties. About noon the "Flying Fish" arrived. Her Commander reported that she had run on the reef off the Island of Nirai, and for several hours was threat ened with total shipwreck. She was finally, however, hauled off, and the only damage sustained was the loss of part of her false keel.

In the course of the 12th, King Tanoa arrived from Ambou, and sent his messenger on board to say to Captain Wilkes that he and his chiefs were coming next day to pay him an official visit. The messenger was instructed to state to the king that we would be prepared to receive him. His majesty disembarked, accompanied by his attendants, and proceeded directly to the Council House, which is the place where all strangers are entertained. Here they seated themselves, and commenced exchanging compliments with the Chief Levuka, and his head men. When this was over, the common people brought food and placed it before the visitors; it consisted of yams, taro, bread-fruit, and a roasted pig; the present was accompanied by a speech from Levuka, to which the King's Prime Minister replied; then came clapping of hands, which is the Fejee mode of expressing thanks. When the meal was over, they all indulged in large potations of ava, which also was furnished by the Levukians.

At 10 A. M., the king and his chiefs visited the ship. They were received with a guard and by all the officers belonging to the "Peacock," Flying Fish," and this ship. The quarter-deck was also dressed off for their reception. When the king came over the side Captain Wilkes took him by the hand, and led him aft on the quarter-deck, where he was invited to take a seat. For a considerable time his majesty said nothing, nor could we conjecture what caused him to be so silent; at length, however, he directed the interpreter, David Whippy, to ask if we were offended with him, adding, that he was led to suppose so, from the fact that we did not fire a salute upon his coming on board. Whippy was directed to assure him that we were pleased to see him, and to add, that it was our intention, before he left the ship, to fire a large salute. The king being satisfied with this explanation, a council was held, which resulted in the adoption of rules and regulations for the intercourse of American vessels, similar to those established at the Navigator and Society Islands.* This business over, Captain Wilkes invited all the company into the cabin, where a collation was prepared. The sight of so many new things as the cabin presented, excited their highest admiration and wonder. In about half an hour the king rose up and expressed a wish to examine the ship; upon which, Captain W. took him around all the decks. He expressed great astonishment at the number and size of our guns and at the ship's wheel, and observed, that he could not understand how we could steer our "big canoe" by such contrivance.

On returning to the spar-deck the salute was ordered to be fired. He was greatly terrified at the firing of the third gun, which had been charged with a stand of grape that he might see their effect, and desired the interpreter to say to Captain Wilkes that he was satisfied, and request him to stop firing. When the company returned to the quarter-deck, the purser made them suitable presents in the name of the government; these consisted of axes, plain-irons, accordions, whales' teeth, shawls, muskets, watches, Windsor soap, tobacco and pipes; they were received with much clapping of hands. His majesty was highly delighted after this on seeing the marine guard go through the manual exercise. In expressing their satisfaction at anything, they repeat the word "vinaka" several times very quickly. Nothing more of importance passed, and shortly after, the king rose to take his leave. The guard was turned

* A copy of these Rules may be seen in the Appendix.

out, and the same honors paid him on his going away, as when he came on board.

Tanoa belongs to the highest order of chiefs and is considered very powerful. He is about 70 years of age, tall and slender; his countenance is pleasing and intelligent; he wore the maro with long ends hanging down before and behind, and the usual head-dress of the chiefs called "Sala." On his breast hung an ornament about eighteen inches in circumference made of ivory, tortoise shell and mother-of-pearl. Upon his arms he had strings of trochus shell ground down so as to resemble rings; his face, beard and moustaches were bedaubed with black paint; his hair, like that of all his people is crispy. He has a great impediment in his speech, so much so, that there are few persons who can understand him. He is a good friend to the whites, and calls those who live in his dominions his children, and causes the other natives to treat them with kindness and respect. His suite on this occasion consisted of twelve chiefs, and several Tonga men who seemed to be great favorites with him. All these chiefs were young looking men, and their countenances indicated shrewdness and intelligence.

Whippy told us, that after they left the ship, they had a great deal to say about their reception; and all seemed to be pleased, and expressed the wish that "big canoes" would often come to visit them.

May 14th. The king paid us another long visit to-day. He came on board, when the colors were hoisted, and did not go away until a few minutes before sunset. He told us he came this time "to see for himself," and asked to dispense with all ceremony. About 1 o'clock two of his people came alongside with his dinner. He sent word to them that he had been invited to dine on board the ship, and to take the dinner on shore again; it was brought in an iron pot, and consisted of yams and taro. On leaving the ship he shook hands with all the officers, and mentioned that he should return to-morrow to Ambou, and in a few days his son Seruh would pay us a visit.

May 15th. This morning the "Peacock" got under-way and stood out to sea. I understand she has orders to proceed direct to Rewa, and make every endeavor to capture the chief Vendovi—it being known that he is deeply implicated in the murders committed on the crew of the brig "Charles Daggett." The details of this horrible transaction are, as near as we can learn, as follows:—The brig, some years since, came among these islands to obtain Biche de Mar.* The captain, (Bachelor,) became acquainted with Vendovi, and having, as he supposed, obtained his good-will, determined to make his island one of the principal stations. They previously took on board, as pilots and interpreters, several white men who were living on the islands. He also took the precaution at first of keeping a chief, as hostage, on board; but who, after a few days, pretending to be sick, was sent on shore. One of the interpreters, who was then at the Biche de Mar house, perceiving this, and observing at the same time some suspicious movements among the natives, became convinced that they had formed the design of taking the vessel, and as soon as he saw the mate told him what he had observed, and cautioned him to be on his guard. The mate immediately came to the same conclusion, and turned to walk to the landing-place, where he had left his boat; but Vendovi, who was in company with him suspected that his treachery had been detected, and he determined to secure him. He took the hand of the mate in a friendly manner, and walked along some distance with him. Then suddenly stopping, he seized both the mate's arms and pinioned

* This animal is sometimes called Sea-Slug. It is found on the reefs, and when prepared, it is sent to China, where it is used as an ingredient in soup.

them to his side. This was the signal for a general assault. Some of the savages beat out the brains of the mate with clubs while he was held by Vendovi, and a large number attacked the house in which the other men were, and killed two of them. The interpreter and a Tahitian escaped with great difficulty by swimming off to a boat. The next day the bodies of the murdered men were obtained by paying a musket for them, and were buried along-side the vessel.

Rewa is situated on the eastern side of the Island of Viti-levu, and contains between two and three hundred houses. Its chief is styled a king, and, like Tanoa, exercises absolute authority over his people.

May 17th. To-day, David Bateman (marine) departed this life. He had been sick some time with an affection of the lungs. He was removed to this ship about ten days ago, from the "Porpoise," and was then very ill. Since our arrival here he was sent on shore, where a suitable place was provided for him, and every attention shown him by the surgeon of the vessel. He was buried in a small garden belonging to one of the white residents.

May 19th. We should judge from the great quantities of fish which have been brought along-side for sale for the past two or three days, that they are very abundant in these waters. They were taken mostly by the women, on the reefs, at low water, by means of hand-nets. It is a very common thing for the natives of the other islands to land on these reefs, and carry off the women for cannibal purposes. I was an eye-witness of an attempt of the kind made yesterday afternoon. About 4 o'clock, a canoe, manned by three men, rounded the southern point off the island, and stood in for the reef. The women immediately threw down their nets and plunged into the water; clubs and pieces of coral were then thrown at them by their pursuers, and at length two of the poor creatures were captured. The canoe, however, soon capsized; and, while the men were employed in righting it, the two women succeeded in making their escape, for their pursuers dared not to follow them very close into the shore, lest they should themselves fall into the hands of the enraged Levukians. It is said that the flesh of women is preferred to that of men; and that they consider the arms and thighs the choicest parts.

This forenoon we received a visit from Tanoa's son, Seruh, and his attendant chiefs. He had the same honors paid him as were shown to his father. He is between twenty-five and thirty years old—has regular features and a good figure. His behavior was proper enough while in our company; but I am informed by the resident whites that he is exceedingly haughty and overbearing towards the natives. He takes advantage of his high position to plunder the lower order of chiefs of their whales' teeth, muskets, knives, or anything else they may have in their possession, which he fancies. Indeed, his eye bespeaks a savage, tyrannical heart. He is the eldest of Tanoa's sons—consequently is the heir to the kingly power. His dress consisted of the tapa turban, a large whale's tooth, which hung pendent on his breast, two armlets made of the leaf of pandanus, resembling light yellow ribbon, and the "Searo," or white tapa, which was wound round his waist four or five times, leaving one end of it trailing on the deck. His hair and beard were jet black, and combed and twisted with great care. The Fejee chiefs pay great attention to this part of their toilet, and have regular barbers attached to their establishments. Seruh had his prophet, or "Ambati," with him, who appeared to be a shrewd, intelligent man. The whole party seemed delighted with the ship, and made us quite a visitation.

May 21st. We hear that the "Peacock" has succeeded in capturing Vendovi. It was effected by seizing his bro'' er chiefs, and retaining them on board the ship until he was delivered up to Captain Hudson.

It is very gratifying for us to learn that a messenger arrived here this afternoon from Ambou, with permission for the Chief Levuka to take the taboo off the cocoa-nut trees. This will enable us to procure the fruit in future. The taboo was laid on a short time previous to our arrival in the islands, and, I am informed, was done out of respect to a high chief, who was drowned in the harbor of Rewa. None but chiefs of high rank can remove the taboo; hence the necessity of waiting in the present instance for the chiefs of Ambou to give orders on the subject. The taboo lasts from two to twelve months in the case of chiefs, according to their rank for a common person, usually about four days. Trees that are tabooed have bands of pandanus or cocoa-nut leaves fastened around them, and a piece of wood is set up in a small mound of earth near by.

May 22d. At sunset we sent eleven men to the observatory, armed with muskets and cutlasses. We were advised to take this precautionary step by Whippy and the other whites residing on the island, who, of course, are well acquainted with the character of the natives. They assured us that Vendovi's friends were watching for an opportunity to avenge themselves upon us; and if we had any property on shore, it could not be too well protected. It is the Fejee custom to attack their enemies under cover of night, when it is not easy to discover their approach. From what I have seen and heard, I think they are the most treacherous and cowardly people on the face of the earth.

May 23d. It is reported here that the greatest excitement prevails at Rewa on account of Vendovi's capture. Shotted all the guns; shifted our berth nearer the Observatory, and at sunset sent 25 men in charge of Messrs. De Haven and Sanford to protect it. We also have Tanoa's son, Seruh, on board as a hostage. Signals were concerted with the observatory in case of an attack, and the battery got ready to give an enemy a warm reception.

May 24th. At an early hour this morning Seruh took his departure for Ambou. To-day one of the sailors stationed at the Observatory, reported a native for stealing his sheath-knife. Levuka immediately had the thief apprehended, and sent on board for us to punish. He is now confined in the "Brig," but he denies having taken the knife in question; yet Levuka wonders that we do not kill him!

May 25th. This afternoon the native prisoner alluded to in the foregoing remarks, was released from confinement, as there was not sufficient proof to establish his guilt. The poor fellow's joy amounted well nigh to a phrenzy. He shouted and clapped his hands, and then running up to the spar-deck, he plunged into the water and swam to the shore. A canoe, which arrived a few hours since from Rewa, reports that the excitement caused by the capture of Vendovi has entirely subsided, and a majority of the people considered him a dangerous individual, and were glad to have him removed from among them.

June 2d. At 1.15 P. M., H. B. M. schooner "Starling," tender to the "Sulphur," Captain Belcher, arrived direct from Rewa. Her commander, Lieutenant Kellet, informed us that the object of his visit was to obtain from us a rudder-pintle for the "Sulphur," she having carried away one of hers by encountering a coral-rock when going into Rewa.

Seruh paid us another visit to-day, and brought yams, pigs, and other provisions, as a present.

June 29th. Nothing of much interest has transpired during the past four weeks. We have been engaged most of the time in surveying the islands and reefs in the vicinity of Ovalau. One day some thirty of Tanoa's wives visited the ship; they were rather good-looking and quite young, excepting one. She, I should judge, was about fifty years of age, and Whippy told me that she was the only one of all the king's wives who bore the title of queen. Her attire was like that of the other females. She wore the "leeku." She had a profusion of shell-ornaments upon her neck and arms, and her body was smeared from head to foot with a mixture of oil and turmeric. Her hair was dressed in a very grotesque manner, and dyed black, white and red—its natural hue being gray.

They made a long visit, and told us that they were coming again next day, but, fortunately for us, they scarcely reached the shore when they received orders from the old king to return to Ambou immediately. Their curiosity was so great as to be very annoying after a little while; they wanted to handle and examine everything they saw.

On the 27th we broke up the Observatory, and proceeded to make preparations for going to sea.

July 3d. We reached Savu-Savu Bay on the Island of Venua-levu.* It is a fine sheet of water, affording a number of good anchorages; among others, the one in which we are now lying, called by the natives, Waicama, (harbor of hot-springs,) from the circumstance of there being springs of that character in its vicinity. It may be described as being a deep cove, surrounded by a highly picturesque country, and so well

* This is one of the largest islands in the Group. It is upwards of a hundred miles long, and from thirty to sixty in breadth. Its general character is mountainous, but the soil is fertile, especially in the valleys. Bread-fruit, cocoa-nut trees, and many others affording food for man, are abundant. Yams and taro are the principal crops.

protected from both sea and wind, that vessels may lie in it at all seasons of the year without the least fear of danger. The hot-springs alluded to are seven in number—two of them issue from a rock, which at high tide is overflowed; the remaining five are located in a small valley, and within a few yards of the margin of a mountain-stream. The temperature of the two first-mentioned springs was 200°, that of the five, 210°, and that of the stream 75°. The rock in the neighborhood is of a volcanic origin, but there is no smell of sulphur; the water is very clear, and has a brackish, or saline taste. It is a common practice for the natives residing about the bay to cook their food in those springs, and I was shown one in which I was told human flesh had been cooked only a few days before. The account the natives give of them is, that they have always been in the same state, and that they are the abode of a spirit which it would be dangerous to offend, as it might at any time destroy the inhabitants by causing the hot waters to overflow the island. There is one priest, who pretends to have communication with the spirit, and there was a "Booree" near by the spring in which their interviews took place.

The natives also informed us that formerly this part of Venua-levu was very populous, but constant dissensions had nearly depopulated it. On the top of a hill about two miles from the beach were the ruins of a very large Fejee fort.

At daylight on the 5th, we were again under way, and by 5 P. M. on the same day, we arrived at Sandal-wood Bay, or Mabua, where we found the "Peacock." Sandal-wood Bay is a large circular basin open to the sea. The neighboring country is not so interesting as that about Savu-Savu Bay, and the sandal-wood tree by which it was once covered, has become almost extinct.

The principal town is situated on a river, and was said to be the theatre of continual broils between two brothers. It contains from sixty to seventy houses, and is surrounded with pallisades formed of trees and other timber, and a ditch. The inhabitants were the most docile* we had ever met in the group, and supplied us with plenty of fresh provisions. In some of the houses graves were observed, which the white residents told us were placed there to protect them from the enemy.

Soon after we let-go the anchor a boat came along-side from the "Peacock" bringing Vendovi† ; the officer who had charge of him informed me that he had acknowledged to Captain Hudson his guilt in causing the murder of part of the crew of the "Charles Daggett," and admitted that he had held the mate by the arms, while the natives killed him with clubs. He is about thirty-five years of age, tall and rather slender, and has a countenance which belies his character—its expression is mild and benevolent. He was placed under the charge of a sentry, with orders not to allow any one to speak to him. At the same time the master-at-arms was called up, and directed to see that he received his meals at the proper hours.

During the 7th, 8th and 9th, we experienced heavy gales, accompanied with a tremendous swell. On the latter day, the purser of the squadron reported the salt provisions as running short, and recommended a reduction to be made in the rations.

On the 12th, between the hours of 2 and 3 o'clock P. M. we descried a small sail standing in the bay. It proved to

* This was to have been expected, for their intercourse with the whites has been more frequent than that of any other part of the group. It is here that such large quantities of sandal-wood have been shipped for the China market.

† Vendovi was taken to the United States, but soon after his arrival he sickened and died in the Navy Hospital at Brooklyn, New York.

be our launch, which, together with the first cutter in charge of Mr. Knox, left the ship a few days previous on surveying duties. It was expected that the first cutter would make her appearance next, but moment after moment passed away without our being able to see anything of her. Some, therefore, believed that she had capsized during the recent storms, others that she had been captured by the natives. At last, the launch reached the ship, when it appeared from Mr. Knox's report, that the latter opinion was correct. He stated that she got on a reef near by Sualib Bay, and while he was endeavoring to get her off, the natives came out in great numbers, armed with clubs and muskets, and claimed the boat and everything in her as their property.* He ordered his party to repel the robbers, but soon discovered he was completely in their power, as all his ammunition was saturated with salt water. He was, therefore, compelled to leave the cutter in the possession of the natives and take refuge on board the launch. After Mr. Knox left, the robbers dragged the boat over the reef and stripped her of everything. They then appeared to be anxiously watching the launch, and even fired their muskets at her. Immediately on receiving the report, orders were given for several boats to be fitted out from the "Peacock" and this ship, with all possible dispatch. About sunset the boats were reported to be in readiness, and Captain Wilkes accompanied by Captain Hudson, proceeded on board the "Flying Fish," and in a few minutes after they all made sail, and stood out the harbor. At an early hour next morning they reached Sualib Bay. After coming to an anchor, the pilot was sent on shore to hold a parley with the natives, and

* Any canoe or vessel when driven on shore is accounted an offering to the gods. All that it contains is considered as belonging to the people of the district where the accident happens.

state to them that if they restored the boat and the things* found in her, they would for this time be forgiven. But the savages would not even comply with these terms, and Captain Wilkes deemed it his duty to chastise them in order that they might be convinced that such outrages could no longer be committed without receiving punishment. Accordingly, a large force, commanded by Captain Hudson, proceeded on shore, fired two of their villages, containing from thirty to forty huts each, and broke up all the canoes. It is not known that any lives were lost on either side. Indeed, our people had no occasion to fire a single shot, as the savages proved themselves to be arrant cowards; the moment they saw Captain Hudson disembark, they fled in all directions, so that when he reached their towns he found them completely deserted.

When the work of destruction was over, our people returned to the beach, launched the captured cutter, and then embarked and proceeded on board the schooner. Soon afterward they set out to rejoin the ships in Sandal-wood Bay, which they accomplished about midnight.

On the 15th, Captain Wilkes left in the "Flying Fish," to take a tour round the islands. Messrs. Alden and Henry in the first cutter, and Mr. Underwood in a boat named "Leopard," also left the ship on surveying duties.

July 21st, we performed the last offices to one who lost his life by an accident that befell him while he was assisting us in our duties; I allude to Mr. Baxter, mate of the ship "Leonidas," of Salem. The particulars are as follows:— When the "Peacock" arrived at Matawata Bay, she found the "Leonidas" there; and there being a great deal of sur-

* The value of these things which consisted of the men's clothing, of books, charts, and instruments of the officers, sails, water casks, oars, &c., was estimated at $1,500. They were never recovered.

veying to be done, and a number of base lines to be measured by sound, she was requested by Captain Hudson to fire her guns as signals. The request was complied with, and Mr Baxter acted as gunner. He had fired the first gun, and was re-priming for the second, when a spark coming from a part of the cylinder which hung in the chamber of the gun, communicated with the powder-horn which he held in his hand, and exploded. This communicated with a cylinder weighing about two pounds, which he carried in the bosom of his shirt, which also exploded, and burned his breast, stomach and face in the most dreadful manner. He was immediately conveyed to the "Peacock," where every attention was shown him. On her arrival at this place he was sent on shore, where a comfortable tent was erected for his accommodation. He was constantly attended by a surgeon, but to no purpose. After forty days and forty nights of the most excruciating suffering, he expired. He was buried on a point near the ships, with a head-stone and suitable epitaph. He was a native of France, and in his last moments communicated to Doctor Guillou his real name, which was Vincente Pierre Boudette.

It is proper to state that the cylinders used on the occasion were made of canvas. Had they been flannel, the usual material, we presume the accident would not have happened.

On the 22d, the "Peacock" got under-way, with orders to proceed to Matawata Bay.

On the afternoon of the 28th, Captain Hudson came on board; and at an early hour the following day, we set out to join the "Peacock"; but the wind fell light and baffling, and we finally were obliged to anchor again off Naloa Bay, to keep from being drifted on the neighboring reef. Naloa Bay is remarkable as the spot where the Chevalier Dillon was attacked by the natives. Here, also, the "Leonidas" had one of her sailors killed by a chief, named Gingi, only a few weeks before. The reason he assigned for the act was, that the sailor had maltreated him when he was to the islands in a previous voyage. We endeavored to seize the murderer, but without success.

We saw some pottery here of an excellent quality, manufactured by the native women. The clay used is of a red color, and is obtained in great quantities on the shores of the bay. Some of the vessels were very gracefully shaped, and had tracings executed upon them by young girls with the fibres of a cocoa-nut leaf. The pots are dried in the open air; and for baking them they use a common wood fire, without any oven; but the tenacity of the clay is such, that even without baking the pottery is sufficiently strong. The different parts are all made separately and afterwards joined; but this is done so well, that it is impossible to discover the joints, especially if the vessel has been varnished.*

About noon next day (29th), we arrived at the place of our destination.

Matawata is a large town, and situated near the beach. The country around it is quite level—has but few trees on it, and the soil does not appear to be fertile; but the town is well built, and has considerable trade in Biche de Mar and tortoise-shell.

The king's name is Tui-Matawata. He is old, and suffers very much from the elephantiasis—so much so, that he can scarcely walk. He has several wives; among others, one called Henrietta, who is a native of Rotuma—has a fair complexion, and is quite good-looking. Our pilot was well

This varnish consists of the resin of a species of piue, mixed with a decoction of the mangrove bark.

acquainted with her history; and one day he related to me the circumstances under which she came, or rather was forced, to marry the old king. She had, while at her native island, married a Tahitian who was residing there, and had gone with him to Tahiti on a visit. Wishing to return to their home, they had taken passage on board of a Salem vessel engaged in the Biche de Mar trade. On arriving at Matawata, they were invited to land and remain with some of her countrymen, many of whom were residing there. Unfortunately, the king saw her, and took a fancy to her; and he immediately killed and feasted on her husband, and then compelled her to become one of his wives. The pilot added, that she was disgusted with the old savage, and if she ever had the chance to run away from him, she would avail herself of it.

We found at Matawata a large number of plants which are not noticed in any of the botanical works.

On the 30th of July we commenced to survey the bay. Next morning all the signals were found missing, the natives having stolen them during the night. As such acts were calculated to delay our operations, Captain Hudson sent an officer to the king to state to him, that if the signals were not restored by 12 o'clock on the same day, he should be obliged to send an armed force on shore to punish the inhabitants. He requested the officer to inform Captain Hudson that it was not his people who had stolen the flags, but the natives who lived in the mountains, and over whom he had no control. We had good reasons for doubting his majesty's veracity, and on re-demanding the signals they were brought on board. This incident shows how little dependence can be placed on the word of a Fejeeian. Indeed, I have been assured that they tell a falsehood in preference, when the truth would better answer their purpose; and adroit lying is regarded as an accomplishment, and one who is expert at it is sure of a friendly reception wherever he goes. When the white residents wish to obtain the truth, they invariably request them not to tell lies.

On the 31st, several of our boats returned from the leeward Islands, bringing the melancholy intelligence of the murder of Messrs. Underwood and Henry by the natives of Malolo. We learned by the same boats of the death of one of the sailors, named Smith, who was attached to the schooner "Tyvity"* as one of her crew.

The following are the circumstances connected with the death of Messrs. Underwood and Henry:—

On the 23d ultimo, Lieutenants Alden and Underwood came to anchor on the reef at Malololie, which is connected with the large island Malolo, by a coral isthmus, bare at low water. Here Mr. Underwood landed alone, and soon encountered a boy with an armful of clubs, who, when asked whether any provisons could be purchased in the neighborhood, answered, "plenty, plenty." Mr. Underwood directed him to lead the way to the place he referred to. On the beach they fell in with a party of men who were quite as much confused at the sight of Mr. Underwood as the boy had been before. At this juncture, Lieutenant Alden recalled Mr. Underwood by signal, and this, perhaps, prevented an attack on him that afternoon. The next morning (July 24th), the "Peacock's" cutter joined the other boats. The scarcity of provisions, and the distance of the schooner, whose own necessities were also pressing, now made it absolutely necessary to obtain supplies ashore. The natives pretended to have an abundance of food at the village of Malolo-levu, but could not be induced to

* The schooner belonged to one of the white men residing on Ovolau, and was hired to go about the islands to procure fresh provisions for the squadron.

transport it across the isthmus, which was impassable for boats, except at high-water. While trying to think of some way of removing this difficulty, a man, who called himself the orator of the town, arrived, and delivered an invitation from his chief to go to Malolo-levu, and take off a present that had been prepared for them on the beach. This story of Fejee manufacture, was little credited, but as there was reason to believe that provisions might be purchased from some of the natives, and the case was urgent, Mr. Underwood, whose boat drew the least water, volunteered to make the attempt. Accordingly, in a few minutes he shoved off; but after pulling a short distance, observing that he had no one with him who could talk with the natives, he returned and asked for a New Zealander, named John Sack. Having taken this man, he again shoved off and pulled for the beach. Mr. Alden followed as soon as the tide permitted, and Mr. Emmons, after taking a round of angles. Lieutenant Alden lost no time, after anchoring off the town, in getting a chief in his boat as a hostage for Mr. Underwood's safety. This native early attempted to escape in a canoe, but Mr. Alden forced him back into the boat, and threatened to shoot him if he did so again. In the meantime Mr. Underwood continued to barter with the natives, and sent off a message to Mr. Alden for muskets and powder, which could not be supplied. Mr. Henry now requested permission to land, and during his absence Mr. Emmons arrived. A second message soon afterwards came from Mr. Underwood, requiring another hatchet to effect his purchase. Lieutenant Alden sent the hatchet, with directions to Mr. U., that as the natives did not appear to be willing to trade, he should lose no time in coming off in his boat. At this moment the hostage jumped overboard, and made for the shore in a diagonal line to avoid being shot at. Mr. Alden immediately leveled his gun at him, and ordered him to stop; he slackened his pace for a moment, and then continued to retreat, upon which a ball was fired over his head, but none at his body, lest it might provoke an attack on Lieutenant Underwood. The escape of the hostage was evidently the preconcerted signal for an attack on the shore-party. The chief immediately gave orders to make fight, by the cry of "Turanga," "Turanga." Mr. Underwood was at this moment knocked down and wounded in the shoulder with a spear, but he recovered from the stunning effects of the blow, and killed the native who threw the spear. At the same time two other natives seized the musket of a sailor, named Clark, and tried to wrest it from him. One of these he stabbed in the breast with his sheath-knife, the other Mr. Underwood struck on the head with the butt-end of his pistol, upon which both relinquished their hold. Lieutenant Underwood now ordered the crew to lose no time in regaining the boat, while he and Mr. Henry covered their retreat. In this effort he killed a native with one of his pistols, and was in the act of drawing the second from his belt, when a blow which he received on the head, brought him to the ground almost senseless. Recovering himself he renewed the contest, and killed another native, but at length received a cut across the forehead with a pole-axe, which terminated his valuable life.

In the meantime Mr. Henry had shot one of the natives with his pistol-knife, and cut another down with the same weapon, but seeing Lieutenant Underwood dead, was hastening to the boat, when a missile struck him on the back of the head and brought him to the ground. Clark, after shooting the man who killed Mr. Underwood, succeeded in regaining the boat, but was severely wounded.

On seeing the attack, Lieutenants Alden and Emmons

steered for the shore with the boats under their charge. When the boats reached the beach, the savages retreated precipitately in the mangrove bushes, carrying with them their dead and wounded. Mr. Alden was among the first who landed, and going up to Mr. Underwood he raised his head, and asked him if he had anything to communicate through him to his poor wife; but, alas! he was too far gone to speak. His skull was literally smashed to pieces. Some hopes were at first entertained that Mr. Henry was yet alive, but when a vein was opened no blood was found to flow. Both bodies had been stripped by the natives, and were laying in the sand, whence they were conveyed to the boats. Mr. Emmons took possession of a canoe that the natives had abandoned, and no enemy being now in sight, the boats, with colors half-masted and union down, sailed across the isthmus and escaped by a passage, where they might have been attacked at great advantage.

The schooner by this time got under-way without suspicion of any disaster. The sensation that was excited when the boats arrived along-side and exposed to view the mangled bodies, can be more easily imagined than described. Captain Wilkes, in particular, wept over them like a child. He kissed his nephew, Mr. Henry, on the face several times, and then turning around to Mr. Underwood, patted him on the breast and repeated the words, "Poor fellow." Every attention was paid to the wounded and dead, that affection and regard could dictate.

There being no doubt from the reports of all parties present, that this outrage was entirely unprovoked, Captain Wilkes determined to inflict the punishment it merited, and this, not because he wished to gratify any feelings of revenge, but for the sake of saving the lives of other whites who might visit the Group after the expedition left.

Accordingly, the first cutters of the "Vincennes" and "Peacock," now in charge of Mr. Eld, were dispatched tc keep guard round the island, and prevent the escape of any of the inhabitants, while the schooner got under-way, and proceeded to a small island to inter the dead. Here they were laid side by side in the same grave. It was a lonely and suitable spot that had been chosen in a shade so dense that scarce a ray of the sun could penetrate it. The grave was dug deep in the pure white sand, and sufficiently wide for the two corpses. Mr. Agate read the funeral service. After the graves had been closed, three vollies were fired over them. Every precaution was then taken to obliterate all marks that might indicate to the odious cannibals, the resting-place of the sacred dead. Places remote from the grave were more disturbed by footsteps and digging than the grave itself, and leaves were scattered over a large space of ground.

The islet where they repose, is called Henry's island, and the cluster to which it belongs bears the name of Underwood's Group.

A single canoe attempted to leave Malolo during the burial of the dead, but was driven back with the loss of one of her people. The natives came to the beach in large numbers, taunting the boats with the cry of "Lagoini, lagoini papa langa;" in English, "Come on, come on, white men;" but the orders expressly forbade a landing, or any other demonstration which might abate their arrogant confidence.

About noon the schooner reached her former berth, and shortly after the "Porpoise" hove in sight. When she anchored, Mr. Emmons boarded her, and communicated the melancholy news to Captain Ringgold. Preparations were now commenced in good earnest to punish the savages; the arms were got in good order, the parties duly organized, and by 10 A. M. next day the whole of the disposable force of the brig and schooner, consisting of eighty men, landed at the west side of the island, while the vessels took commanding positions off the reef. After landing, the men were formed in three divisions, and took up their line of march, the whole commanded by Captain Ringgold. On arriving at the principal town, they found it to be of a large size, well fortified with strong posts, driven into the ground close together, and the intervening spaces filled up with a kind of wicker-work, and the whole surrounded by a deep ditch, filled with water.

When within a few yards of the entrance, which was a small low gate, scarcely large enough to admit one person, the principal chief came out, and made the following taunting speech: "Come on; I and my people are ready for you; Fejee men are good to eat, but white men are better, and intend this night to have some of you for supper. Fejee men like to eat white men; we are glad to see you; yes, we are glad to see you." He then rallied his men, and ordered them to fire at our people from behind the fortifications.

Captain Ringgold now made a signal for two of the divisions, which had been sent to destroy the yam-patches, and cut down the cocoa-nut trees, to join him, which they did with great alacrity. He then formed the whole in one line, and marched up to the intrenchments, under a heavy shower of spears and arms. He next directed several rockets to be set off in hopes of firing the town, and thus compel the savages to abandon their intrenchments; but this did not produce the desired effect, and he therefore opened his fire upon the fortification. Now was seen what many of those present had not before believed, the expertness with which these people dodge a shot at the flash of a gun; still our men took plenty of time in firing, and the number of killed and wounded of the enemy was immense. Upwards of twenty were seen to fall at the first volley. In this manner was the contest kept up until the principal chief was shot dead, a circumstance, which, together with the half-burned state of the town—for the rockets eventually set a large hut on fire—spread a great panic among them, and they fled through a gate, which was intentionally left unattacked, carrying their dead and wounded on their backs. At this moment a volley of musketry might have greatly increased the destruction of lives; but as women and children could be distinguished amid the throng of fugitives, the order was given to cease firing, and they were allowed to escape.

Our people now marched into the town, and threw upon the flames whatever they found that might be valuable to the enemy. This involved the destruction of the whole wealth of the island, which had been centered here on account of its great strength. This fact serves to show that the savages were not ignorant of the consequences that were likely to follow their foul deed, and had made timely preparations for defending themselves.

Several things that had belonged to Mr. Underwood were seen among the ruins. A little child, who seemed to have lost its parents, and whom our people endeavored to avoid shooting during the conflict, was burned to death in one of the houses. The dead that the natives had been obliged to leave behind, were all found shot through the head. Many lay beside a mound which had been but recently raised for additional security.

While Captain Ringgold and party were thus employed on shore, Captain Wilkes and Messrs. Alden and Emmons were not less active on the water. Scarcely had the action commenced with the town, when two large canoes were seen stand ing over from Vita Leva. Immediately the signal to intercept them was made, and Mr. Emmons reached them first, and made signs to them to heave-to; but they stood on their course to Malolo. Upon this Mr. Emmons announced his intention to destroy them. Several were killed at the first fire, and the rest jumped overboard and made for the shore. Mr. Emmons continued to fire at the fugitives until he fell in with Captain Wilkes, who directed him to spare the lives of the survivors, but make them prisoners. Lieutenant Emmons had already rescued a little child, and now attempted to save its mother. This woman had at first been taken for a man, and fired upon from Captain Wilkes's boat, but when the error was discovered they ceased firing, and hastened to her rescue. In her alarm, however, she mistook the design, and continually dived to avoid the boat, so that they were obliged to abandon her, and she swam towards Vita Leva, ten miles distant. We heard afterwards that she had safely arrived there. The other prisoners taken by the boats were the head-chief's wife, two girls, each about sixteen years of age, and a boy about five years old. After taking the prisoners to the brig, where they were kindly treated by both officers and sailors, all the boats proceeded to the leeward part of the island to destroy another town. When they had almost reached the place, the shore-party hailed, and informed them that five canoes had been seen to put off from the western-side of the island. Mr. Emmons was forthwith dispatched after them, while the other boats remained to destroy the town, which they speedily accomplished.

After a very long and fatiguing pull, Mr. Emmons overtook the fugitives. They were at first some distance apart, but as he approached them they closed their line, and stood ready for an attack. Their numbers were partly concealed behind a breastwork of baskets, filled with roots, which they had thrown up for the occasion. Mr. Emmons wished to pull to windward to avail himself of a light breeze, but he had only got a few yards off when some of the canoes appeared disposed to commence the attack, and executed a manœuvre by which they expected to get his boat on the reef when she might be carried by boarding. But Mr. Emmons brought his blunderbuss to bear upon the natives, and ordered them to change their course, which, strange to say, they had the folly to do. Being now where there was plenty of water, Lieutenant Emmons opened fire upon the canoes. Large numbers were killed and wounded, and the rest leaped overboard. During the pursuit which followed, several of the fugitives gained a canoe which had drifted out from the shore, and put off to seaward, passing over a reef upon which there was not sufficient water for the boat to float. Three of the captured canoes were cleared of their "lumber," and taken along-side the "Porpoise." The fourth being badly stove, was left on the reef until next morning, when she was also secured.

Subsequent investigation confirmed the opinion, that these canoes had left the island with the express intention of cutting off Mr. Emmons. Their known loss was twenty-seven men; but there is good reason to believe that it was much greater. Our own party had the good fortune to escape with a few slight wounds.

It was Captain Wilkes's intention to renew the attack next day, (27th,) but early in the morning one of the women who had been liberated the preceding day, came down to the beach, and begged for mercy to the survivors, describing in moving terms the misery to which they had been reduced.

Captain Wilkes told her to return to those who sent her, and state that he would not listen to the mediation of women;

but a little while after he dispatched two boys, who had been captured by Mr. Emmons, to order all the people on the island to assemble by noon on a certain hill, and receive our terms. The prisoners were directed to add, that, if the order was not obeyed, hostilities would be renewed. At 11 A. M. the whole party of men who had been on shore the previous day landed, and formed into a hallow-square, to await the approach of the natives; but none appeared. Twelve o'clock arrived, and they still kept away. At last they began to appear, moving slowly on their hands and knees, and filling the air with their wailings.

When yet a considerable distance off they halted, and sent messengers to say that they were afraid to approach nearer; but the messenger was ordered to tell them that they must do as they had been directed in the morning. On receiving this answer, they resumed their wailings, and at the same time moved towards the hill. Every now and then they would stop and raising their faces from the ground send up a piteous cry. In this way did they manage, until at last they reached the spot where Captain Wilkes was standing, when they threw themselves at his feet.

After a minute or two, one of their old men began in a tone of the deepest humility to supplicate forgiveness, and to promise that the people of Malolo would never again kill white man. He added, that they acknowledged themselves conquered and that the island belonged to us; that they had lost everything; that the two great chiefs of the island and all their best warriors had been killed; all their provisions destroyed, and their houses burned; that they were now convinced that the white men were better warriors than the Fejee men. During the whole time he was speaking, all the others remained bent down with their heads touching the ground.

They were asked many questions, and among others, what had induced them to commit the murder. They admitted that Lieut. Underwood and Mr. Henry had done nothing to offend them, and that they had been killed without the slightest cause.

Captain Wilkes now told them that he would grant them pardon, but they must supply the squadron with water and provisions; with which conditions they agreed to comply.

The next day they appeared on the beach and fulfilled their agreement. This was according to their custom, that the conquered should work for the victors. They acknowledged their loss to be about one hundred persons; we did not lose in the combat, a single life, and only very few were wounded. These wounds were inflicted with spears and arrows, for their fire-arms were rendered harmless by being over-charged. It is said to be their practice to put charges into them according to the size of the person they intend to fire at; they almost fill the barrel with powder when they shoot at a large man.

Thus ended this affair, an awful and a severe lesson to the savages, but not more so than they deserved. It must be remembered that the murderers were looked upon by their own countrymen as a set of pirates. I think it would be a blessing to the whole race if the United States or some other civilized nation would conquer them into subjection and order. It would at once put an end to their dissensions and barbarities, and afford encouragement to commerce and safety to person and property.

The moment Captain Hudson received intelligence of the melancholy disaster, he directed the ship's colors to be half-masted, and issued the following order:—

"Information having been received from the commander of the expedition, of the death of Lieutenant Joseph A. Underwood and Midshipman Wilkes Henry, on the 12th instant, who were treacherously murdered by the natives of Malolo, one of the Fejee Islands, the officers of the United States ships "Vincennes" and "Peacock" will wear the usual badge of mourning for thirty days, as a testimony of regard for the memory of their departed brother officers, who have been suddenly cut off from their sphere of usefulness in the expedition, while arduously engaged in the performance of their public duty.

(Signed) "WILLIAM L. HUDSON,
"Commanding U. S. Ship 'Peacock.'

"*Fejee Islands.*"

On the 2d of August, the whale-ship "Triton," fifteen months from the United States, arrived; as also the schooner "Tyvity," with three thousand yams. The latter likewise brought as passengers, the second-mate and cooper of the American whale-ship "Shylock," which was lost on a reef * off Turtle Island, a few weeks since. It appears from their account that the loss of this fine ship is to be attributed to the negligence of the man who had the "look-out" forward at the time the accident occurred. They charge him of going to sleep, and not knowing the danger the ship was in until she had struck.

The captain and the first-mate have proceeded to Hobart Town in an English brig. The second-mate has shipped on board the "Triton," and is said to have behaved in the most shameful manner, refusing to assist the surviving sufferers,

* The position of this reef was afterwards determined by the brig "Porpoise." It lies in latitude 19° 48′ 00″ south, and longitude 178° 35′ 00″ west. The reef is six-and-a-half miles long, and has an illiptical form. Turtle Island is about nine miles in circumference, and has a few inhabitants, whose manners and customs are similar to those of the Tonga people.

and left them on the wreck, exposed to the cruelties of the natives.

August 7th, the "Porpoise" came in and anchored. She left Ovalau on the 4th instant. Captain Wilkes was there in the "Flying Fish," and was to follow the brig in a few days.

During the afternoon of the 8th, a meeting was held on board the "Peacock," when Captain Hudson was called to the chair, and Lieutenant R. E. Johnson appointed secretary. The chair announced that the object of the meeting was to obtain a joint expression of feeling in relation to the death of Lieutenant Joseph A. Underwood and Midshipman Wilkes Henry, who, on the 24th day of July last, were treacherously killed by the natives of Malolo.

On motion, a committee, consisting of Lieut. Johnson, Dr. J. C. Palmer, Mr. William Rich (botanist), Passed Midshipman Blunt, and Midshipman Blair, were appointed to draft resolutions befitting this melancholy occasion.

The committee retired, in obedience to their instructions; and after a short recess, the meeting was called to order again, and the chairman of the committee reported the following resolutions, which were unanimously adopted:—

Resolved, That amid the toils and dangers which the officers of this expedition have been called upon to encounter, they could have incurred no deeper calamity than the untimely death of their beloved coadjutors, Lieutenant Joseph A. Underwood and Midshipman Wilkes Henry.

Resolved, That the loss of these gentlemen is most deeply mourned, not only on account of their personal worth, but from our sincere interest in the expedition, which has been deprived of two of its most efficient officers.

Resolved, That the energetic and persevering manner in

which the lamented dead performed all duties, however arduous, afford an example worthy our emulation; and that the strongest terms of sympathy with their friends at home are inadequate to the expression of our regret.

RESOLVED, That, as a mark of affection and respect for our lost associates, we cause a monument, designed among ourselves, to be erected to their memory in the cemetery at Mount Auburn.

RESOLVED, That a copy of these resolutions be transmitted to the bereaved relatives of Lieutenant Underwood and Midshipman Henry.

It was further resolved, that a committee of nine persons be appointed to carry the foregoing resolutions into effect; and that this committee consist of the following gentlemen, to wit:—Captain William L. Hudson, Lieut. James Alden, Lieut. H. L. Case, Dr. J. C. Palmer, Mr. T. R. Peal, (ornithologist), Passed Midshipman S. F. Blunt, Purser Wm. Speiden, Midshipman George W. Clark, Midshipman J. L. Blair.

It was next moved and resolved, that the sum of two thousand dollars be appropriated for the erection of the monument; and that the pursers of the expedition be authorized to charge the said sum to the officers and scientific corps, in proportion to the rate of their several salaries.

The subject of an inscription was referred to a future meeting, and the committee were instructed to select a model from the designs which they might hereafter receive.

The meeting then adjourned.

On the 9th of August, the "Flying Fish" arrived, and Captain Wilkes rejoined the "Vincennes."

Next day, it being Sunday, the chaplain of the squadron delivered a sermon on the death of Messrs. Underwood and Henry. The following portions of it may be interesting:—

Lieutenant Joseph A. Underwood, was born July 15th, 1811. He entered the Navy of the United States in 1829, and since that time had been almost constantly employed in active service. He was one of the officers earliest attached to the expedition in which we are embarked, and had been nearly four years connected with it, at the time of his decease. With some of you, he encountered the dangers and hardships incident to a passage round the stormy Cape and of Noir Island; saw and endured with manly exposure the more appalling prospect that tried men's souls. For a year previous to his death, with us who survive, he shared the risks in the ship, in the boat, and on shore, peculiar to a passage among the reefs and islets that thickly stud this southern sea. With health unbroken, he sustained the blighting heat and piercing cold of the torrid and the frigid zones, as we passed rapidly from clime to clime. He bore unmoved, the arduous toils, privations, and perils of our southern cruise, when, amid the ice-islands of the Polar Ocean, we threaded our devious and often dangerous way. With us he visited these barbarous islands, and had been repeatedly engaged in the arduous and perilous duty in which he met his melancholy and untimely fate. Our lamented friend had been married but a few weeks, when he left his native land, and had completed his twenty-ninth year, only two days previous to his leaving the ship for the last time. While I recognize the charitable sentiment—"Nought of the dead, but good," I am happy to assure you, that in relation to our departed friends, it will be in perfect accordance with that sentiment to say, "Nought of the dead but truth." With the Roman orator, I can say, I come to bury our fallen friends, not to praise them. And if a year's acquaintance can give me an opportunity to judge, I can testify to his amiability and worth. His deportment was distinguished by a studious regard to propriety and decorum, and in his conversation and conduct, he respected the feelings and sentiments of those with whom he was associated. His manners and address were those of an accomplished gentleman. There was no affected distance or reserve, or any manifest consciousness of superior understanding. His politeness was not merely external, but that of the heart. In his intercourse with men of every condition, his conduct was dictated by benevolence and regulated by that great law of moral equity, "To do unto others as you would wish them do unto you," and in all that intercourse his intentions were just, kind, generous and noble. In forming his opinions he was independent—in maintaining them he was firm. "Decision of character was in-wrought in the very texture of his mind." He was afraid of no man. When he had assumed a position, dictated by wisdom and prudence, he maintained it unawed by any opposition which might be brought against him. His temperament was ardent, but under discipline; of that kindness and principle which led him to respect the feelings and prejudices of others, it had been chastened, and subdued. In the performance of any duty, he was remarkable for untiring diligence, and unceasing perseverance. In a highly creditable knowledge of his profession he added various collateral attainments and polite accomplishments. His acquaintance with pure mathematics, as applicable to astronomy, navigation, and surveying, was known to you all. He was familiar with several of the modern languages of Europe; and who has not seen the chaste, beautiful and faithful productions of his pencil, with which his portfolio was enriched? In regard to his intellectual character, he possessed a mind of the first order. His conceptions were clear, concise and vivid; his judgment was remarkably correct; he reasoned with calm deliberation, and examined a subject with a prodigious grasp of mind in all extensive bearings. If it embraced numerous and various particulars, he directed his attention to each, and suspended his decision until he had examined them all.

Having thus with a well-balanced mind looked through a subject, he rarely had occasion to retrace his steps, or renounce the conclusions to which he had arrived. A correct and refined taste enabled him to see and appreciate whatever was sublime, and beautiful in art or nature; and his memory retained with fidelity that rich variety of facts and sentiments which his reading and observation had committed to its charge. Such, my hearers, were some of the principal traits which distinguished the character of our lamented companion and friend. With his immediate relations I had not the happiness of being acquainted; but from all I can learn, he was a dutiful and grateful son, a kind brother, and a faithful and affectionate husband to the now widowed partner of his bosom.

I have thus briefly and imperfectly touched upon the character of the lamented Underwood.

It only remains to say of the much-loved companion of his untimely fate, that many of the traits which Underwood possessed, belonged to Henry, with a due reference between them in age and experience in the service. The loved and lost Henry—the cherished object of affection of his widowed mother—was deservedly dear to us all. He was a youth, manly beyond his years. He possessed in an eminent degree, that propriety and dignity of demeanor which commanded the respect of all his inferiors, and won and retained the esteem and confidence of his superiors and associates. He was distinguished for zeal and devotedness to the service, disinterestedness, fortitude and courage—a varied combination of excellencies—which rendered him an honor to his profession, and afforded high hopes of future distinction. His memory is precious, and will not be forgotten; and to you, the junior officers of the squadron, so lately his youthful companions and compeers, I would say, embalm his excellencies of character by imitating them in your lives; and if you have not chosen a better maxim for your guidance through life, take this from one who loves you all—"Dare always to do right, and only dread to sin against God."

On the 11th of August, at an early hour, we bade adieu to the Fejee Islands, and stood for Honolulu.

CHAPTER XIV.

FEJEE GROUP.

The Fejee Group is composed of one hundred and fifty-five islands, of which number one hundred are uninhabitable, on account of their sterility and want of water; the remaining number possess an excellent soil, and abound in mountain streams—for the islands are of a mountainous character, some of the peaks having an altitude of nearly five thousand feet. The valleys are beautiful, and in some places well cultivated. Yams and dry taro are the principal crops; sugar-cane grows spontaneously and of an excellent quality. The natives do not make sugar, but manufacture large quantities of molasses, and they use the leaf of the plant to cover the roofs of their houses.

The principal towns are Rewa and Ambou, situated on the east side of Vitilevu; they contain about four thousand inhabitants each, and, as I have before observed, the latter is the residence of King Tanoa, the most powerful chief in the group.

The climate, though warm, is pleasant and salubrious. During our long stay at Ovalaou, we experienced very little rainy weather. The mean temperature on board the ship was 76°. The population, according to the best information obtainable at this time, is about one hundred and twenty thousand. It is utterly impossible to have precise data on this subject, for the white men residing in the group, have not had access to all the islands, nor can we depend on native inform ation as each chief is anxious to swell the number of his fighting men. They are evidently a distinct race from the rest of the Polynesians. They are of a color almost black, while their hair is frizzled or crisped, though not so much so as the Africans; the nose is broad and flat, and the eyes are jet black, and have a wild, restless expression. They are personally well-formed, muscular, and of good size. The men have a custom of bedaubing their faces and bodies with a mixture of lamp-black and cocoa-nut oil, which gives them a disgusting appearance.

In character, they are cruel, deceitful, passionate, and treacherous. We had repeated proofs of the latter in their various attempts to surprise and cut off our boats, while employed in surveying duties. Another universal trait in their character is covetousness, and is the incentive to stealing, and many other odious acts. They are also great cannibals; indeed, they carry this revolting practice to a greater extent than any other savages yet known to the civilized world. The bodies of enemies slain in battle do not satisfy their appetite for it. Violence, stratagem, and sacrifices to the gods, are resorted to for this horrible purpose. The chiefs are fond of giving entertainments, and, on such occasions, human flesh, either roasted or boiled, is handed round to the guest. When a new spirit-house is built, several human beings are slaughtered, and the bodies eaten by the Abati, or priest, and his friends.

The usual dress of the men consists of the maro, and of the women, a sort of apron or girdle about eighteen inches in width. Children of both sexes, until they arrive at the age of puberty, go entirely naked. Women only are tattooed—the operation is performed by persons of their own sex—and the parts thus ornamented are those concealed by the dress, and sometimes the lips and fingers. The women firmly believe that to be tattooed is a passport to the world of spirits, so much so, that if a girl dies before the operation is performed, they paint a semblance of it, by which means they expect to deceive the gods.

It is the custom for grown persons of both sexes to powder their hair with the soot collected from the smoke of the wood called "tooi-tooi," or else with lime. In using either of these substances they diffuse it plentifully in a large calabash of water, in which they dip their heads frequently. When they have got on a sufficient quantity, they place themselves before a mirror, and with a sort of comb and a stick about twelve inches long, and pointed at both ends, they work the hair up, until it has acquired the size and appearance of an immense peruke. The natural color of their hair is black, but by the use of lime and carbon and other coloring matter, they make all the various shades between black and red; many of which colors, in numerous instances, decorate the same head. Some are white in front, black behind, and red on the sides. Those who have been deprived of their hair by nature or accident, supply the defect by wigs, which are so skillfully made as scarcely to be distinguishable from the genuine natural growth.

They eat with their fingers; and in serving up their food, they always sweep off the mats or lay down new ones, placing the victuals upon fresh leaves. They take their principal meal in the evening, over which they spend much time. In drinking, they throw their heads back, hold the vessel six or eight inches from the lips, and allow the water to run into the mouth, as if from a spout. The white residents speak highly of the cooking, and say, they have seen at the feast given by the chiefs from twenty to thirty different sorts of dishes.

Their language is copious and pleasing to the ear. The missionaries are endeavoring to reduce it to writing. It furnishes words for expressing every emotion of the mind. They have also distinctive names for all the plants, trees, and other subjects of the vegetable kingdom that grow under their climate. The language affords various forms of salutation, according to the rank of the parties. When the common people approach a "duowa turanga," or a chief, they cry out, "Duowa," to which the chief replies, "Wa." If the chief is on his route, they turn out of his path, squat on their haunches, and lower their clubs to the ground. Women make their salutations in words different from those employed by the men. They have also forms of expression equivalent to our "No, sir," and "Yes, sir."

Their mode of sending messages is peculiar:—The messenger is furnished with as many sticks or reeds as the message contains separate subjects. The sticks are of various lengths, in order to distinguish them from each other. When the messenger arrives at his destination, he delivers the reeds successively, and with each of them repeats the purport of the message of which it is a memorial. The reply is conveyed after the same manner.

Women are treated as inferior beings; they are prohibited from entering the spirit-houses or eating human flesh. The girls of the lower classes of a tribe, are entirely at the disposal of the chief, who may sell them to transient strangers, or do anything else with them he pleases. Wives, besides taking care of their children, and doing the work about the house, are obliged to assist the men in cultivating the soil; if they misbehave they are tied to a tree and flogged.

At the age of fourteen, boys undergo the operation of circumcision, which is performed after the manner of the Jews. Young girls allow their hair to grow in long locks, and usually decorate them with flowers of various colors. They are also fond of painting their noses and cheeks with vermilion. After marriage the curls are cut off, and the hair is kept short and frizzled.

Polygamy, in its greatest extent, is practised—some of the chiefs having from ten to one hundred wives. The woman, however, who is of the best family is always looked upon as the principal wife—all the others being required to yield implicit obedience to her. The daughters of chiefs are usually betrothed early in life. If the betrothed husband dies before the girl grows up, the next brother takes his place. The parties may be frequently seen walking arm-in-arm after they are engaged. Among the lower classes, however, marriages are mere matters of bargain, and wives are looked upon as property. The usual price is a musket or a whale's tooth. If detected in infidelity, they may be killed by the husband, or sold into slavery; but I was told that Fejee wives are generally faithful. On the death of the husband, his favorite wives are strangled and buried with him in a common grave.*

When a member of a family is dangerously ill, one or more of the other members cut off his little finger as a sacrifice to the gods for his recovery; if the sick person is afflicted with a lingering disease, his relatives kill him, that he may escape all

* We learn that among the Fejee Islanders, the chiefs have from twenty to a hundred wives, according to their rank, and at the interment of a principal chief, the body is laid in state upon a spacious lawn in the presence of an immense concourse of spectators. The principal wife, after the utmost ingenuity of the natives has been exercised in adorning her person, then walks out, and takes her seat near the body of her husband, when a rope is passed round her neck, which eight or ten powerful men pull with all their strength, until she is strangled and dies. Her body is then laid by that of the chief. This done, a second wife comes out and seats herself in the same place. The process is repeated, and she also dies. A third and a fourth become voluntary sacrifices in the same manner, and all of them are then interred in a common grave—one above, one below, and one on either side of the husband. The reasons assigned for this are, that the spirit of the chief may not be lonely in its passage to the invisible world, and that by such an offering, its happiness may be at once secured.
Missionary Enterprises in the South Sea Islands.

further misery. The little finger is also often cut off on the death of a great chief. The usual symbol of mourning for men is short hair or beard—they seldom cut both. The women burn themselves to blisters on the neck and breast; this is done by holding a piece of ignited tapa over the part to be burned. Funerals among the higher classes are invariably followed by feasts and ava-drinking.

The government is decidedly despotic. The will of the chief is the law, and instant death would be dealt out to any one found opposing it. The common people are looked upon as slaves, and may be sold and destroyed by their masters without remonstrance or appeal. The victims offered as sacrifices to the gods are generally selected from this class. They are also slaughtered in great numbers when a great chief dies, in respect to him.

Their religious creed* is in substance as follows:—That there is one Great Spirit who sees and knows all things, and who has the power of dispensing good and evil to mankind, according to their merits; that there are many other spirits besides who have the same power, but not in so great a degree; that dogs, cats, guns, stones, trees, canoes, rivers—in fact, everything—has a soul as well as man; that certain persons are inspired; that there are no future rewards and punishments, but that punishment for crime will be received in this world only, and the future is one of perfect and eternal happiness. They also firmly believe that omens are indications from the gods themselves to man, and spells and charms are effective means of getting the gods to accord to the wishes of the maledictor. The priests are called "Ambatis," and exercise great influence over the lower classes. They are

* There are missionaries residing at Rewa and Somu Tomou, but as yet they have made no converts.

generally companions of the chiefs, and are present at all the feasts and ava-drinking. One of the principal duties of a priest is to perform the marriage ceremony.

Their account of the origin of the races is this:—All mankind, say they, sprung from one father and mother. The Fejee was first born, but acted wickedly, and was black; the Tonga was next born—he acted better than the Fejee—was whiter, and had some clothes given him; white man came last—he behaved well—was liked by the Great Spirit, who made him white like himself, and gave him clothes and everything he could desire.

During our stay at Ovalaou, I witnessed the performance of two dances. On both occasions the men and women danced together. They kept time to a monotonous chant, in which they all occasionally joined; their motions were stiff and inelegant. Both boys and girls are instructed in the dance by masters and mistresses.

Their knowledge of medicine is limited to a few plants and the bark of two or three kinds of trees. In surgery they are more skillful. The most common surgical operation among them is that of blood-letting, and is performed by making a small incision with a shell or a knife in various parts of the body for the relief of pain, inflamed tumors, &c., &c. By the same means they open abscesses and ulcers. They also cut off their toes to cure sores in the legs, elephantiasis, and leprosy. In cases of hard tumors, they apply hot bread-fruit, so as to produce a blister, and ultimately a purelent surface. In cases of sprains they rub the part afflicted with the dry hand, or with a mixture of oil and water. Of gun-shot wounds they lay the wound open that they may be able to extract the ball, should it still remain. Midwifery is a distinct profession, exercised by females only, and they are said to be very skillful.

Their arms consist of clubs, spears, bows and arrows. There are two kinds of clubs—one kind about four feet long, and five or six inches in circumference; the other about eighteen inches long, and fashioned like a drum-stick. The latter sort are intended for throwing, and are said to be a very formidable weapon. Every man is furnished with two of these when he goes into battle; some of them are beautifully carved.

Their manufactures are mats, tapa, baskets, &c. This is exclusively the work of women. The tapa is made, as at the other islands, from the Chinese mulberry, and by a similar process. They make some that is very neatly and tastefully printed. On several of the islands they also manufacture large quantities of pottery; they make it into pots, jugs and lamps, and it appears to be of as good quality as that which is manufactured for common use at home. The men have the reputation of being the best native mechanics in the South Seas. Their canoes are constructed with much judgment and ingenuity; I saw some that were upwards of one hundred feet in length, and proportionally wide. The double-canoes are capable of carrying from one hundred to two hundred men each.

As they are unacquainted with the use of money, they barter commodities chiefly for muskets, powder, whales' teeth, cotton cloths, hatchets, knives, scissors, razors, glass bottles, and red paint. Among themselves, mats and tapa-cloth form the principal currency and personal property. They wear the whales' teeth around their necks as ornaments, which are highly prized.

The foreign trade with these islands is much more limited than it was some twenty years ago. Sandal-wood is now exhausted, or only found in small quantities; tortoise-shell is so scarce as to be of small account, and these, with the smaller articles, such as clubs, spears, mats, and shells, are mostly picked up by the white residents on speculation and sent to Sydney, New South Wales, from whence they are forwarded to England, and sold as native curiosities. The merchant-traders, therefore, are confined chiefly to the article of bech-de-mar, which is still found in considerable quantities, and is in great demand in the China market.

The general character of the Fejee Islanders may be gathered from the preceding remarks. The dark side of the picture presents them as unprincipled, cruel, rapacious, deficient in courage as well as in human feelings, and indifferent to the commission of crime. This melancholy catalogue of vices arises from the disadvantages in point of religion, of government, and the general structure of society, under which they live. There is no doubt that under a better form of government they would become quite a different people.

The resident missionaries represent them as being, in point of natural abilities, superior to any of the other Polynesians.

CHAPTER XV.

SANDWICH ISLANDS.*

SEPTEMBER 30th. About noon this day, we made the Island of Oahoo; and by 5 P. M., came-to in the roads off of the town of Honolulu. Soon after, we communicated with the shore, and had the satisfaction of receiving letters from our friends at home.

The appearance of Oahoo, when viewed from the roads, is by no means inviting. The plain on which the town stands is almost treeless, while the mountains to the eastward are a mass of naked rock. These mountains are composed of basalt and tufa; and, doubtless, what is termed by the foreign residents the "Devil's Punch Bowl," was once a volcanic crater, vomiting forth the strong entrails of the nether world.

Early in the following morning, we hove-up the anchor, and towed the ship to a berth in the harbor, where we found about a dozen other vessels, mostly American, and engaged in the whale-fishery. The channel is narrow and tortuous, but the harbor is perfectly secure and convenient. Vessels of four to five hundred tons can lay along-side any of the wharves, and discharge or receive their cargoes. It is defended by a fort mounting some twenty guns.

At 10 A. M., our Consul, P. A. Brinsmade, Esq., visited

* These islands were discovered by the celebrated Captain Cook, who named them after Lord Sandwich, the then Lord of the Admiralty. There are nine in number, and bear the following native names :—Hawaii, Oahoo, Maui, Kauai, Molokai, Lanai, Hamakua, Kakoolawe, and Niihau.

the ship, and in the course of the afternoon, many of the foreign residents; and among others the English and French Consuls.

October 2d. To-day I visited the town. It is regularly laid out in streets, and contains many houses built in the European style. It also contains several churches and two hotels. The natives' houses are well adapted to the climate, and are pleasant, convenient residences—some cover a great extent of ground; there is a small yard before each, inclosed by a wall built of *adobes*. The houses belonging to the better classes have their floors covered with mats, and are furnished with chairs, beds and curtains.

The king's palace stands facing the harbor, and has an air of snugness and comfort rather than elegance. It is a single-story building, constructed of wood, and painted white. Several of the stores owned by foreign residents are large and appeared to be doing good business; indeed, Honolulu is the New York of the group. The merchants of the other islands come here to purchase their goods. The population is estimated at 7,000.

The natives have healthy, athletic forms, and in complexion are a shade darker than the Tahitians. They have made much greater progress in civilization than any of the Polynesian nations. They are well acquainted with weights and measures, and the value which all articles ought to bear in exchange with each other. Their currency is gold and silver. The chiefs are well clothed in the European style; but the masses are not more than half-dressed, and some still wear nothing but the maro. The apparel of the women consists of a long loose-gown, made of calico, and a fancy-colored silk handkerchief, thrown over the neck and shoulders. Most of the old people of both sexes have from one to three of their front teeth knocked out. This seems to have been an old religious custom, and was considered as a propitiatory sacrifice to the gods, to avert their anger.

Of the white residents the Americans are the most numerous. Most of the foreign trade is in their hands, and several are reputed to be quite wealthy. The town bears many evidences of their enterprise. Their dwelling-houses and stores are the largest and handsomest in the place. They have also a neat chapel of their own, and support a weekly newspaper.

There is a regular market here, and all kinds of provisions can be had as cheap as we get them at home. The beef comes chiefly from the Island of Hawaii, and is fat and well-flavored. Oranges, pine-apples, plaintains and bananas are also abundant, and of an excellent quality.

When it became so dark that I could no longer see the town to advantage, I repaired to the principal hotel, where I got a very good supper. There is a billiard-table connected with this establishment, which I found well patronized by the foreign residents and chiefs; several of the latter were noble-looking men, and spoke very good English.

On the 20th, two natives were hung at the fort, in the presence of a great concourse of people, for poisoning a woman, wife to one of them. Their trial took place about a fortnight before, and was conducted, we were told, in a very impartial and dignified manner. The governor was the presiding judge, and the king and high chiefs were present. The accused were allowed to challenge a jury, which consisted of twelve of the most intelligent and respectable natives. They were also allowed to choose counsel. One of the criminals was a chief of high rank.

October 27th. This morning I went to witness an examination of the native children. I found them assembled at the

Rev. Mr. Bingham's church, to the number of 700. The examination lasted several hours, the exercises being spelling, reading, writing, arithmetic, singing, grammar and geography; and it is certainly speaking moderately to say, the evidences of improvement exhibited on the occasion were very creditable to both teachers and pupils. The Governor, and Captains Wilkes and Hudson made short addresses, which were listened to with much attention. The scholars were then marched through the town to the Rev. Mr. Smith's church, each school bearing a banner, and the whole procession headed by the young chiefs.

It was upon the whole one of the most interesting spectacles I have witnessed for a long time, and spoke well for the missionaries. Besides the school just mentioned, there are three others in Honolulu—one of which is under the superintendence of the Catholic bishop.* It is the opinion of the missionaries, and other foreign residents, that the native children are not inferior in intellect, or in other respects, to white children having equal advantages.

October 28th. Having visited every object worthy of notice in the town of Honolulu, I determined to-day to ride out to the Pali. Strangers visiting Oahoo, ought by all means to take this drive—it is impossible to conceive a more interesting one. After proceeding about two miles from the principal hotel you enter a valley, through the centre of which winds a beautiful stream, whose banks are lined with taro plantations, meadows and gardens, and dotted with cottages, while the sides on either hand are bounded with a range of hills, covered to their summits with verdure. The eye cannot turn but to banquet on some lovely or romantic object. Every cottage is

* Formerly the Protestant was the only religion tolerated by the government, but now all creeds are tolerated, and the Catholics have numerous converts in Honolulu.

a picture, and the industry and happiness of man seems to co-operate with the beneficence of the soil and climate. In no part of the United States have I seen more agricultural neatness and industry. All the stone fences, dividing one field from another, are kept in the highest order. As you advance you feel the air becoming more bracing, for the valley rises with a gradual ascent from the sea to the Pali. The bottom of the valley is more undulating, the hills grow higher and steeper, and the vegetation more varied. After a ride of about four miles through such country as has just been described, you enter a grove of *hibiscus* and other tropical trees. In a few minutes you come again into open space, and after turning round a pile of rocks the Pali suddenly bursts upon your view, filling you with wonder and astonishment. On either hand immense masses of volcanic rock rise to the perpendicular height of between six and seven hundred feet; while looking down beneath the fearful precipice, you behold in one view plantations, trees, villages, meadows filled with cattle grazing, the town of Honolulu, with its harbor and shipping, and the blue bosom of the Pacific. Painters, poets, and romance-writers would find here ample materials for contemplation and study. My guide, who was an elderly man, pointed out the place where two stone idols stood, before the coming of the missionaries to the islands, to which, he said, every native who intended to descend the precipice made an offering of tapa and flowers, in order to render them propitious to his descent. He also showed me the identical spot where the last king of Oahoo and his warriors were driven down headlong and dashed to pieces, by Tamahamaha I.,* and his

* In viewing Tamahamaha I., says Mr. Turnbull, my imagination suggested to me, that I beheld in its first progress one of those extraordinary natures which, under other circumstances of fortune and situation, would have ripened into the future

victorious army. The precipice is at least three times the height of Dover cliffs, and it is really fearful and dizzy to cast one's eyes over the horrid boundaries,—

> "The murmuring surge
> That on the unnumbered idle pebbles chafe,
> Can scarce be heard so high."

On my way back I met great numbers of native women, who were riding out on horseback for pleasure. They were evidently in high spirits, for such chattering and giggling I have seldom heard. They fairly made the hills and valleys ring again. They also appeared to be very fond of showing off their horsemanship, and the mettle of their steeds. Running and leaping over every fence and wall that could be seen on their path was the order of the day. Indeed, horse-riding* is a favorite amusement of the Honoluluians, and there is not a Saturday afternoon in the year which is not devoted to it, and the more break-neck and wild the animal is the better.

On entering the town my horse took fright at the sight of a group of urchins who were playing in the street, and, after running about half a mile, threw me, and bruised my side to such a degree that I was immediately obliged to go on board the ship, and have it attended to. But for this mishap I

hero, and caused the world to resound with his feats of enterprise. What other was Philip of Macedon, as pictured by the Grecian historians, a man who overcame every disadvantage, and extended the narrow sovereignty of Macedon into the universal monarchy of Greece, and under his son, of the then known world. He is both a warrior and a statesman, and his subjects have already made considerable progress in civilization, but are held in the most abject submission, as Tamahamaha is inflexible in punishing all offences which seem to counteract his authority. His palace is built after the European style, of brick and glazed windows, and defended by a battery of ten guns. He has European and American artificers about him of almost every description. Indeed, his own subjects, from their intercourse with Europeans, have acquired a great knowledge of several of the mechanical arts, and have thus enabled him to increase his navy—a favorite object with him.

* The females ride like the men.

should be tempted to look upon this day as one of the happiest I have enjoyed during my earthly pilgrimage.

On the 2d of December the "Peacock" and "Flying Fish" sailed for King's Mill Group, thence to Columbia River.

December 4th. At 1.40 P. M. we took our departure for Hawaii—P. A. Brinsmade, Esq., and Dr. Judd, physician to the mission, taking passage with us.

During our stay at Oahoo, much was accomplished in the way of science. The artists of the expedition also were continually employed, and took many views of scenery, and portraits of the chiefs and common people. The harbor of Pearl River, was, for the first time, accurately surveyed, and found to be commodious and convenient for shipping, with twenty-three feet of water over the bar, off its entrance. The roadstead and harbor of Hanolulu were also thoroughly sounded out. The Salt Lake of Ewa* which heretofore was supposed to be connected with the sea, and to be influenced by the tides, was examined, and the salt was found to be a mineral production; salt was found nearly two hundred feet above the surface of the lake. This examination also settled the question with regard to its depth. Instead of being fathomless, its depth was no where found to be more than two feet.

Meteorological and magnetical observations were daily taken, both on board the ship and at the observatory, in short, nothing was neglected that could add to the natural history of the island.

December 5th. At an early hour this morning we came in sight of the mountains of Hawaii. Their immense

* This is a small circular lake situated about seven miles to the west of Honolulu, so impregnated with salt, that between five and six hundred barrels of fine hard chrystalized salt are taken out annually. It belongs to the king, and is a source of considerable revenue—large quantities of the article being sold to the Hudson's Bay Company, and used for curing salmon and hides.

height excited our astonishment and wonder; the summits rose far above the highest clouds, and for several thousand feet down were covered with snow, which, when the sun rose, glistened and sparkled with a degree of brilliancy that almost blinded the beholder. This mighty scene recalled the following effusion to which Moore was excited on a similar occasion:

"No, never shall I lose the trace
Of what I've felt in this bright place;
And should my spirit's hope grow weak,
Should I, O God! e'er doubt thy power,
This mighty scene again I'll seek,
At this same calm and glooming hour,
And here at the sublimest shrine
That nature ever reared to thee,
Re-kindle all that hope divine
And feel my immortality!"

At sunset the natives* assembled on the forecastle, and at our request gave us a specimen of their wrestling. Forming a ring, one of them stepped in the centre with his arms extended; he was immediately approached by another from the opposite side, not in the usual step, but by crossing the legs alternately; he then brought both feet together, and commenced making a variety of motions with his hands. After this, which lasted about five minutes, each seized the other by the wrist and neck, and by a variety of movements made by the arms and feet, continued to struggle until one of the parties was thrown.

During the night, many meteors were observed. It is impossible for language to paint the glories of the firmament in clear moonlight nights among these islands. They surpass any I have ever witnessed in other parts of the globe.

* While at Oahoo, numbers of these people were shipped on board the different vessels of the squadron, for the purpose of employing them in the boats.

December 9th. At 3.30 P. M., we reached the harbor of Waiakea, or Byron's Bay, and anchored in three and a half fathoms of water. The entrance into this bay is so easy that a pilot is altogether unnecessary, for you have only to keep the western shore aboard until the reef, which makes off the mouth of the bay, is passed, and then haul up for Cocoa-nut Island, off which is the best holding-ground.

We had no sooner let-go the anchor, than the king's agent came on board to welcome us to the island, and to make Captain Wilkes a present of some mullet, which had just been caught in the king's fish-pond.* He was neatly and respectably dressed in the European style, and from having been brought up in Mr. Bingham's family spoke our language perfectly well.

* The Hawaiians take great pains to have fine fish. They take them from the sea when very small, and put them into ponds of salt water, where they remain several months; thence they are carried into brackish water, and finally are introduced into ponds of fresh water, where they are carefully attended.

CHAPTER XVI.

HAWAII.

The aspect of this part of the island of Hawaii is one of surpassing beauty. The country gradually declines from the base of the mountain Mouna Loa, some thirty miles inland, to the coast, where it boldly and precipitately terminates. The soil appears to be of the best quality, not overgrown with forests and thickets, as is generally the case with those islands we have heretofore visited, but extending out in a kind of meadow-patches, enlivened by numerous streams, and beautifully diversified with clusters of bread-fruit trees, so as to give the whole a picturesque and at the same time an easy cultivated prospect. In entering the bay, the neatly-thatched huts of the natives, situated among groups of venerable bread-fruit and other trees, become more numerous, and on arriving at the anchorage the scene is perfect; for here, in addition to the beauties nature has so bountifully bestowed on the surrounding country, the taste and art of advancing civilization can be seen.

The missionary families established here have built themselves houses in the European style. There are also one or two stores, a neat chapel, and a mill or two for grinding cane. owned by a China man.

December 10th. This morning we sent the scientific instruments to the Observatory. This building is situated on the south-eastern side of the bay; it is thirty feet long, by fifteen wide, and was, I am informed, erected expressly for our use by an order from the king. There were numbers of persons still employed in leveling off the ground around it, and in platting down the grass with which it is covered.

Dec. 11th and 12th. These two days have been spent in making preparations for the excursion to the top of Mauna Loa.

On the 14th, Captain Wilkes and party left for Manua Loa. The expedition set out from the Observatory, and, besides Captain W., consisted of Messrs. Budd, Eld, Pickering, Judd, Brinsmade, Brackenbridge, and Elliott, Serg. Stearns, twelve of the crew, and one hundred and fifty natives, or kanakas. It was Captain Wilkes's intention to have started at a much earlier hour, but in this he was disappointed by a circumstance which could not be foreseen. No sooner was the order to march given than thirty of the natives laid down their loads and declared they were sick, and could not go the excursion. Others were engaged to take their place, but not without much persuasion and great additional expense. They positively refused to go unless they received double the pay which had been offered those whom they were to relieve—that is, eight dollars.

The party will spend one night in the vicinity of Kilauei, which will be on their way. On reaching the summit of Mauna Loa, they will immediately go on erecting the tents. This done, the natives are to be discharged, with orders to return again when their services are needed. As soon as the instruments are up, Captain Wilkes and Messrs. Budd and Eld will proceed with the observations, and continue them until a sufficient number are obtained to form the data from which the proper results are to be obtained. Such are the objects of this enterprise, and we do most sincerely wish it all the success imaginable. No observations, we believe, have as yet been made by any one at so great an altitude with instruments like those with which the party are provided; and as all of them would be highly interesting and useful, it would give us particular pleasure to have the honor of making them secured to our own country.

There are some, however, who are of the opinion that the whole affair will fall through, from the fact of the natives not being able to stand cold, which is said, after an elevation of ten or twelve thousand feet, to be intense.

December 15th. To-day I visited the shore, in company with a brother officer. We landed on the western side of the bay. A clump of cocoa-nut trees was standing within a few yards of the water's edge. Passing this we came to two avenues, of about half a mile in length, lined on either side with cane-plantations, taro-patches, and interspersed with trees loaded with flowers of the most gay and beautiful colors. One of the avenues, e were told, was entirely the work of those females who had violated the seventh commandment, and, like that at Tahiti, was distinguished by the name of "Broom-rood." After making a short call on one of the missionary gentlemen, who resides in a very neat and comfortable house situated at the termination of the road just mentioned, we repaired to Mr. Pittman's. This gentleman is a native of Boston, and the principal merchant in Hilo. While we were sitting in his store, several natives came in, and made a number of purchases, which, we remarked, consisted chiefly of cotton-stuffs. We next set out to visit a brother-officer and messmate, who had taken up his residence on shore on account of ill-health. Pursuing a path which lay through fields overgrown with bushes, we soon arrived at the banks of Waikea. This river rises among the mountains in the interior, and previous to the introduction of Christianity was regarded by the natives as an object of great veneration.

The remains of many of the temples that were dedicated to its god are still to be seen on its banks. The bed over which it flows is composed of black volcanic rock, and in some places is full of fissures and chasms. A little to the right of the spot where we struck it, there are two very beautiful cascades. The Waikea was also distinguished in olden times for the great number of fairs that were held on its banks. We had scarcely crossed this beautiful stream when we reached the house which our friend occupied. It is the property of Mr. Pittman's son, and, besides being shaded by magnificent trees, it commands a noble view of the harbor. After spending a few hours with our friend, we set out to return on board. Many native houses were scattered along our path, some of which we entered. They were not so large nor so cleanly as those we had seen at Oahoo.

We reached the ship just as the eight o'clock gun was fired.

December 17th. During these twenty-four hours the air has been uncommonly keen, on account of the wind blowing from the westward. This wind blows down the mountains, and is more dreaded by the natives than any other. Both day and night, during its continuance, they keep large fires burning in their houses, and gather round them as closely as they can. It is, in fact, to them, what the northeast wind is to us in the winter season.

December 18th. Several letters have been received to-day from the Mouna Loa party, and among others, one from Captain Wilkes, addressed to the first Lieutenant, in which, he directs that fifty of the crew should be sent to him. One of the letters stated that about thirty of the natives had given out.

The swell is running very heavy. We have stood it out, however, thus far, with only one anchor and eighty fathoms cable.

December 19th. At early dawn, Lieut. Alden and Mr. Sanford left here with the fifty men sent for by Captain Wilkes.

It is justice due to those men to state, that not one cf them waited to be ordered; they came forward and volunteered their services the moment they learned they were needed. During the night the reflection from the Volcano Kilauea, was uncommonly vivid, insomuch that we concluded some new eruption had taken place.

December 21st. In the afternoon we hauled the seine, and in two hauls captured fish enough to supply every mess in the ship for several days to come. Both hauls were made near the beach, and the last one in the presence of a great number of the Kanakas, and it was amusing to see the astonishment which they expressed.

They have seines of their own, but they are of such miserable construction as to be of very little use. There are many varieties of fish found in the bays of Hawaii; but the mullet is considered superior to all others in point of flavor.

December 22d. More letters have been received from the Mauna Loa party, and they all state, that the natives are giving out hourly; one cause of complaint is, that the loads which they are required to carry, are too heavy, which, no doubt, is too true; we should think that fifty pounds was altogether too much for any one man to carry, especially on so long a journey, and one beset with so many natural difficulties. It would have been better, we believe, to have had the loads lighter, and employed more people.

December 23d. To-day the Headman of Hilo, and family, and the King's agent and his lady, dined in the ward-room. The former is a large man with European features and of dignified manners. He also bears the reputation of being a man of great energy of character. The females were neatly dressed after the European fashion, and, considering their opportunities, conducted themselves remarkably well.

Storm on the Hawaiian Coast.

In the evening, Mr. Williamson, gunner, reported that he saw on shore, Mr. Sanford and a man named McDonald, who was so lame as scarce to be able to walk.

December 24th. This morning Mr. Sanford and McDonald came on board. Mr. Sanford stated that he was obliged to return on account of his suffering from the asthma, after leaving the volcano. In the evening Mr. Elliott arrived with orders to the first Lieutenant, from Captain Wilkes, to keep up a constant communication between the ship and the mountain. Mr. Elliott reports that he left the party about fifteen miles, or two days' walk, from the top of the mountain; that the ascent thus far had been difficult and painful, and that one of the crew named Longly (an excellent man) was found missing. He also tells us that they had suffered a great deal from cold, and want of provisions and water; the latter article being so scarce, that upwards of two dollars had been paid for a gallon of it.

In the course of the afternoon, two white men came on board to say to the Purser, that they had been dispatched by Captain Wilkes to tell him to send two hundred natives up the mountain with wood. These men report that Captain Wilkes, and about half a dozen others had reached the summit.

December 26th. At an early hour, one hundred and thirty natives left town with wood and water, for the use of the party on Mauna Loa. The Headman of Hilo went with them, and will hereafter stay at what is termed the half-way house, and superintend the natives, who are to be constantly kept carrying wood and water up to Mr. Alden's tent.

December 27th. We are gratified to learn that Longly has been found. The poor fellow was laying under a rock speechless, and already in a state of delirium preceding a final dissolution; but he is now doing well.

CHAPTER XVII.

VISIT TO THE GREAT VOLCANO—ARRIVAL AT MAUI—DESCRIPTION OF LAHAINA—VISIT FROM THE KING.

On the morning of the 24th of January, Messrs. M——, H——, and myself, applied for permission to visit Mount Kilauea. As the permission was granted, we set about making the necessary arrangements for the tour. We directed our steward to put up provisions for six days, and in the afternoon went on shore, and engaged horses from the Headman of Hilo to take us up to the crater. We also engaged a white man, named Smith, to act as guide to the party, and several natives, who were to carry our baggage.

We told Smith we should be ready to set out the next day, and should expect him and the natives to meet us at an early hour at the Observatory, that being the starting-point. Accordingly, the following morning, we repaired to the Observatory, where we found Smith and the natives; and by six o'clock, all preparations being made, we took our departure. Pursuing a westerly course, we soon came to the River Wikuea, which we crossed near the Headman's house. In a few minutes after, we reached the road which leads to the volcano. We had only traveled a short distance on this road, when we entered a track of country which was entirely covered with fern, and but thinly inhabited. It was here that I took the resolution to return my horse to the Headman and take to walking. Smith informed me that there were but few horses on the island, and those have been brought over from Oahoo, and are generally old and broken down.

At 1 o'clock it commenced to rain, but it turned out to be only a shower. The road now laid through a dense forest, in which we observed growing in great abundance the Teutui-tree, from the nut of which the natives extract an excellent oil. On emerging from this wood, we found ourselves in a country similar to that we passed over before. About 4 o'clock we reached the house where Captain Wilkes and party spent their second night while on their way to the summit of Mouna Loa. It is a large native building, standing a few hundred yards from the road, with some cultivated land around it. We now came to a region of country entirely composed of lava and producing no other vegetation than what grew in the crevices. This lava was of a dark brown color and very hard, and with a surface ruffled like that of the sea at the first springing up of a breeze. It was a highly interesting scene both for the geologist and mineralogist. After a walk of between three and four miles over this volcanic region, we passed on our left a cluster of cottages, surrounded apparently by a rich soil, and shortly after reached what is called the "half-way house," where we proposed to spend the night. Upon entering, the inmates immediately retired to one of the out-houses, thus giving us possession of the entire building. It appeared to be newly erected and better constructed than any building we had seen on the way. In the centre of the floor was a cheerful fire, the sight of which we hailed with joy, for we were both wet and cold. Around its gladsome blaze we seated ourselves, enjoyed its genial warmth, dried our clothing, and then proceeded to partake our repast. When the repast was over we once more gathered around the fire, and, after comfortably warming ourselves, retired for the night.

January 26th. At 8 o'clock we resumed our journey. It was a bright sunny morning, and the neighboring woods were enlivened with songsters of various colors and species. Few birds are to be seen along the shore, but in the interior of the island they are numerous, and the notes of three or four kinds are exceedingly sweet.

Between 11 and 12 we reached the two shanties situated about eight miles from the volcano. Here we halted for the baggage men to come up. Scarcely had we got seated when a girl about sixteen years of age, entered, and took a seat by us. Upon inquiry she informed us that she belonged to the opposite side of the island and was going to visit some of her friends who were residing near Hilo. She was evidently one of the lower class, yet her manners were pleasing and even graceful. Perceiving she was without provisions, we offered her some of our own, but she declined the offer, and shortly after rose up and proceeded on her journey.

The scantiness of vegetation, the presence of disrupted volcanic masses, and the appearance of columns of steam issuing from the rents intersecting the ground over which we were passsing, convinced us that we must be near the crater Kilauea.

At length, about 4 o'clock, we came in sight of the monarch of all volcanoes—but the light of day, robbed it of much of its splendor; still the eye of man never beheld a more sublime and terrific scene. Before us was a cavity between six and seven miles in circumference and upwards of a thousand feet in depth; within this were to be seen lakes of varied size and form, filled with burning matter, and emitting columns of flame and vapor.

It is remarkable that this crater should present an external aspect so entirely dissimilar to that of Etna and Vesuvius, or any of the volcanoes of South America. Those are characterized by an elevated cone, out of which are ejected igneous rocks and ashes. Kilauea, on the contrary, is an immense depression in the midst of a vast plain with nothing to warn you of a near approach but the signs which I have before spoken of.

We now directed our course toward the cluster of shanties erected on the brim of the crater by Captain Wilkes's party, which we soon reached, and found one occupied by Dr. Pickering, who came round by the sea-shore. The remaining shanties were in the possession of about fifty natives, who had come from a town near the coast to take away a large canoe which they had made in the neighboring wood, some time previous.

After supper we proceeded in company with Dr. Pickering to a place about half a mile to the eastward of the shanties to obtain a view of a small crater which was represented to be unusually active. We could not possibly have selected a more eligible position. We stood on a pile of rocks which commanded a bird's-eye view of the fiery lake. It was several thousand feet in circumference, and nearly round in form. The color of its burning contents was that of a cherry-red or deep crimson, and it was in a state of terrific ebullition. Sometimes the fiery fluid was ejected many feet into the air, at other times it was seen to overflow the edges on the circumjacent lava, for many yards distant. We continued to gaze upon the scene about an hour, and then returned to our lodgings, where we soon had opportunity of observing another phenomenon of a character not less grand and splendid. We were reclining on our mats, with our eyes directed towards the largest of the lakes, when a portion of the bank forming one of its sides, was seen to give way and fall into the liquid lava beneath with a frightful crash. The whole surface was in the most violent agitation; billows were formed as high apparently as any we had ever seen on the ocean, and dashed against the side of the crater with such violence as to throw the fiery spray sixty or seventy feet high. The sight of this spectacle alone would have repaid us for the trouble of coming thus far. When the surface of the fiery stream became quiescent again, we wrapped ourselves in our blankets and sought repose.

When breakfast was over, we proceeded to visit the bottom of the crater. After a brief walk in the direction of the Sulphur Springs, we turned to the left, and suddenly commenced descending by a steep and rugged path; columns of vapors smelling strongly of sulphur were issuing from crevices and pits lining either side of the road. We estimated some of the latter to be upwards of two hundred feet in depth. After a descent of about one quarter of a mile, we passed on our right a crater which bore unmistakable signs of having long since become extinct; it was everywhere covered with shrubbery, and trees of considerable dimensions. Another walk of about fifteen minutes brought us to what is called the "Ledge." It was not until then that we formed an adequate idea of the magnitude and sublimity of this wonderful crater. On whichsoever side we cast our eyes, we beheld a wall of solid lava of a thousand feet, or more, in altitude, and from six to seven miles in circumference. This ledge surrounds the crater; thus forming a kind of natural gallery several hundred yards in width. The surface is but little broken, and presents a uniform appearance, being of a dark brown or iron color.

At length we reached the bottom. The path leading to this was also very abrupt and dangerous; we were in danger every moment of being killed by the falling of fragments of rocks, or of being precipitated down the fathomless pits. The descent did not exceed four hundred yards, but we were upwards of twenty minutes in accomplishing it.

Dr. Pickering and myself remained at the bottom of the crater upwards of an hour. It varies in its character much; in some places the surface is so hot as to be painful to the feet, and the gurgling sound of the liquid lava beneath warned us that we were treading on dangerous ground; in others it was broken and twisted into every imaginable shape; in others it was thrown up in the wildest confusion, resulting, no doubt, from the sudden cooling and contracting of the lava; in another place there were lakes of fire and smoke, and in others again it presented a smooth glassy-like surface, and so fragile as to frequently break through, and precipitate us several feet before we gained a sure footing. I received several falls, and bruised my hands and knees dreadfully.

We approached within a few yards of the largest of the lakes. It is situated to the northeast, and ranges in a direction nearly east and west, and we estimated its circumference at upwards of three-quarters of a mile, it being oval in shape; at the east end the lava flowed in gentle waves—at the west it was in a much higher state of action—it was there boiling and thrown up into the air to the height of hundreds of feet, and then descending again in showers of spray. The heat was so intense as to burn our hands and faces many yards distant, and the glare so strong as to be painful to the eyes. Thick black columns of smoke rose from the centre. The wind roared like thunder, as it rushed by us to fill the vacuum produced by the intense heat, while at intervals the bank on which we stood, cracked and shook in the most frightful manner. The idea of falling into some of these fissures was by no means agreeable, and really, I, for one, felt very much relieved when we turned our eyes from the scene to retrace our steps.

On our regaining the ledge, we fell in with Mr. H., who had gone to collect some specimens of what is called Pele's hair. He succeeded, and beautiful specimens they were. There seems to be some doubt as to the manner this is produced. My opinion is, that it is formed simply by the sweeping of the wind over the surface of the lava while in a liquid state. It is to be found all over the ledge, and on the bushes growing around the brim of the crater; it very much resembles tufts of fine flax. On the leeward side of the crater, Mr. H. found it so abundant that the ground in places appeared as if covered with cobwebs.

Pele, according to the mythology of the natives, is the goddess of Kilauea, and it is believed that many of them still worship her in secret. It is said that they never approached it previous to the introduction of Christianity, without the greatest fear and veneration, and then only to deliver their offering by casting it into the burning lake.

When about half way back we met Mr. Lyman, one of the resident missionaries, and Mr. Elliott, our chaplain. At 3 P. M. we reached our lodgings, and, as might be expected, were hungry, thirsty, and very much fatigued. After dinner I accompanied Mr. H. to the Sulphur Banks to procure some specimens, but in this we were disappointed, as we saw none that were worth the trouble of preserving. There were some forming, however, which promised to be very fine. The edges of several of the crevices from which the gases issued that produced the sulphur, were lining with crystals of the most beautiful shape and brilliancy. We estimated the length of these banks to be two hundred yards, and their height from ten to thirty feet. Many caverns and chasms were observable in their vicinity.

The ensuing night harmonized well with the glorious scenes witnessed during the day:—

> "As when the moon, refulgent lamp of night,
> O'er heaven's clear azure spreads her sacred light,
> When not a breath disturbs the deep serene,
> And not a cloud o'ercasts the solemn scene:
> Around her throne the vivid planets roll,
> And stars unnumber'd gild the glowing pole;
> O'er the dark trees a yellower verdure shed,
> And tip with silver every mountain's head."

January 28th. At an early hour I bade adieu to Kilauea, and set out to return to Hilo, taking the route by which Dr. Pickering had ascended. After a walk of about five miles I overtook the party of Kanakas whom we found at the volcano on the evening of our arrival. They were compelled to bear the canoe on their shoulders, as the road was too steep and rugged to allow the use of rollers. At 11 o'clock I came in sight of Mount Popii, and by noon reached the summit, from which I had a view of the crater on the western side. It appears very ancient, as everywhere it is covered with trees and shrubbery. It resembles a funnel in shape, and I estimated its depth to be four hundred feet.

Leaving Mount Popii, I turned off to a path diverging to the left, which soon brought me to another crater. The bottom of this was overflowed with fresh lava; but it did not materially differ from the one above mentioned. This lava had doubtless run in during the recent eruption, and worked its way from the crater Kilauea by some subterranean passage; its color was nearly that of clay, and the surface appeared highly glazed—the aperture through which it run in may still be seen. It bore from where I was standing about northwest, is several feet in circumference, about fifty yards from the top of the crater, and one hundred yards from the bottom.

Pursuing the same path I next came to the bed of lava, which owes its origin to the same eruption as that just alluded to; this presented the most singular spectacle. Many of the trees with which the whole country was formerly covered are still standing, overlooking the scene of desolation. The lava was in that state which it generally assumes after it commences to cool. Throughout its whole length and breadth it was split and broken into pieces of various shapes and sizes; gases were escaping from several of the rents which smelt strongly of sulphur, insomuch that I became aware of their existence an hour or two previous to my reaching them. It was from these fissures that the liquid mass made its appearance. One of them is nearly three feet in width, another two feet, and a third eighteen inches. From the summit of Mount Popii a fine view of the stream may be obtained. It is about three miles long, and from three to five hundred yards wide. The appearance of the surface is uniform, being of a color nearly black, and full of glittering crystals. The average height above the adjacent ground is four feet. No one can see all this, and yet question the theory of the igneous fluidity of the centre of our globe. All combustible causes that we are aquainted with are totally inadequate to produce such an effect.

It was my intention to have visited another crater, which I was told to be still larger than any I had seen, except that of Kilauea; but having missed the path leading to it, and it being also near sunset, I deemed it best to endeavor to reach a house about two miles off, where Smith said I would find good lodgings, and which I succeeded in reaching about dusk.

Smith was right; we had excellent accommodations, and our sleep was sweet and refreshing.

January 29th. The landscape was still glittering with the dews of night when I resumed my journey. The morning is the proper time to travel here, as the air is then cool and delicious. After a short walk I reached a village, containing between twenty and thirty houses. As I passed through, many of the inhabitants came out of their dwellings to inquire where I was going, and from whence I came. The Hawaiians are naturally a very curious and inquisitive people. The land in the vicinity of this village appeared fertile, and was in a high state of cultivation. Among other productions, I observed the coffee-tree and sugar-cane. The average height of full-grown coffee trees is about nine feet; they arrive at their full growth in four or five years, and continue to bear from ten to fifteen years. The coffee-blossom is a beautiful and highly fragrant little white flower, and the berry, when fully ripe, is of a pale red color. I came next to a field of lava, which, like those I passed yesterday, had been torn and shattered, either by the expansive force of the air underneath at the time the lava was in a semi-fluid state, or by some violent convulsion of nature. The traveling over it was excessively fatiguing, as the lava was both very rugged and brittle.

Leaving this barren and solitary waste, I soon passed on my left several conical hills, which were once craters, but now are overgrown with bushes and other vegetation.

At 3 o'clock I stopped at a shanty, erected by the side of the road, to prepare dinner, and to allow the natives, who carried the baggage and specimens, to come up.

Having refreshed ourselves, we pursued our way. The path now lay through an open country, covered with light yellow soil producing nothing but grasses, and a few whortleberry bushes.

Another two hours' walk brought us to a pool of rain water; here we filled up our water bags and calabashes. There are but few springs in this part of Hawaii, and no rivers—so that the inhabitants are obliged to have recourse to the method of catching rain-water in calabashes, which they keep suspended in great numbers around the roofs of their habitations at all times. Nature is boundless in her resources, and the more we inquire and examine, the more we are lost in wonder and admiration at the great scheme for carrying on the designs of the Creator. Though some parts of these islands are left for six months together without rain, yet an ample provision has been made to counteract the ill-effects of so long a drought. Vegetation, which, with us, would speedily perish without an abundant supply of rain, is there sufficiently nourished by that moisture, which plants, as they bud and blossom and produce their fruit, have the power of hoarding up and retaining from one rainy season to another, and by the heavy dews that nightly fall upon their large expanded leaves.

About sunset, we arrived at Waiiha, where I determined to spend the night. This is a pleasant village, situated within a few miles of the sea-shore. The inhabitants appeared to be in very comfortable circumstances; their houses were large and well furnished, after the native manner. The dwelling in which I took lodgings, was the property of the principal magistrate of the place. He himself was absent, but his wife gave me a cordial welcome; she received me with many expressions of kindness, led me into the house, and immediately set about to prepare a repast. We had two dishes, which deserve notice, as I believe they are peculiar to the natives of these islands; the names under which they are best known, are Poi and Poi-dog—the former is made of boiled taro, pounded up and mixed with water into a paste; it is served up in calabashes, and conveyed to the mouth with the fingers, by all ranks and ages. People who live on the sea-coast, eat with it a small fish in a raw state, resembling the sardine.

The Poi-dog is not one of our common curs, but a dainty animal, fed entirely on vegetable food, generally on taro made into a poi, and hence the name—(a Hawaiian would no more eat one of our kind of dogs than we would)—the animal is sometimes roasted before the fire just as we roast beef; but more generally it is "lau-ude," that is, after the skin is taken off, the animal is wrapped up in leaves and put into a hole made in the earth, of several feet in circumference, and about two feet in depth; when in, some more leaves are spread over the animal, hot stones are then placed on the leaves, and a covering of nine or ten inches thick, formed of leaves and earth, is spread over the whole. In this state the animal remains about three-quarters of an hour, when the hole is opened and the animal taken out. The many eulogies passed on the dish by my kind hostess, and my curiosity in the matter, conquered my prejudices against the name, and really had I not known to the contrary, I should have thought I was partaking of a piece of roast pig.

January 31st. At an early hour I took leave of the kind family, with whom I passed the night. The Hawaiians are a hospitable people, and there are many of them who, if they had only one fowl or pig in the world, would cheerfully take it to furnish a repast for a friend or a stranger.

After a brief walk I reached the sea-shore, which I found thickly sprinkled with cottages. At 10 o'clock I halted at a house which was deserted, to partake of some breakfast. This house, I was told by the guide, had been the residence of a chief, and was deserted during the recent eruption, when it was believed that it, like many others, would be destroyed by the liquid lava. It was large and well built, and commanded a fine view of the ocean.

When breakfast was over, I proceeded to visit the place where the stream of lava run into the sea during the eruption just alluded to, also the three hills, said to have been formed at the same time. The direction of the stream was northeast, and is said to be between twenty and thirty miles in length, and from one to nine thousand yards in width. When first discovered it was supposed that a new crater had been formed; but it is now ascertained that it worked its way from the old Volcano Kilauea. The depth of the stream, as seen down the rents, was from five to twenty feet. At first it flowed smoothly, and after remaining so for some ten days, broke up into its present rough and confused state. I estimated its breadth, where it run into the sea, to be two thousand feet. The lava, as far as the eye could reach, was of a jet-black color, and excessively brittle. I ascended two of the highest hills; they stood within a few yards of the beach, and parallel to each other—were formed of sand, scoria, and ashes—and I found their height to be two hundred feet. It is not likely they will remain permanent, as the surf is continually beating against their sides and gradually washing them away. Near these hills were two sand-beaches, which owed their origin to the same eruption. The sand was composed of a substance similar to that of the adjoining lava, and was probably formed by the igneous stream coming in contact with the sea. The lava suddenly cooling, flew into small pieces and particles, and was thrown back upon the land by the agitated waters.

I now walked along the coast, sometimes keeping so near the edge as to be wet with the spray of the surge which broke violently against it. The houses thickened, and about 4 o'clock I reached a hamlet, consisting of some dozen or fifteen cottages. After another two hours' walk I arrived at the last village within the district of Puna. The appearance presented by this village was very inviting. The houses were mostly built among shady groves, while the country in the vicinity was beautifully laid out in plantations and gardens. It had an air of freshness and comfort which was very gratifying, especially after coming from the desolate scene above described. The inhabitants, though not so well dressed, or perhaps not so far advanced in the scale of civilization as those about Hilo, were very kind and hospitable. Many of them invited me to their houses, and made me presents of cocoa-nuts and bananas.

After walking a mile or two farther I came to a piece of wood, the traveling through which was exceedingly fatiguing and dangerous, as at almost every step I sank ankle-deep into mud, or fell into some hole, which the darkness of the night rendered invisible. But as I was aware that the wood was of no great extent, and that when through it I should be near my journey's end, I pushed on, and about eight o'clock I had the satisfaction of finding myself in the open country about Hilo. I directed my steps to the Observatory, and on reaching it found there one of our boats, which conveyed me to the ship, and so ended this interesting jaunt. It afforded me both amusement and instruction; and it is not likely that some of the impressions it has left upon my mind will ever be effaced while on this side of the grave.

During my absence nothing worthy of particular notice transpired, except the return of the expedition which set out to ascend Mauna Loa. Indomitable perseverance eventually overcame all obstacles, and the "Stars and Stripes" waved upwards of a week over one of the highest mountains in the world. The success of the undertaking was as complete as could be wished. The altitude of the most elevated point of the mountain was measured, and found to be 13,500 feet above the level of the ocean.

The following observations, extracted from Mr. Eld's journal, will give some idea of the character of the mountain, and of the hardships experienced by our people during their continuance on its summit. He says—

"I never in all my life have witnessed so perfect a scene of desolation as the upper region of this mountain presents. There is not a tree on it, nor shrub, nor any other kind of vegetation, to refresh the eye. You behold nothing but a mass of lava that at one period has been ejected in a liquid state from the terminal crater. To appearance it is of different ages, some of very ancient date, though not yet decomposed. In some places it is smooth, in others it appears in the form of clinkers, which occasionally are raised from five to thirty feet above the surface of the surrounding lava. There are several extinct craters in sight, one of which is even larger than that of Kilauea."

"December 25th. This is the most uncomfortable Christmas-day I have ever experienced. The only way we had of keeping warm was to wrap ourselves in pea-coats and blankets. We had not wood enough to cook our food, and I had to content myself with some sea-biscuit and a piece of raw pork."

"December 27th. The cold this day to our feelings was intense, although the thermometer did not stand lower than 26°. All our exertions in carrying stone for the wall which is to surround our tents, for the purpose of protecting them from the violent winds, and other exercises, such as running and jumping, could scarcely keep us from freezing. We also found it very difficult to breathe, on account of the rarified state of the air. On examination it was also found that our pulses varied, and were very easily excited—mine fluctuated from 80 to 120 beats."

"December 28th. This has been a pleasant day for these regions. At sunrise the effect of horizontal refraction on the sun was very perceptible. It seemed quite small as it appeared above the sea, forming a long horizontal ellipse of two and a half diameters, first enlarging on one side and then another."

"On the 31st the temperature at noon in the sun was 92°, in the shade at 55°, and after dusk it was as low as 13°. In the afternoon I had an attack of the Mountain Sickness. I was sick at the stomach, and had a severe pain in the head."

"The night was favorable for observations, and we made many."

On the morning of the 5th of February we got under-way, and shaped our course for Maui.

The following day, at 2.45 P. M., the Island of Kaloolawe bore west north-west. This is a small, barren island, and used by the Hawaiian Government as a place of exile for convicts, who depend on rain-water for drink, and glean a scanty subsistence from potatoes, which they manage to raise on one or two fertile patches. At 4 P. M. we descried the Island of Maui; it appeared at a distance like two distinct islands. The coast was generally bold and steep, and intersected by numerous valleys, or ravines. Many of these are apparently formed by streams from the mountains which flow through them into the sea. The rocks along the coast were composed of very hard compact lava, or a kind of basalt.

The habitations of the natives appeared in clusters at the openings of the valleys, or scattered over the sides of the hills. It is a beautiful island.

About sunset we came-to off Lahaina, the principal town.

February 8th. This forenoon we were honored with a visit from his Hawiian majesty, Tamahameha III. As we had the chronometers on board we did not salute him, but paid him, however, every other mark of respect. Tamahameha III, or Kamme, as he is familiarly called, is a son of the celebrated Tamahameha I., and a brother of Liho-Liho, during whose reign idolatry and the taboo system were abolished. He is probably twenty-seven years of age, of a middle height, and rather inclined to be corpulent. His complexion is dark olive, his hair of a jet black and straight, and his countenance mild and interesting. In disposition, he is frank, kind and generous. The people always speak of him as a good man. His manners are perfectly free and agreeable. He was educated under the surveillance of the missionaries, and, besides reading and writing his own language, can speak English and Spanish intelligibly. About two years since, he married the daughter* of a chief of the second rank, but, as yet, he has no children. He is generally attended by a number of favorites who join in all his amusements and occupations. His dress on state occasions, consists of a blue coat with epaulettes, white pantaloons and vest, a chapeau, and a sword. At other times, he generally appears in a blue jacket and a blue cloth cap with a gold band around it. He is very fond of the sea, and has a schooner belonging to himself, in which he spends much of his time. He is also fond of all kinds of athletic exercises, is an excellent rider, and a good shot. He made us a long visit, and examined every part of the ship. He appears to entertain a high opinion of Americans, and I understand he frequently consults them upon matters of state. The Rev. Mr. Richards, who acts as his private secretary,

* It is said he married her from love, after the chiefs refused to allow him to marry one of his sisters—a practice which in former times was not considered improper.

and who accompanied him on the present occasion, is a native of New England.

February 9th. To-day I visited the town. It is built near the sea-shore, and the principal street is about a mile long. Near the landing-place is a fort in good repair and well adapted for defence. Many of the houses have gardens attached to them, in which are growing taro, plantains, bananas, cabbages, onions, and a great variety of other vegetables. The king's palace is not yet finished, and he resides at present in a grass house built after the native style. The material employed in the construction of the new building is coral, brought from the neighboring reefs. The town contains several stores, a chapel, and a reading-room. It has considerable trade with whaling vessels.

The inhabitants are numerous, and as well-dressed and well-behaved as any we have seen in the group. The surrounding country is very romantic and beautiful. The whole valley in the rear of the town is a perfect garden. The habitations of the natives are seen peeping through the leaves of the trees; a fine stream takes its course from one end of the valley to the other—in some places flowing along gently and smoothly—at others, rushing down a fall of several feet, and dashing and breaking against the rocks that intercepts its progress; while the sides of the hills which bound the valley towards the interior, are covered with verdure. An excellent view may be obtained of this charming landscape from the summit of the hill on which the high-school is located. There, as you stand, nearly three hundred feet high, you behold in one view the whole scene in which there are beauties that words cannot describe.

> "But who can paint
> Like nature? Can imagination boast
> Amidst its gay creation, hues like her's?

And lay them on so delicately fine,
And lose them in each other, as appears
In every bud that blows? If fancy then
Unequal, fail beneath the pleasing task,
Ah! what shall language do?"

Want of time prevented my visiting the High-school, but, I understand, it is not in a very flourishing condition. The missionary gentlemen connected with the institution are, it is said, unfitted for the management of its operations. From this school, of late years, have been taken all the native teachers, and most of the young men employed on the part of the government. On returning to the beach, I found it thronged with native children, who were amusing themselves in the surf. This seems to be a favorite sport, not only with children, but men and women, and it is a novel and a beautiful sight to see them coming in on the top of a wave moving with a velocity that would overtake the swiftest of our race-horses.

Sometimes they will suddenly disappear, and thus remain until another roller comes along, and dashes them upon the beach. They will not engage in the sport unless the surf is running high. The surf-board which they use is made of some light wood, and is about six feet in length and twenty inches wide. It appeared to me to be a very dangerous amusement, especially for children; but they seemed not to mind it. I continued to gaze on the scene until our sun-down boat shoved off to return to the ship.

In the course of the afternoon Messrs. Budd and May left the ship to survey the shoal off the Island of Kaloolawe.

March 10th. Several boats have been employed to-day in surveying and sounding the harbor, or, more properly, the

roadstead; the best anchorage is abreast of the King's Flag Staff.

March 13th. This afternoon Mr. May and his boat's crew returned in canoes paddled by natives, the boat having gone to pieces at sea the same day he left the ship. It was very fortunate that Mr. Budd was near at hand with his boat. Seeing their situation, he immediately pulled up to them, and conveyed the crew ashore. He then returned to the wreck for the instruments and Mr. May, who he found had drifted, in the meantime, two or three miles out to sea.

After landing, they walked some twenty miles before they reached the settlement, where they were hospitably entertained by the chief, and furnished with canoes to bring them back to the ship. Mr. May might have gone ashore with the men, but he generously declined to leave the wreck until the crew were taken off first.

In the evening, Mr. Budd arrived with the instruments; he stated that bad weather had prevented him from carrying out the instructions, in regard to the survey intrusted to his charge.

March 15th. At an early hour this morning, Mr. Budd and Mr. Sanford left with two boats to join the king's schooner, the use of which his Majesty had offered to Captain Wilkes until the shoal off Kaloolawe could be surveyed.

The following day we ascertained by triangulation, the elevation of the highest peak on Maui. It is six thousand three hundred feet above the level of the ocean. At a height of two thousand feet from the base of this mountain, both the climate and soil are said to be well adapted to the growth of wheat and Irish potatoes.

About noon we got under way, and stood over towards Kaloolawe under all sail. We "lay-to" during the greater part of the night.

March 17th. At daylight wore ship, and stood in for Kaloolawe, and soon after fell in with the king's schooner. As she had not yet completed her surveying duties, we called away all our boats, and sent them to assist her. About 9 A. M., the boats returned, and we filled away and stood for Oahoo, while the king's schooner stood back for Maui.

The shoal here alluded to is situated about two miles from the shore, has two fathoms water on it, at low tide, and is composed of a number of rocks, all within the circumference of three hundred feet. Ships passing through the channel between Hawaii and Maui, intending to anchor in Lahina Roads, must give Kaloolawe a wide berth, and steer for the Peak of Lanai until the High-school of Lahaina bears to the eastward of east northeast, when they may haul in, and steer directly for it.

The principal object in returning to Oahoo, is to replenish our stock of provisions and stores.

On the morning of the 19th, we anchored in Honolulu harbor. We found our friends and acquaintances all well, and apparently delighted at our return. Received an official visit from the Governor of the island. He was received with all due respect. Governor Kekuanaoa is a noble, intelligent looking man, and possesses great energy of character. He is one of the chiefs who accompanied King Liho-Liho in his visit to England, and speaks the English language quite well. He married the daughter of Tamahameha I., and his son Prince Alexander I., is now the heir to the Hawaiian throne.

On the 22d, Lieutenant Alden, with two boats in charge, left the ship to re-sound, and re-survey the harbor off Pearl River, on account of some doubts being expressed by the inhabitants of Honolulu, as to the accuracy of the former survey.

March 25th. This evening, Lieutenant Alden returned from Pearl River, and reported two of his crew as having deserted. He states that he found every part of his former survey correct.

CHAPTER XVIII.

NORTHWEST COAST OF AMERICA.

HAVING completed our surveying and scientific duties at the Sandwich Islands, on the morning of the 5th of April we sailed for the northwest coast of America. As light winds prevailed during this and the following day we did not make much progress on our course.

On the evening of the 7th, we passed the Island of Kauie. This is another of the Sandwich Islands; it is about forty miles in length and twenty-three in breath. The population is estimated at 12,000. Its valleys are fertile, and produce sugar-cane, yams, and taro.

On the 19th, we experienced a great change in the weather; the wind shifted from the southward and eastward to the northward, and we had some violent squalls, which compelled us to reduce sail to reefed-topsails. In a few minutes after the wind shifted, there was a very sensible change in the temperature, and we found it necessary to put on our woolen clothing to keep comfortable. At noon our latitude was 33° 12′ 00″ north, longitude 152° 28′ 00″ west.

During the 20th, 21st, and 23d, we must have sailed through hundreds of acres covered with the Villula, or little man-of-war, as they are commonly called by sailors, from their resemblance to a vessel under canvas. They all had their little sails expanded, and were steering in the same direction as our ship. Their sail is a thin, semi-transparent membrane, extending diagonally from one side of the animal to the other. When examined in a bucket of water in the open air, it appeared to be almost white, but in certain lights, and in its native element, its edges are tinged by the most brilliant blue and crimson reflections. From the body are suspended numerous hair-like tentacula, or feelers, that are constantly engaged in entangling the food upon which the animal lives. It was an interesting sight to see these delicate little creatures mounting securely over the lofty billows, though a brisk breeze was carrying us along at the rate of eight or nine knots an hour.

On the morning of the 28th of April we made Cape Disappointment, off the mouth of the Columbia River, but, as the weather was boisterous, and the sea broke with great violence on the bar, we did not deem it prudent to attempt to enter the river. Next morning the prospects of getting in were no better; indeed, the chances seemed to be still more against us, as the wind during the night had hauled round to the southward and westward with increased strength; we therefore concluded to stand for Puget Sound, to the northward. About 10 A. M. on the 30th, the "look-outs" reported "breakers a-head"; immediately all hands were called, and the ship was brought by the wind. After standing a few minutes on this course the weather cleared, and we discovered Destruction Rocks not more than half a mile off, and exactly in the direction where the breakers had been reported to be. It was in fact a very narrow escape from shipwreck and certain destruction, for even if we had succeeded in getting ashore, we should in all probability have been murdered by the savage natives. A few years ago a Russian brig was wrecked near the same place, the vessel went to pieces, but the crew got safely on shore. They were immediately attacked by the natives and massacred. Another time they attacked the boat of an American vessel that was engaged in the fur-trade, and killed several of the crew. The savages pretended at first that they had come to trade. Our pilot, who has been much among them, also represents them as being a treacherous and savage set.

This circumstance goes to show that we must have been under the influence of a strong current setting to the eastward, for we had been steering all the preceding night northwest, a course which gave the rocks a berth of between thirty and forty miles.

At 3 P. M. we passed between the two outer Flattery Rocks, carrying ten fathoms all the way through, and between 4 and 5 o'clock passed Cape Flattery proper.

We now sailed close along the starboard-shore, which gave us an opportunity of forming some idea of it. A chain of small islands and rocks run parallel with it some eight or ten miles after passing the Cape. It had but little beach, became high and broken in the interior, and was covered with a dense forest, apparently composed of the fir-tree.

A little before sunset several canoes put off from a small bay and pulled toward us, evidently with the intention of paying us a visit, but we had no time to wait for them to get along-side, and after following us some time they turned back. In two of the canoes we observed several women, who seemed to take as active a share in the labors of the paddle as the men. They were all dressed in skins and blankets, and their heads were covered with a green-looking straw-hat of a conical form, with a very broad base, much resembling those which the Chinese are represented in pictures as wearing.

The weather during the night was very disagreeable.

May 1st. The weather continues cold and rainy. The shore we have passed to-day has been divided into steep cliffs and heads, with intermediate beaches. At 9 A. M. a large canoe, paddled by nine Indians, boarded us. They were all small in stature, and far from being good-looking, having broad, flat faces, with high cheek-bones and low foreheads. They were also very dirty about their persons, so much so that it was difficult to make out the color of their skin. One of them was dressed in corduroy pantaloons, and a jacket made of scarlet cloth, and could speak a little English. Their own language was harsh and disagreeable, seeming to be made up principally of gutterals, and the sounds *cluck* and *click* They wore as ornaments a small silver tube stuck through the partition of the nose, and small brass bells suspended around the rim of their ears. They had with them some eight or ten otter skins, but were unwilling to sell them. It seemed as though they had come merely to look at the ship, she being the largest they had ever seen. They remained on board several hours and then went along-side the "Porpoise."

May 2d. This morning another canoe, manned by seven men and one squaw, boarded us. They brought with them some fish, which they readily exchanged for a few pipes and some tobacco. The woman was seated in the bow of the canoe, and was not permitted by the men to come on board. At 3.30 P. M. we passed Point Dungenness, a low, woody tongue of land. After passing this point, our progress was greatly impeded by a very strong ebb-tide. It run between three and four miles an hour. We observed as we sailed along this part of the coast a great number of tall poles, which our pilot informed me, were stuck up by the Indians for the purpose of suspending nets to them, in which they take geese and other wild fowl that frequent these shores at certain seasons of the year. About sunset we reached Port Discovery, and anchored for the night. Numbers of men, women and children came running down to the beach as soon as we made our entrance, and some of them got into their canoes and came along-side. They were no better looking nor more cleanly than those we had before seen, and we were very glad to purchase the fish they brought for sale, in order to get them out of the ship as soon as possible.

This harbor is a superb one, being easy of access, free from rocks or shoals, eight miles long, and from one and a half to two miles wide—possessing the very best kind of bottom, and with sufficient depth of water for the largest vessel to lay within two hundred yards of the shore. The country in the vicinity is not mountainous, but rises into hills of moderate elevation, covered all over with pine and spruce trees of the largest dimensions.

May 3d. The following General Order was issued this afternoon, and passed round to be read:—

"The undersigned informs the officers and crews under his command, that the duties upon which they are about to enter, will necessarily bring them at times in contact with the savage and treacherous inhabitants of this coast, and he therefore feels it his duty, to enjoin upon them the necessity of unceasing caution, and a restrictive and mild system in all their intercourse with them.

"In my General Orders, of July 13th, 1839, my views are expressed fully, respecting our intercourse with savages, and I expect that the instructions therein contained, will be strictly regarded.

"With a knowledge that many of the misfortunes that have befallen previous voyagers on this coast, have arisen from an unrestrained and unguarded intercourse with the natives, he deems it important to order officers in charge of boats, and those having men under their direction, to make it their especial duty to govern them so as to avoid any disputes, or maltreatment of the Indians; and that force is never to be resorted to, but in cases of self-defence.

"No officer or man will be allowed to visit the shore, without arms; and boats' crews upon surveying, or other duties, will be furnished with such as are necessary for their protection.

"United States ship 'Vincennes,'

"CHARLES WILKES."

We had a grand feast to-day, on fish and clams, which we bought from the natives along-side. The latter are not so large as those found on our own coast, but they are more tender, and much better flavored. They may be obtained in any quantities, any where along the beach. The fish were of the salmon and cod kinds. It is yet rather too early in the season for salmon, but they are very fine notwithstanding, especially when broiled.

May 5th. Several of the boats have been employed to-day in surveying the harbor.

In the forenoon I visited the shore. The beach abreast the ship was covered with Indian huts; they were constructed in the rudest manner imaginable, consisting of a few mats and rushes spread out on poles, and offering little or no protection against either the wind or rain. The fire was kindled upon the ground near the centre, and the interior of the building was filled with smoke. I was almost blinded by venturing into one of them, and was very glad to get out again into the open air. A mat or two spread on the ground near the fire, was used for sitting and sleeping upon. This was the only furniture to be seen, and the only article which could conduce to comfort. The owners of these wretched dwellings called themselves Clalams, and were the most singular looking people we had ever seen. The top of their heads was as flat as a board. This was caused by compression when they were very young. I was surprised to find them so poorly clad, in weather that was almost cold enough to freeze water; none had on more than one blanket, and some of them were to be seen going about in a state of perfect nudity. I never before had seen a people who seemed to have so little shame.

The children seemed to give their mothers but little trouble; the infants were tied to a piece of bark which hung to a pole, and was kept in motion by a string fastened to the toe of the mother. The little creatures were perfectly naked.

I observed the men were well supplied with muskets, fowling pieces, and knives, which they procure from the Hudson's Bay Company in exchange for furs. They had also bows and arrows, and the latter were pointed with iron.

The roofs and sides of many of the huts were hung with fish, strung on poles or sticks. There can be no want of food here, as the waters abound with excellent fish, and the forest with game of all kinds. Deer and bear-tracks are to be seen in every direction, and the natives have only to go a few yards from their huts, to kill enough to feed on for weeks together.

I spent several hours in wandering about in the neighboring woods. They were composed almost exclusively of pines, many of which were of immense diameter and height. I measured several that were twenty-five feet in circumference, and upwards of two hundred feet in height. The underbrush was not thick, and the principal impediment to clear walking was the vast number of fallen trees, over which I was obliged to climb. I saw numerous tracks of quadrupeds and one or two flocks of wild geese. The natives say the proper time for killing deer is early in the morning, at which time they resort to the springs to drink. Occasionally I encountered extensive thickets of rose-bushes, through which some large animal appeared but recently to have passed.

On returning to the beach I passed a burial-ground. It was surrounded with stakes to prevent the wild beasts from entering it, and the corpses instead of being interred were wrapped in mats, and placed upon the ground in a sitting posture.

May 6th. Having completed the survey of the harbor, we again spread our sails to the breeze and stood out into the Sound, followed by a great number of canoes, which had for sale fish, clams, and venison. We laid in a large supply of these; and the articles preferred in exchange were, as usual, powder, fish-hooks, clothing, and paint. The fish were the largest we had seen of the kind—some of the cod weighing between forty and fifty pounds. Towards evening the wind became so light we could not stem the tide, and so we stood into Port Townsend, and anchored in ten fathoms water. This is another excellent harbor.

A short walk from the beach here brings you to a beautiful lawn, ornamented with a great variety of pretty flowers. It extends several miles into the interior, and abounds in small lakes, around which hovered vast numbers of ducks and geese. The wood which skirts the green is composed of the same kind of trees as that about Port Discovery.

The Indians inhabiting the surrounding shores are clad in blankets and skins of wild beasts, and appear friendly. They are passionately fond of smoking, and will exchange anything they have for pipes and tobacco. The principal ornament worn by the women is a round piece of white bone, of about two inches in length stuck through the cartilage of their noses.

May 7th. At 1 P. M. we proceeded to get under-way, but were obliged to come-to again soon after on account of light variable winds. Mounts Reinier and Baker are visible from this point. They both rise to a great altitude, and their summits are covered with perpetual snows. There were no natives to be seen at this place, nor any evidences of any ever having been here. The weather during the night was boisterous, and as the anchorage is not well protected, the ship rolled heavily, so much so that we could scarcely walk the decks.

May 8th. Early in the morning we sent the boats out to survey, although the weather was by no means favorable for such duties. Several of the boats narrowly escaped being swamped. We finished about noon, when we made sail and beat to the southward and eastward along Admiralty Sound, with a fresh breeze and a heavy head-sea till about 7 P. M., when we again let-go our anchor within a quarter of a mile of the shore. The water here was deep, and the coast on either hand bold and rugged, and apparently uninhabited. We named this place Pilot Cone, from the circumstance of our receiving there two pilots in the employ of the Hudson's Bay Company, to take the Squadron up to Nisqually.

May 10th. We have enjoyed beautiful weather all this day, and I cannot conceive a more magnificent picture than the Mountains Rainier and Olympus presented as the rising sun illumined their lofty peaks, and dispersed the mists that still floated in fleecy clouds over the tranquil valleys around their bases. The altitude of the latter mountain is stated to be eight thousand feet. At 2.30 P. M. we got under-way. The Sound now became quite narrow, being in some places not more than half a mile wide. Some Indians were observed to day, followed by their dogs, which were small, and had a head and ears strongly resembling those of the wolf. At sunset we came-to under the western shore to wait for day-light. It was a rich treat to behold the sublime prospect around us through all its transitions of sunshine—purple hues, mellow twilight, and evening shades—until there was nothing else to be seen but the dark masses of Rainier and Olympus, uplifting themselves against the clear and starry skies of this region.

May 11th. At an early hour we were out surveying as usual. When finished we again spread our canvas, and made the best of our way for Nisqually, distant about twelve miles. After running about an hour we reached the narrowest part of the Sound, which, at this point was less than 400 yards wide ; the shores on either side were high and precipitous, and the tide run like a sluice. Just before we arrived at the narrows, above described, we passed on our left what appeared to be a large arm of the Sound. We also passed several small conical-shaped islands. About dusk we at length reached our port, and anchored in twenty-two fathoms water. We found here a steamer belonging to the Hudson's Bay Company, and kept to run about the coast to collect furs from the Indians. The Sound is here divided into a great number of arms, some a mile or two wide,and apparently thirty or forty miles in length.

May 12th. Hauled-in close to the shore and moored ship, as we are to remain here some weeks, and perhaps months. Sent all the scientific instruments to the Observatory, except the pendulum. Lieutenant Johnson has been temporarily detached from the "Porpoise," and ordered to take charge of a party that is to examine the interior. Received orders to hold myself in readiness to proceed with Lieutenant Case to Hood's Canal, for the purpose of surveying the same. In the afternoon a large number of natives came on board, among them were some women, who were very good-looking and better dressed than any we have before seen. They came to exchange some moccasins and baskets for red paint and looking glasses. The moccasins were neatly and even tastefully made, and found ready market among the officers, who wished to preserve them as specimens of Indian ingenuity and taste.

July 3d. We reported our return from the so-called Hood's Canal, having been absent from the ship upwards of three weeks; it was found to be an arm of Puget Sound. Its shores are nowhere more than one hundred feet in height, and are formed of stratified clay, with a light gravelly soil, covered with pine and spruce. At Tskutska Point the Canal divides into two branches—one taking a direction nearly northerly, while the other pursues its course to the southwest. At the southern extremity of the canal there is an extensive inlet, called "Black Creek," by which the Indians communicate with the Columbia and Chickelees Rivers. The water in the centre of the canal is too deep for anchorage, but there are several good harbors, of all of which surveys were made.

We fell in with Indians almost every day, and had considerable intercourse with them in the way of trade—they supplying us with venison and fish, and we giving them in exchange powder, fish-hooks, red paint, and cotton handkerchiefs. The venison, in particular, was sold very cheap—five of the ordinary musket charges of powder being the price of a whole carcass.

Though these Indians seemed to understand each other, they informed us that they belonged to different tribes. One party called themselves Squamish, another Socomish, and a third party Toandos. The Squamish appeared to be the most numerous, and, according to their own account, could muster two hundred fighting men. The Toandos were the best-looking, and they assured us that they inhabited the mountains, and were now paying a visit to their friends the Socomish. All these tribes, in their habits and manner of living, resemble those about Nisqually. On leaving the ship we were warned to be on the watch for them, as they were arrant thieves, but I am not aware that they ever attempted to take anything from us, except one of the eye-pieces belonging to the Theodolite. This seemed to excite their attention more than anything else connected with the expedition, and they frequently asked us if it could speak, and whether it had not something to do with the "Great Spirit."* The women are not very good-looking, and the whole burden of domestic occupation is thrown upon them.

They have no permanent settlements; and there were several families who followed us wherever we went, and became familiar with some of the sailors. The men possess muskets, spears, and bows, and arrows. The bows are short and small, but have great elasticity, and when in their hands will do good execution.

The Canal does not terminate where Vancouver's charts would lead one to suppose, but extends ten miles further to the northward and eastward, and approaches within two miles of the waters of the Puget Sound, from which point we communicated with the "Vincennes," the second week out, and obtained a fresh supply of bread and other provisions. There is plenty of fresh water along the shore, and we found several streams large enough to turn mills. Generally speaking, the soil is not rich, and the climate is similar to that experienced at this place.

* The eye-piece was finally recovered through the kindness of Mr. Anderson, the principal agent of the Hudson's Bay Company at Nisqually, by threatening the tribe who had it, the Socomish, with the destruction of their villages and canoes, if they did not give it up by a certain day.

July 5th. Yesterday was the "Glorious Fourth," but being also Sunday, it was very properly agreed that the celebration should be postponed until to-day; accordingly, at an early hour this morning, all was bustle and preparation on board the ship. By nine o'clock all the crew were mustered in clean white frocks and trowsers, and I was directed to take charge of them for the day. Soon after we landed abreast of the ship, and walked up to the Observatory. Here we formed into a procession, and marched off with drums and fifes playing, and the Star-spangled Banner waving, for Fort Nisqually, Vendovi bringing up the rear. Vendovi was dressed "a-la-Fejee," and appeared to enjoy the occasion quite as much as any one present.

On arriving abreast of the fort we halted, and gave three cheers, which were promptly returned by Mr. Anderson and people. We next marched to a piece of open ground, distant about half a mile from the fort. This was the place chosen for the dinner and amusements. There were a great many Indians gathered here, looking at us silently and with much astonishment. At the usual time, dinner was piped by the boatswain and his mates, and we all repaired to partake of the ox which had been purchased from Mr. Anderson, and barbacued for the occasion.

So far, everything had contributed to make the day a very pleasant one. But as there can be no such thing as perfect happiness in this sublunary world of ours, so now a circumstance occurred which for a time threw a gloom over the party. When the salute was fired, one of the men, named Whitehorn, had his arm seriously injured by the sudden explosion of the gun. The wound was dressed as well as it could be, and a litter was made, on which he was conveyed to the ship, under the charge of his messmates.

When dinner was over, the amusements of the morning were exchanged for the excitement of horse-racing—the horses having been engaged from the Indians for that purpose. Sailors like this sport better than almost any other, though very few are able to ride well; but, on this occasion, fortunately, no one was hurt, although a good many were thrown by their steeds.

All the officers, together with Captain McNeil, Dr. Richards, and Mr. Henderson, dined at the Observatory, with Captain Wilkes. Captain McNeil and Dr. Richards are native Americans. The Captain came here a number of years since, and engaged in the fur business, and succeeded so well in it, that the Hudson's Bay Company were glad to buy him off. He is now a trader in the Company's service, owning stock, and receiving a share of the dividends. He is married to a half-breed, and resides in the fort, with Mr. Anderson.

Dr. Richards is attached to the Methodist Mission, and appears to be a kind, gentlemanly man; his residence is situated near the Observatory, and I called there, in the course of the afternoon, to pay my respects to his lady, who received me very kindly.

The doctor informed us that the Mission had but recently been established, and so far, it had not been able to accomplish much; and it was his honest opinion that it never would answer the expectations of its friends at home.

After the rejoicings were ended, I returned the men on board the ship, in the same good order as they had landed, and, I dare say, it will long be remembered by us all, as one of the most pleasant celebrations we have ever experienced.

July 6th. We received, this morning, a visit from Dr. McLaughlin. The doctor is the Chief Factor and Governor of the Hudson's Bay Company. He left Vancouver about a week since, and he expressed his regrets at not being able to reach Nisqually in time to be present at the celebration of the Fourth; he lost his way, when about a hundred miles from the fort. He is a tall, dignified-looking man, with a fair complexion, and I should judge his age to be nearly seventy. He is of Scotch extraction, but by birth a Canadian. He has been in the employ of the Company upwards of forty years, and is said to be pre-eminently fitted for the situation he occupies, being a man of great energy of character, and much talent.

Captain Wilkes conducted him around the ship, and he seemed much pleased.

On his leaving, to return to the shore, the yards were manned, and three cheers were given him, in a manner which showed that we appreciated his kindness towards us; they were three very hearty cheers.

July 16th. To-day, Mr. Johnson and party returned from the interior. They speak favorably of the country passed over, and of the Indians they fell in with. At a place called Chimikane, they found two missionaries, Messrs. Walker and Eel, whose labors had been attended with remarkable success. Among other duties, they had taught the Indians the art of cultivation, and many of them now subsist entirely on the produce which they raise on their lands.

As nothing has yet been heard from the "Peacock," which, on leaving the Sandwich Islands, was ordered to visit the King's Mill Group, and then meet the rest of the squadron at the Columbia River, fears are entertained by many, that she has met with some serious accident.

CHAPTER XIX.

FROM NISQUALLY TO COLUMBIA RIVER, BY LAND.

JULY 17th. I received orders to-day, to join Mr. Eld in an expedition, which has for its object, the exploration and survey of Chickelees River and Grey's Harbor. These orders came rather unexpectedly, and at a very late hour. The ship was already under-way, and I was at my station, when I received them. It seems, that when the expedition was first planned by Captain Wilkes, he designed having Lieutenant Johnson take charge of it, and Mr. Eld to accompany him as his assistant; but Mr. Johnson found fault with his written instructions, whereupon Captain Wilkes took the command from him, and gave it to Mr. Eld, and I am ordered to fill Mr. Eld's former place.

As soon as I was able to get together my instruments and bedding, we shoved off from the ship, and landed on the beach at the foot of Nisqually Hill, where we pitched our tents for the night, as it was almost sunset before we left the vessel, and we had considerable to do before we could proceed on our journey. Among other things, it was absolutely necessary we should see Mr. Anderson, as he was to supply us with the "trade" which we required, to make our purchases from the Indians. Indeed, our instructions do not require us to leave Nisqually before the 19th instant. The following are the other individuals composing the party:—Mr. Brackenridge, assistant botanist, sergeant Stearns, two marines, named

Dismond and Rogers, two sailors by the names of Brooks and Ford, and a half-breed boy, named Joseph, who is to act as interpreter.

About the time we reached the shore, we saw the "Vincennes"* weigh her anchor, and stand down the Sound; the breeze was favorable, and having all sails set, we soon lost sight of her.

8 P. M., we have just seen a Squaw Chief, of the Sachal tribe, who has promised to meet us at the first "Portage," and act as our guide to the Sachal River.

At early daylight Mr. Eld and myself walked up to the fort, and handed Mr. Anderson a list of the articles of trade required, which he at once directed to be put up, and conveyed to our tents. After this we went, by invitation, on board the Company's schooner, and breakfasted with her commander, Captain Scarborough, whom we found to be a very intelligent man, and from whom we received a good deal of information, respecting the Company's affairs. From the schooner, we returned to Nisqually, to take leave of Mr. Anderson and Captain McNeil; after which, we repaired to the beach, caused the tents to be struck, and in a few minutes more we were on our way to the first Portage. We had not proceeded far, however, before we discovered that both our canoes were leaking in all directions, and in order to prevent their being swamped, it was necessary to keep one man in each, constantly bailing. Everything fore and aft was wet through, and the bread and flour were almost ruined. Owing to this circumstance, which of course, checked our progress, we have not been able to reach the first Portage to-day, as we had hoped doing when we first set out.

It is not very probable that we shall have occasion again, to

* She left for San Francisco, California.

return to Nisqually. I will, therefore, here offer all the additional observations which I have to make, regarding it. Its situation is a bad one for trade, as the anchorage is so small that only a few vessels can be accommodated within a proper distance from the shore; and the long hill which it is necessary to ascend, in order to get to the fort, is a serious objection to its becoming a place of deposit for merchandize, as it would very much increase the labor and expense of transportation. Many better places than Nisqually could be found, for a location of a town in the same part of the Sound, and it is a matter of wonder to me, why they were not preferred.

The fort is constructed of pickets, inclosing an area of about two hundred and fifty feet square, with four corner bastions. Within this space are the Agent's stores, and about half-a-dozen log-houses. The fort, when constructed, was thought to be large enough, but since it has become an agricultural post, as well as a trading one, it is found too small, and Mr. Anderson thought it would be enlarged in the course of a year or two. I was in the garden several times, and found it to be under good cultivation; the onions, turnips, peas, &c., &c., all looked very thriving.

The surrounding country is said to be very healthy, and the winter to be mild and of short duration. The Indians in the neighborhood are not numerous, perhaps the whole number not exceeding three hundred. They belong to the tribes who compress their heads, and they are vicious and exceedingly lazy; I have frequently gone into their tents in the middle of the day, and found every member of the family asleep. They are also inveterate gamblers, carrying the vice to the extent of staking their wives and children, and even themselves, for years of slavery! their clothing consists of a blanket, a pair of skin breeches, and moccasins.

They are all of wandering habits, and change their residences in search of their food, which consist, principally, of fish and clams; the latter may be seen in great quantities in their tents, strung on sticks, upon which they have been preserved by smoking and drying. They likewise store up for winter use the camass root and smoked salmon; but generally, however, they are not well fed, as they are too lazy to exert themselves for a supply of food, unless they are in actual want.

In the winter several families live together in lodges constructed of plank; when warm weather returns they break up, and resort in small parties to those places where they can obtain their food most easily. They all understand the Chenook language, but when speaking to each other, they use a language which they call their own, and which differs materially from the Chenook.

The mean temperature during our stay was found to be 59°, and during the same period, the barometer averaged 29.30 inches.

The following morning, at the request of Mr. Eld, I proceeded to the portage, for the purpose of seeing the Chief Squaw before mentioned, and making arrangements with her for Indians and horses to carry the party across the Portage. I arrived there after a pull of ten or fifteen minutes, and shortly after saw an Indian, who informed me that he had been sent by the chief woman to say, that she could not afford us the promised assistance that day, but would to-morrow without fail. I requested the Indian to show me to her house, as I imagined that by seeing her in person I could persuade her to change her mind, but he assured me that she was absent, and would not return home until late in the evening. It was vexatious to meet with so many impediments at the very outset of the expedition

On the following day we made an early start, and by 8 o'clock we reached the Portage. The chief woman was there awaiting us, with her horses, five in number; they were large fine-looking animals, and in excellent condition, which is not generally the case with Indian horses. She also brought with her ten men, who were to assist in carrying the small canoe. The large one, she declared, was too heavy to transport, and if we would let her have it, she would give us a smaller one in return, when we arrived at the Sachal River, which offer we very thankfully accepted. In less than an hour all the arrangements had been completed, and we proceeded on our journey, the Indians bringing up the rear.

It is due to the Chief Squaw to say, that we owe this dispatch principally to her; though her husband was present, she made all the bargains, and gave the Indians their directions. She is a woman of great energy of character, and exercises greater authority over those around her than any man chief I have met with since I have been in the country. She is about fifty years of age, and dresses very neatly for an Indian woman.

We were three hours in accomplishing the Portage. It is between four and five miles long, over a gently rising country thickly covered with maple and spruce trees. The soil is composed of vegetable mould, and seemed to be entirely free from rocks or stones.

Soon after passing the Portage, we came to a small lake, called by the Indians, Sachal, which we examined and found to be three miles in circumference. The soil around it was light brown, sandy loam, and the forest extends down to the water's edge. In the deepest part of the lake, the water appears to have a reddish tinge, but on examining it in a tumbler, it looked as clear as crystal. The Indians informed us, that there was another lake to the northeast, and next day Mr. Eld and myself set out to visit it. We arrived there after a walk of several hours, and the supposed lake proved so insignificant as to hardly deserve the name of a pond; it was not more than one hundred and fifty yards in diameter, nor more than four feet deep, and was overspread with water lilies.

On our return we struck the tents, and, embarking in our canoes on Lake Sachal, we steered for its southern end, where we entered the river bearing the same name. We now made very slow progress, owing to the sinuosity of the river and a variety of other obstructions. Every few minutes we either came in contact with drift-wood, or became entangled among the branches of trees and bushes, covering the banks of the river, and from which it was impossible to clear ourselves otherwise than by cutting them down with our hatchets.

We lost some time also through a trick played us by two Indians, who had been following us for some time in a small canoe, and were anxious to pass us. Having come where the river branched off, we were unable to decide which way our course lay. We therefore inquired of the Indians in the canoe, and they motioned to us to turn off to the right; we did as they directed; but after pulling for more than an hour, we met other Indians, who assured us that we were steering the wrong way, and offered to accompany us back to the main stream, and put us on the proper course, an offer which we very gladly accepted. We did not at first like the idea of being thus outwitted by savages, but, after awhile, when all the trouble of getting right again was over, we were willing to admit that it was a capital joke, and perhaps had as many a good laugh over it as the Indians themselves.

It was past 9 o'clock when we stopped to encamp, and still

we found that we were only six miles from where we entered the river.

At an early hour the following day we were again underway. The drift-wood was still very plentiful, so much so, that in one place the stream was completely choked up by it, and we were compelled to land and carry our canoes around the place. On re-embarking, we used poles in lieu of paddles, and found it a more successful mode of navigating the river. About sunset we reached the town belonging to the Sachal tribe of Indians, and we concluded to stop and spend the night with them.

After supper, Mr. Eld proceeded to visit the chief of the town. He received him kindly, and gave him considerable information respecting his own people and other Indian tribes. Mr. E. was desirous that he should accompany us down the river, but he declined, giving, as a reason, that we should soon meet the Chenooks who were a "bad people," and he was afraid to go among them. According to the chief's account, the Sachals are not more than forty in number, and live chiefly on the camass root and salmon, which fish they capture in great quantities in the rivers Sachal and Chickelees. They have tents similar to those of the Indians in Puget Sound, but they appeared more cleanly and industrious than the tribes of that region.

The country about this town afforded good pasturage, and we observed numbers of horses grazing. At sunrise we resumed our course. The river now had more breadth, and the country on each side became quite interesting; it presented an undulating surface, and was well wooded. In the afternoon we were compelled to make two long portages, in order to pass portions of the river which were filled with rapids and bars. In making these portages we observed several deserted huts.

About 5 P. M., we were overtaken and passed by our old friend, the Squaw Chief, and her husband. She informed us that they were going to pay a visit to a sister, who was residing on the banks of the Chapel River. Her canoe was large and handsomely painted, and was paddled by five slaves, two of whom were women. The following night was a pleasant one, and Mr. Eld and I availed ourselves of it to obtain observations for ascertaining our latitude and longitude.

The next day (25th) we arrived at the point where the Sachal and the Chickelees unite, and we encamped on the banks of the latter stream. The country, as far as we could see, appeared to be well adapted for cultivation, and we observed for the first time since leaving Sachal Lake, some large stones or rocks.

About dusk we had a visit from some Chenooks, who had encamped three or four miles further down the river. We had attracted their attention, they said, by the smoke of our fires, and at first supposed us to be some of their own people. They were all young and rather good-looking, and much better dressed than any Indians we had yet met on the route.

At early dawn the following day, Mr. Eld, with sergeant Stearns, Brooks, and the interpreter, Joe, set out to examine the Chalap, a branch of the Chickelees. They were absent two days and a part of a third, during which time I remained with the rest of the party at the same encampment. The weather continued pleasant, and Mr. Brackenridge made several botanic excursions. He spoke favorably of the country, and thought it well adapted to yield crops of corn and wheat. In the course of the second day several Indian families visited us, and we bought from them a quantity of smoked salmon and some blackberries, which are found in great abundance in the neighboring prairies. These Indians behaved very properly.

with the exception of two girls, who could not have been more than fourteen years of age. That they were ladies of easy virtue, no one, I think, could deny, who had an opportunity of witnessing their conduct.

Shortly after Mr. Eld took his departure, one of the men who remained with me reported that he had just come in from a short walk, and had found a place where there were a number of Indian images. I repaired to the place with him; it was a small pine grove, situated not many yards distant from the encampment. The images were six in number, cut out of plank, and painted with a kind of red pigment. Some of the figures had two heads, one above the other, and one appeared to be intended as a representation of the Sun. We had met with nothing of the kind before, and we could learn nothing now on the subject from the Indians who visited us. There is reason, however, to believe that they had something to do with their notions on religion. Mr. Eld found the Sachal to be a small stream, and utterly impenetrable on account of the bushes and a kind of long grass overgrowing it; he was therefore obliged to leave his canoe and take horses. His guide turned out to be a grand scoundrel, and he caught him in the act of stealing a blanket and some other property, belonging to the party.

On the first day out he met some Indians of the Squamish tribe, who were anxious that he should encamp with them, but as he saw enough of their character to convince him that they were not to be trusted, he declined the invitation, and went on some distance further. He also kept strict guard during the night. He passed over some flats, but, generally speaking, his route lay through a rough, hilly country, thickly covered with pine, several of which he measured and found to be upwards of two hundred feet in height, and from twelve to eighteen in circumference.

On Mr. Eld's return to the camp, the whole party again embarked, and steered down the Chickelees. After a pull of a few miles, the banks of the river on both sides became higher and so steep as to render it quite difficult to land. The "log" was thrown frequently to ascertain the strength of the current, which was found to be one-eighth of a mile per hour. We met this day only two Indians. They were Chickelees; yet, when the interpreter asked them some questions in their tongue, respecting the navigation of the river further down, they pretended not to understand him, and their whole bearing went to show that they were not kindly disposed toward us.

We encamped this day on the left bank of the river, and could hear very distinctly the sound of breakers, a circumstance which convinced us that we must be near the sea-coast.

At 9 A. M. the following morning, we resumed our course down the river. For two or three miles the channel was nearly of the same breadth as it was on the preceding day, but after that it became several hundred feet wider. The country, as far as the eye could see, varied in character—that on the left bank was low, with only here and there a tree—that on the right bank, high and well wooded.

At length, at 9.30 A. M. we made our entrance into Grey's Harbor. It had been our intention to encamp on the south-eastern shore, that being near the scene of our operations; but the wind, sea, and tide, all three being against us, it was impossible to make any progress. Indeed, my own canoe came very near swamping, several times. We therefore bore away for the southwest, or lee shore, where we finally succeeded in effecting a landing, but found it an exceedingly uncomfortable position. It was an extensive bed of brush, roots, and half-decayed logs, that had been thrown up by the tides. Notwithstanding this, we would have been compelled to remain there, that night at least, had it not been for the Chief Woman I have before so often mentioned. Knowing all the while which way we were bound, she had for some days past been looking out for us, and now that she beheld us in this pitiable situation, she hastened to our assistance. "I come," said she, "expressly to convey you to the opposite shore, where you will find a suitable place for encampment, and also be less exposed to the wind." We, of course, accepted the offer, and I at once transferred all my things to her canoe, and Mr. Eld did the same with a portion of his baggage; with this reinforcement, and partly by keeping before the sea, we made very good weather, and at last reached the opposite shore, where we found quite a large encampment of Chickelee Indians.

So soon as the tents were erected, Mr. Eld and myself went among the Indians, for the express purpose of negotiating for a canoe, to take the party around to the Columbia River. After going about some time, I found an Indian, who said that he had a large canoe, which he would sell me, and take his pay at Fort George, as he wanted to be paid in blankets, an article which we had not with us. I went with him to examine it; it was sufficiently capacious, and nearly new, and I told him that he might consider the bargain closed, and I proceeded to give directions about having the canoe launched. It had hardly reached the water, however, when he told the interpreter to say that he was not satisfied with my terms, and the canoe could not be taken away unless I would pay for it on the spot. The reason why I could not pay down, was again stated to him, but to no purpose; and as Mr. Eld had been equally unsuccessful in his negotiations, we concluded to let the matter drop for that day, and return to our encampment. No one who has not had dealings with these people, can form any idea of the degree of patience it requires, to get along with them; they are as changeable as children, and the word "honor" seems not to be in their vocabulary.

After breakfast, next day, I went again to the Indian encampment, to see about purchasing a canoe, and succeeded, finally, in procuring one from a Chief. I likewise succeeded in engaging six men, who promised to remain with us until we reached Astoria. And to make them still more contented, I gave them leave to take their wives with them.

On returning to the camp, I proceeded to get my instruments, and then went in search of Mr. Eld, who, I understood, had commenced operations at the opposite side of the harbor. Not being able, however, to find him, I went on surveying alone; at length I saw a canoe at a distance, which I supposed to be his. Accordingly, I at once put up the instruments, and directed the Indians to pull for the canoe; instead of doing this, however, they commenced complaining, and finally pulled in for the camp. Here they disembarked, and declared that they would not remain in our employ another minute, if I did not give them some powder and tobacco, which I positively refused to do. The women now commenced to pack up their things, and carry them towards the canoe, a circumstance which induced me to believe that the party intended to take the canoe, and return to their encampment. I therefore directed sergeant Stearns to seize the mens' muskets, and put them in one of the tents. This the sergeant did, but the moment we turned our backs to the tents, one of the Indians drew his knife, rushed into them, and brought out the guns, one of which he handed to a woman. After a short struggle, we succeeded in retaking the muskets, upon which an Indian, who acted as spokesman to the party, came up, and said that they intended to adhere strictly to the bargain which they had made with me in the morning, and were ready to go to work at any moment I thought proper. I told them it was my wish, they should go forthwith; the order was obeyed, and I directed them to pull for the place, where I thought I had seen Mr. Eld. The canoe, however, had not proceeded more than two hundred yards, when they began to raise new objections—one complained of being sick, another that he was very hungry, and a third said that he had a sister, who was unwell, and he must go and see her before he could go any further. I reminded them of their promises, and even offered to make them a present, if they would go on, but to no purpose. They ran down to their encampment, and when abreast of it, stood in. On reaching the beach, they landed, and then hauled up the canoe, and I expected nothing less, than being told that I was to consider myself their prisoner. Such, however, was not the case; they said nothing about my remaining with them; and when I remarked that I wished to return to our camp, they even furnished me with a small canoe, to ferry me over the stream, which separated the two encampments.

The following day, the owners of the muskets came to the camp, and begged that they might be returned to them, and we finally yielded to their wishes. Owing partly to these troubles with the Indians, and partly to bad weather, we had made but little progress in the survey of the harbor as yet. Some days it stormed so furiously, that we could not venture out at all.

On the 6th of August, we shifted our camp about six miles toward the Capes. After staying here a few days we selected another place at the South Head. Our greatest difficulty now was the want of provisions. All our stores had been exhausted, and for some days past we had been living on dead fish we picked up on the beach, and some cammass root which we had bought from the Indians. This state of things lasted until the 13th of August, when Lieutenant De Haven who had been sent by Captain Wilkes to afford us relief, arrived with a supply of provisions. This enabled us to go on our usual ration, and in a few days we all regained our strength, and were able to proceed with our surveying duties.

From Mr. De Haven we learned for the first time the loss of the "Peacock" on the bar off the mouth of the Columbia River.

On the 24th the survey was completed, and we set out for Astoria, where the Squadron was now lying.

The soil in the vicinity of Grey's Harbor is of an inferior quality, and the harbor itself seems to offer but few facilities for commercial purposes. The channel is narrow, the width being from one-half to two-thirds of a mile, with dangerous breakers on both sides. The depth of water is from five to seven fathoms. The space after entering is extensive, but the greatest part of it is filled up with mud flats which are bare at low water, and confine the harbor for the anchorage of vessels to a few hundred yards. The River Chickelees before entering into the harbor, increases in width some six or seven hundred feet and is navigable for vessels drawing ten or twelve feet of water for several miles above its mouth.

Fogs prevail in the summer season, and some days during our stay we found them so dense as to render it impossible for us to proceed with our surveying duties.

The tides are irregular and influenced by the winds; the time of high water at change and full was found to be 11 hours 25 minutes.

The Indians, who inhabit the shores of the harbor, call themselves Chickelees, and their number is about two hundred; they construct their huts after the manner of the Squamish

Astoria.

tribe, and, like them, live principally by fishing. We found them well supplied with blankets, muskets and knives. They are excessively fond of tobacco, and invariably swallow the smoke, and oftentimes retain it so long in the stomach as to throw them into convulsions. They enjoy high reputation as warriors, for which reason they are much dreaded by their neighbors, the Sachals and Sachaps, who are of a more peaceable character. Their amusements are similar to those of the tribes residing about Nisqually.

On the day of our departure (24th) for Astoria, the surf ran very high, and our Indians* instead of paddling the canoes preferred tracking them along the beach inside of the surf. This is the mode they always adopt when they are journeying along the coast, to prevent accidents from the surf, of which they have great dread. We made very good progress, and at sunset arrived within fifteen miles of Shoal-Water Bay. Near this day's encampment we found a Chickelees Chief who sold us another canoe, and who promised to act as our guide around to the Columbia.

About noon next day, we reached Shoal-Water Bay. Here, by reason of not understanding the guide, Mr. Eld and myself separated, he pursuing the course leading to the eastern Portage, I the one leading to the western, and did not see each other again until we arrived on board the "Flying Fish." The western Portage is the one preferred by the Indians; it is between four and five miles long, and lays through a flat marshy country.

On the 27th, the schooner got under-way and landed us at Astoria, where we received written orders from Captain Wilkes, requiring us to join him at Vancouver.

* The day previous to our leaving Grey's Harbor, Mr. Eld succeeded in engaging six Indians who were to take us as far as Shoal-Water Bay.

At Astoria, we had the pleasure of meeting the "Peacock's" officers and crew, who appeared to be in good health and fine spirits, and all spoke of the kind treatment they had received from Mr. Birnie, the agent of the Hudson's Bay Company at Astoria, and I take this occasion to say, that his treatment to Mr. Eld and myself also, was such as to merit our warmest thanks. From what I could learn, both from officers and crew, I inferred, that the loss of the "Peacock" was an unavoidable occurrence, and that through the whole disaster, Captain Hudson's behavior had been that of a good officer and an able seaman.

During our stay at Astoria I also had the pleasure of becoming acquainted with an American missionary and his lady, Mr. and Mrs. Smith. They had arrived in the country two years previous with a party which crossed the Rocky Mountains, and, for the last fifteen months, had been stationed at a place called Kamia. But the Indians having left there, and the climate not agreeing with Mrs. Smith's health, they had determined to leave the country and proceed to the Sandwich Islands; they expected to sail in a few days for Oahoo. They both gave very unfavorable accounts of the Indians among whom they had been residing, and deemed it quite useless to send missionaries among them.

Astoria is situated on the south bank of the Columbia River, and distant about fifteen miles from Cape Disappointment. The location is a beautiful one; it forms the crest of a hill which rises some hundred feet above the level of the river, and in pleasant weather, the waters of the Pacific Ocean, Point Ellice, Tongue Point, Katolamet Range, with many other striking objects, are in sight.

As for the town, it is a sorry one. Indeed, ever since the period fixed on by the Hudson's Bay Company to make Vancouver the principal trading port, Astoria has been suffered to decline ; and, now, all it can boast of is some half-dozen log houses, and as many shades, which, of course, is a great falling off, if the accounts of its former size and prosperity be true.

There are many Indians hanging round Astoria ; most of them belong to the Clatsop tribe, whose principal town is situated near Point Adams. They have an American missionary among them, by the name of Frost, and I should judge they had need for many more, for certainly they are the most degraded set of beings we have seen since our arrival in the country. They will sell anything they have for rum, and while it lasts they are never sober; they are likewise much addicted to lying and stealing. It is also said of them that they are very belligerent; there is scarcely a tribe on the coast with which they are on friendly terms. A white man, however, can travel through any part of their territory quite as safely as he can in any other, for the Hudson's Bay Company are sure to punish all murders, or robberies, with death; and the severity, as well as the certainty of the punishment, is sufficient to prevent the commission of such crimes more frequently than they occur in civilized countries. About a year since, a white man was murdered for his property by a slave belonging to a Chief; the instant the murder was made known to the Company, the slave was seized, and hung in presence of all the tribe.

We performed our jaunt to Vancouver in a flat-bottomed barge, furnished by Mr. Birnie. These boats are, from their light draft of water, exceedingly well adapted for the navigation of the river. They are used by the Company to carry freight up and down the river, and are capable of carryiug large cargoes, and when well-manned can make quite as much headway as a canoe.

The breadth of the river gradually diminishes as you approach Vancouver, and at the lowest ebb the channel is deep enough for vessels drawing fourteen feet water. The current does not appear to be very strong, and the water as it flows past looks turbid, but when it is taken up, it is perfectly clear. The country on both sides rises gradually to the height of some thousand feet, and is well timbered. We saw on both banks many Indian villages, some of which were at the time without inhabitants. This last feature was attributed to the ravages of the fever and ague, and the appearance of the burying-grounds in the vicinity served to confirm the statement; they were large, and thickly studded with graves. The first case of the kind occurred in the year 1830, when an European vessel, commanded by Captain Dominis, was lying at anchor in the river, and the Indians have always believed that he brought the disease among them. In the opinion of the physicians of the Hudson's Bay Company, the disease would not prove so fatal if they would adopt the European mode of treating it, but this they will not do; they prefer their own treatment, which consists in taking a series of cold baths. The manner of disposing of the dead does not appear to be the same at all the burial grounds. In some, the coffins (which were canoes planked over) rested on limbs of trees, while in others they stand in an upright position, with about one-third of their length buried in the ground. The coffins are all painted red, the favorite color, and have hung around them mats, baskets, bows and arrows; in short, everything supposed to be of use to the departed on their journey to the world of Spirits and future Hunting Grounds.

On the third day out, about 4 P. M., we passed the brig "Porpoise," employed in surveying the river, and in about half an hour more we landed at Vancouver, and reported to Captain Wilkes, who congratulated us upon our safe return, and also complimented us upon the result of our labors.

On leaving Captain W. we took a walk in and about the famous fort, and then repaired on board the "Porpoise."

September 1st. This morning I received other orders, namely, to be ready to join the Overland Expedition to California, commanded by Lieutenant Emmons. It is already organized and encamped on the banks of the Willamette River, and will, I am informed, consist, besides myself, of the following individuals:—Lieutenant Emmons, Mr. Eld, Dr. Whittle; Mr. Peale, naturalist; Mr. Rich, botanist; Mr. Dana, geologist; Mr. A. T. Agate, artist; Mr. Brackenridge, assistant-botanist; sergeant Stearns; corporal Hughes; privates Smith and Marsh; seamen Sutton, Doughty, Merza, Walthan; Batist Guardipee, guide.

I understand the object of the Expedition originally was to explore the country as far as the Shaste Mountains, and then return to Vancouver by a different route.

Mr. Emmons is here attending to the procuring of stores, and will return to the camp to-morrow.

The following sketch of a life at Vancouver, by one who spent some weeks there, may be interesting:—

"Fort Vancouver is the depôt at which are brought the furs collected west of the Rocky Mountains, and from which they are shipped to England, and also the place at which all the goods for the trade are landed, and from which they are distributed to the various posts of that territory by vessels, batteaux, or pack-animals, as the various routes permit. It was established by Governor Simpson in 1824, as the great centre of all commercial operations in Oregon; is situated in a beautiful plain on the north bank of the Columbia, ninety miles from the sea, and stands 400 yards from the water's side. The noble river before it, is 1670 yards wide, and from five to seven fathoms in depth. The whole surrounding country is covered with forests of pine, cedar, fir, &c., interspersed here and there with small open spots, all overlooked by the vast snowy pyramids of the President's Range, 35 miles in the east.

"The fort itself, is an oblong square, 250 yards in length, by 150 in breadth, inclosed by pickets, twenty feet in height. The area within is divided into two courts, around which are arranged thirty-five wooden buildings, used as officers' dwellings, lodging apartments for clerks, store-houses for furs, goods and grains, and as workshops for carpenters, blacksmiths, coopers, turners, wheelwrights, &c. The building near the rear gate, is occupied as a school-house; and a brick structure as a powder magazine.

"Six hundred yards below the fort, and on the bank of the river, is a village of fifty-three log houses; in these live the Company's servants; among them is a Hospital, in which those of them who become diseased, are humanely treated. Back and a little east of the fort, is a barn, containing a mammoth threshing-machine, and near this are a number of long sheds, used for storing grain in the sheaf. And behold the Vancourer farm, stretching up and down the river, three thousand acres, fenced into beautiful fields, sprinkled with dairy-houses and herdsmen's and shepherd's cottages! A busy place is this. The farmer on horseback at break of day, summons one hundred half-breeds and Iriquois Indians from their cabins to the fields; twenty or thirty ploughs tear open the generous soil; the sowers follow with their seed, and pressing on them, come a dozen harrows to cover it. And thus thirty or forty acres are planted in a day, till the immense farm is under crop. The season passes on, teeming with daily industry, until the harvest waves on all these fields. And then sickle and hoe glisten in tireless activity, to gather in the rich reward of this toil—the food of seven hundred people at this post, and of thousands more at the posts on the deserts in the east and north. The saw-mill, too, is a scene of constant toil; thirty or forty Sandwich Islanders are felling the pines, and dragging them to the mill; sets of hands are playing two gangs of saws by night and day; three thousand feet of lumber per day—900,000 feet per annum—constantly being shipped to foreign ports. The grist-mill is not idle; it must furnish bread-stuffs for the posts and the Russian market in the northwest; and its deep music is heard daily and nightly, half the year.

"But we will enter the fort. The blacksmith is repairing ploughshares, harrow-teeth, chains, and mill-irons; the tinman is making cups for the Indians, and camp-kettles, &c.; the wheelwright is making wagons, and the wood part of plough sand harrows; the carpenter is repairing houses and building new ones; the cooper is making barrels, for pickling salmon and packing furs; the clerks are posting books and preparing the annual returns to the board in London; the salesmen are receiving beaver, and dealing out goods. But, hear the voices of those children from the school-house! they are the half-breed offspring of the gentlemen and servants of the Company, educated at the Company's expense, preparatory to being apprenticed to trades in Canada; they learn the English language, writing, arithmetic, and geography. The gardener, too, is singing out his honest satisfaction, as he surveys from the north gate, ten acres of apple-trees, laden with fruit, his bowers of grape-vines, his beds of vegetables, and flowers. The bell rings for dinner; we will see the 'hall,' and its convivialities.

"The dining-hall is a spacious room, on the second floor, ceiled with pine above and at the sides. In the southwest corner of it, is a large close stove sending out sufficient caloric to make it comfortable.

"At the end of a table, twenty feet in length, stands Governor McLaughlin, directing guests and gentlemen from neighboring posts, to their places; and chief-traders, traders, the physician, clerks, and the farmers, slide respectfully to their places, at distances from the Governor, corresponding to the dignity of their rank in the service; thanks are given to God, and all are seated. Roast beef and pork, boiled mutton, baked salmon, boiled ham, beets, carrots, turnips, cabbage and potatoes, and wheaten bread, are tastefully distributed over the table, among a dinner-set of elegant Queen's ware, burnished with glittering glasses, and decanters of various colored Italian wines. Course after course goes round, and the Governor fills to his guests and friends, and each gentleman in turn vies with him, in diffusing around the board, a most generous allowance of viands, wines, and warm fellow-feeling. The cloth and wines are removed together, cigars are lighted, and a strolling smoke about the premises, enlivened by a courteous discussion of some mooted point of natural history, or politics, closes the ceremonies of the dinner-hour at Fort Vancouver. These are some of the incidents of life at Vancouver."

CHAPTER XX.

EARLY HISTORY OF OREGON.

"Take the wings
Of morning, and the Barcan desert pierce,
Or lose thyself in the continuous woods
Where rolls the Oregon, and hears no sound
Save his own dashings."

NORTHWESTERN AMERICA is divided from the other portions of the Continent, by the Rocky Mountains, which extend throughout its entire length, in a north-westerly direction, in continuation of the Mexican Andes, to the shores of the Arctic Ocean. Between this great chain of mountains and the Pacific Ocean, a most ample territory extends, which may be regarded as divided into three great districts. The most southerly of these, of which the northern boundary line was drawn along the parallel of 42°, by the Treaty of Washington, in 1819, belong to Mexico. The most northerly, commencing at Behring's Straits, and of which the extreme southern limit was fixed at the southernmost point of Prince of Wales Island, in the parallel of 54° 40′ north, by treaties concluded between Russia and the United States of America, in 1824, and between Russia and Great Britain, in 1825, forms a part of the dominions of Russia; whilst the intermediate country is not as yet under the sovereignty of any power.

To this intermediate territory, different names have been assigned. To the portion of the coast, between the parallels of 43° and 48°, the British have applied the name of New Albion. Since the expedition of Sir Francis Drake, in 1578-'80, and the British Government, in the instructions furnished by the Lords of the Admiralty, in 1776, to Captain Cook, directed him to proceed to the coast of New Albion, endeavoring to fall in with it in the latitude of 45°.* At a later period, Vancouver gave the name of New Georgia to the coast between 50° and 54°, whilst to the entire country, north of New Albion, between 48° and 56° 30′, from the Rocky Mountains to the sea, British traders have given the name of New Caledonia, ever since the Northwest Company formed an establishment on the western side of the Rocky Mountains, in 1806. The Spanish government, on the other hand, in the course of the negotiations with the British government, which ensued upon the seizure of the British vessels in Nootka Sound, and terminated in the Convention of the Escurial, in 1790, designated the entire territory as "the Coast of California in the South Sea."

If we adopt the more extensive use of the term Oregon†

* See Cook's Voyage to the Pacific Ocean, 1782.

† The authority for the use of the word Oregon, or Oregan, has not been clearly ascertained, but the majority of writers agree in referring the introduction of the name to Carver's Travels. Jonathan Carver, a native of Connecticut, set out from Boston, in 1766, soon after the transfer of Canada to Great Britain, on an expedition to the regions of the Upper Mississippi, with the ultimate purpose of ascertaining the breadth of that vast Continent, which extends from the Atlantic to the Pacific Ocean, in its broadest part, between 45° and 46° of north latitude. Carver did not succeed in penetrating to the Pacific Ocean, but he first made known, or at least established a belief in the existence of a great river, termed, apparently, by the Indian nations in the interior, Oregon, or Oregan, the source of which, he placed not far from the head waters of the river Missouri, "on the other side of the summit of the lands that divide the waters, which run into the Gulf of Mexico, from those which fall into the Pacific Ocean." He was led to infer from the account of the natives, that this "Great River of the West" emptied itself near the Straits of Anian, although it may be observed, that the situation of the so called Straits of Arian themselves, were not at this time accurately fixed. Carver, however, was misled in this latter respect, but the description of the locality, where he placed the source of the

territory, as applied to the entire country, intermediate between the dominions of Russia and Mexico, respectively—its boundaries will be the Rocky Mountains on the east, the Pacific Ocean on the west, the parallel of 54° 40′ north latitude on the north, and that of 42° north latitude on the south. The entire superficies would thus amount to 501,600 geographical square miles. If, on the other hand, we accept the north-western limit, which Mr. Greenhow has marked out for "the Country of the Columbia," namely, the range of mountains which stretches north-eastward, from the eastern extremity of the Straits of Fuca, about four hundred miles, to the Rocky Mountains; separating the waters of the Columbia from those of Frazer's River, it will include not less than 400,000 square miles in superficial extent, which is nearly half of all the States of the Federal Union.

Such are the geographical limits of the Oregon Territory, in its widest and in its narrowest extent. The Indian hunter roamed throughout it, undisturbed by civilized man, till near the conclusion of the last century, when Captain James King, on his return from the expedition, which proved so fatal to Captain Cook, made known the high prices which the fur of the sea-otter commanded, in the markets of China, and, thereby attracted the attention of Europeans to it. The enterprise of British merchants was in consequence of Captain King's suggestion, directed to the opening of the Fur trade,

Oregon, seems to identify it either with the Flatbow, or with the Flathead, or Clark's River, each of which streams, after pursuing a north-western course, from the base of the Rocky Mountains, unites with a great river, coming from the north, which ultimately empties itself into the Pacific Ocean, in latitude 46° 18′ 0′0′. The name of Oregon has consequently been perpetuated in this main river, as being really the "Great River of the West," and by this name it is best known in Europe; but in the United States, it is more frequently spoken of as the Columbia River, from the name of the American vessel, the "Columbia," which really first discovered it in 1792, and anchored off Astoria, distant about ten miles from the mouth of the river between the native hunters, along the northwest coast of America, and the Chinese, as early as 1786. The attempt of the Spaniards to suppress this trade, by the seizure of the vessels engaged in it, in 1789, led to the dispute between the Crowns of Spain and Great Britain, in respect to the claim to exclusive sovereignty, asserted by the former power over the Port of Nootka and the adjacent latitudes, which was brought to a close by the Convention of the Escurial, in 1790.

The European merchants, however, who engaged in this lucrative branch of commerce, confined their visits to stations on the coasts, where the natives brought from the interior the produce of their hunting expeditions; and even respecting the coast itself, very little accurate information was possessed by Europeans before Vancouver's survey. Vancouver, as is well known, was dispatched in 1791 by the British Government to superintend, on the part of Great Britain, the execution of the Convention of the Escurial, and he was at the same time instructed to survey the coast from 35° to 60°, with a view to ascertain in what parts civilized nations had made settlements, and likewise to determine whether or not any effective water-communication, available for commercial purposes, existed in those parts between the Atlantic and Pacific Oceans. A Spanish Expedition, under Galiano and Valdes, was engaged about the same time upon the same object; so that from this period, namely, the concluding decade of the last century, the coast of Oregon may be considered to have been sufficiently well known.

The interior, however, of the country had remained hitherto unexplored, and no white man seems ever to have crossed the Rocky Mountains prior to Alexander Mackenzie in 1793. Having ascended the Unjigah, or Peace River, from the Athabaska Lake on the eastern side of the Rocky Mountains to one of its sources in 54° 24′ 00″, Mackenzie embarked upon a river flowing from the western base of the mountains, called by the natives Tacoutche Tesse. This was generally supposed to be the northernmost branch of the Columbia River, till it was traced in 1812 to the Gulf of Georgia, where it empties itself in 49° latitude, and was henceforth named Frazer's River. Mackenzie having descended this river for about 250 miles, struck across the country westward, and reached the sea in 52° 20′ 00″, at an inlet which had been surveyed a short time before by Vancouver, and had been named by him Cascade Canal. This was the first expedition of civilized men through the country west of the Rocky Mountains. It did not lead to any immediate result in the way of settlement, though it paved the way by contributing, in conjunction with Vancouver's survey, to confirm the conclusion at which Captain Cook had arrived, that the American continent extended in an uninterrupted line north-westward to Behring's Straits.

The result of Mackenzie's discoveries was to open a wide field to the westward for the enterprise of British merchants engaged in the fur-trade; and thus we find a settlement in this extensive district made not long after the publication of his voyage, by the agents of the Northwest Company. This great association had been growing up since 1784, upon the wreck of the French-Canadian fur-trade, and gradually absorbed into itself all the minor companies. It did not, however, obtain its complete organization till 1805, when it soon became a most formidable rival to the Hudson's Bay Company, which had been chartered as early as 1670, and had all but succeeded in monopolizing the entire fur-trade of North America, after the transfer of Canada to Great Britain. The Hudson's Bay Company, with the characteristic security of a chartered company, had confined their posts to the shores of the ample territory which had been granted to them by the Charter of Charles II., and left the task of procuring furs to the enterprise of the native hunters. The practice of the hunters was to suspend their chase during the summer months, when the fur is of inferior quality and the animals rear their young, and to descend by the lakes and rivers of the interior to the established marts of the Company, with the produce of the past winter's campaign. The Northwest Company adopted a totally different system. They dispatched their servants into the very recesses of the wilderness to bargain with the native hunters at their homes. They established "wintering partners" in the interior of the country to superintend the intercourse with the various tribes of Indians, and employed at one time not fewer than two thousand *voyageurs*, or boatmen. The natives being thus no longer called away from their pursuit of the beaver and other animals, by the necessity of resorting as heretofore to the factories of the Hudson's Bay Company, continued on their hunting-grounds during the whole year, and were tempted to kill the cub and full-grown animal alike, and thus to anticipate the supply of future years. As the nearer hunting-grounds. became exhausted, the Northwest Company advanced their stations westwardly into regions previously unexplored, and in 1806 they pushed forward a post across the Rocky Mountains, through the passage where the Peace River descends through a deep chasm in the chain, and formed a trading establishment on a lake now called Frazer's Lake, situated in 54° north latitude. It is from this period, according to Mr. Harnon, who was a partner in the company, and superintendent of its trade on the wertern side of the Rocky Mountains, that the name of New Caledonia had been used to designate the northern portion of the Oregon Territory.

The United States of America had in the meantime not remained inattentive to their own future commercial interests in this quarter, as they had dispatched from the southern side an exploring party across the Rocky Mountains almost immediately after their purchase of Lousiana in 1803. On this occasion Mr. Jefferson, then President of the United States, commissioned Captains Lewis and Clarke "to explore the River Missouri and its principal branches to their sources, and then to seek and trace to its termination in the Pacific, some stream, whether the Columbia, the Oregon, the Colorado, or any other which might offer the most direct and practicable water-communication across the continent for the purpose of commerce." The party succeeded in passing the Rocky Mountains towards the end of September, in 1805, and after following, by the advice of their native guides, the Kooskookee River, which they reached in latitude 43° 34′ 00″, to its junction with the principal southern tributary of the Great River of the West, they gave the name of Lewis to this tributary. Having in seven days afterwards reached the main stream, they traced it down to the Pacific Ocean, where it was found to empty itself in latitude 46° 18′ 00″ north. They thus identified the Oregon, or Great River of the West of Carver, with the river to whose outlet Captain Grey had given the name of his vessel, the Columbia, in 1792, and having passed the winter among the Clatsop Indians in an encampment on the south side of the river, not very far from its mouth, which they called Fort Clatsop, they commenced with the approach of spring the ascent of the Columbia on their return homeward. After reaching the Kooskookee, they pursued a course eastward, till they arrived at a stream, to which they gave the name of Clarke, as considering it to be the upper part of the main river which they had previously called

Clarke at its confluence with the Lewis. Here they separated at about the forty-seventh parallel of latitude. Captain Lewis then struck across the country northward to the Rocky Mountains, and crossed them so as to reach the head-waters of the Maria River, which empties itself into the Missouri, just below the Falls. Captain Clarke, on the other hand, followed the Clarke River towards its source, in a southward direction, and then crossed through a gap in the Rocky Mountains, so as to descend the Yellow Stone River to the Missouri. Both parties united once more on the banks of the Missouri, and arrived in safety at St. Louis in September, 1806.

The reports of this Expedition seem to have first directed the attention of traders in the United States to the hunting-grounds of Oregon. The Missouri Fur Company was formed in 1808, and Mr. Henry, one of its agents, established a trading post on a branch of the Lewis River, the great southern arm of the Columbia. The hostility, however, of the natives, combined with the difficulty of procuring supplies, compelled Mr. Henry to abandon it in 1810. The Pacific Fur Company was formed about this time at New York, with the object of engaging in the fur commerce between China and the northwest Coast of America. The head of this association was John Jacob Astor. He had already obtained a charter from the Legislature of New York, in 1809, incorporating a Company, under the name of the American Fur Company, to compete with the Mackinaw Company of Canada, within the Atlantic States, of which he was himself the real representative, according to Mr. Washington Irving—his board of Directors being merely a nominal body. Mr. Astor engaged nine partners in his scheme, of whom six were Scotchmen, who had all been in the service of the Northwest Company, and three were citizens of the United States.

Having at last arranged his plans, he dispatched in September, 1810, four of his partners, with twenty-seven subordinate officers and servants, in the ship, "Tonquin," commanded by Jonathan Thorne, a lieutenant in the United States Navy, to establish a settlement at the mouth of the Columbia River. They arrived at their destination in March, 1811, and erected a fort and other necessary buildings on the south side of the river, about ten miles from the mouth, to which the name of Astoria was given. The Tonquin proceeded in June on a trading voyage to the northward, and was destroyed, with her crew, by the Indians in the Bay of Clyoquot, near the entrance of the Strait of Fuca.

In the following month of July, Mr. Thomson, the agent of the Northwest Company, descended the northern branch of the Columbia, and visited the settlement at the mouth of the Columbia. He was received with friendly hospitality by the Superintendent of the Pacific Company, and shortly took his departure again. Mr. Stuart, one of Mr. Astor's partners, accompanied him up the river as far as its junction with the Okinagan, where he remained during the winter, collecting furs from the natives. The Factory at Astoria, in the meantime, was reinforced in January, 1812, by a further detachment of persons in the service of the Pacific Fur Company, who had set out overland early in 1811, and after suffering extreme hardships, and losing several of their number, at last made their way in separate parties to the mouth of the Columbia. A third detachment was brought by the ship "Beaver" in the following May. All the partners of the Company, exclusive of Mr. Astor, had now been dispatched to the scene of their future trading operations. Mr. Mackay was alone wanting to their number; he had unfortunately proceeded northwards with Captain Thorne, in order to make arrangements with the Russians, and was involved in the common fate of the crew of the "Tonquin."

The circumstances, however, of this establishment underwent a great change upon the declaration of war by the United States against Great Britain, in 1812. Tidings of this event reached the Factory in January, 1813, through Messrs. McTavish and Laroque, partners of the Northwest Company, who visited Astoria with a small detachment of persons in the employment of that Company, and opened negotiations for the dissolution of the Pacific Fur Company, and the abandonment of the establishment at Astoria. The Association was, in consequence, dissolved in July, 1813, and on the 16th of October following, an agreement was executed between Messrs. McTavish and Mr. John Stuart, on the part of the Northwest Company, and Messrs. McDougal, McKenzie, David Stuart, and Clarke, on the part of the Pacific Company, by which all the establishments, furs, and stock in hand of the late Pacific Fur Company, were transferred to the Northwest Company, at a given valuation, which produced, according to Mr. Greenhow, a sum total of 58,000 dollars.

The bargain had hardly been concluded when the British sloop-of-war, the "Racoon," under the command of Captain Black, entered the Columbia River, with the express purpose of destroying the settlement at Astoria; but the establishment had previously become the property of the Northwest Company, and was in the hands of their agents. All that remained for Captain Black to perform was to hoist the British Flag over the Factory, the name of which he changed to Fort George. There have been no changes in the Territory since 1813, worthy of particular notice.

CHAPTER XXI.

FROM VANCOUVER TO SAN FRANCISCO, CALIFORNIA.

At 11 A. M., September 2d, Messrs. Eld, Dana, Brackenbridge and myself, embarked in a canoe paddled by four Indians, to join the Expedition I have before spoken of. At 2, we reached the mouth of the Willamette River, which we entered. It is here about 800 feet in breadth, and its banks are low and uninteresting. After ascending a few miles we met the Rev. Mr. Cone, who was on his way to Vancouver. He spoke of our party encamped in the valley, and stated that several of the scientific gentlemen were suffering from the attacks of the ague. Mr. C. is connected with the Methodist Mission in Oregon. At sunset we encamped near an oak grove on the left bank of the river.

At an early hour the following morning, we resumed our journey, and after pulling about eight miles, reached the Klackamus, where we found five Americans building a schooner, in which they intended to engage in the sea-otter trade. They informed us that they had been in Oregon nearly a year, and had crossed the Rocky Mountains. They did not speak favorably of the country, and stated, that they intended to leave for California as soon as they could make a little money in the fur business. The Willamette River is navigable at the lowest stage of water as far as the Klackamus. After ascending another three miles, we arrived at the Falls. As we approached these, the breadth of the river rapidly diminished, and the water shoaled; the banks were also higher and more precipitious. There is a mission station here under the charge of Mr. Waller. The Hudson's Bay Company have likewise a trading post near by, and pack a great many salmon, which the Indians catch in large quantities. It is said to be the best salmon fishery on the river. The Falls are between twenty and thirty feet in height, and, when the country becomes settled, they will be invaluable for their water-power. An American by the name of Moore, told us, that the western side of the Falls had become his property, he having bought the land on that side of the river from an Indian chief.

Our progress now was much slower than before, owing to the strength of the current, and we crossed and re-crossed the river frequently in order to take advantage of the eddies. This part of the Willamette is considered very dangerous when the water is high, and the Indians, in passing, invariably make to it a propitiatory offering of some of their food, that they may have a safe passage.

The night was clear and pleasant, and we continued to pull until we reached Champooing village, which was as far as Mr. Eld and myself intended to proceed by water.

On the following morning, we breakfasted by invitation, with Mr. McKoy, one of the most noted individuals in this part of the country. Among the trappers, he is the hero of many a tale, and he entertained us during our stay with an account of several of his adventures with the Indians, which certainly showed him to be a man of great nerve and shrewdness. He is about forty years of age, tall, and straight, and has a countenance expressive of great firmness and daring of character. His crops had just been gathered, and he informed us that the average yield of the wheat would be twenty-five bushels to the acre. His house stands on the margin of a small stream, and answers both for a dwelling and a grist-mill.

When breakfast was over, our friend furnished us with horses, and we rode on in the direction of the encampment. We passed many farms of from thirty to one hundred acres, belonging to Canadians who had been in the service of the Hudson's Bay Company; they liked the country, and appeared very comfortable and thriving. We saw a large mumber of cattle, horses, and sheep, grazing in the surrounding fields. From 12 to 1 P.M., we halted, to partake of dinner and rest the horses; another short ride brought us to the American settlement. There were many things here to remind us of home; among others, a good road, well inclosed fields, a blacksmith-shop, and a school-house. This is the largest and most prosperous settlement in all Oregon. It is situated on the banks of the Willamette River, on a fertile plain of many miles in extent; the soil is adapted to the growth of wheat, rye, and Irish potatoes; horned cattle and sheep also, thrive here admirably. The climate of this portion of Oregon is so mild that stock is never kept up during the winter months, and barns are only used for storing the grain. The Methodists have a Mission Station here, and some of the best lands are owned by it.

Near the settlement we forded the river, and shortly after we arrived at the encampment of our party. We were glad to find that the sick alluded to by Mr. Cone, had recovered, and in the course of a day or two we should be able to set out on our intended journey.

On Sunday, the Rev. Mr. Leslie performed Divine Service at his residence, on the opposite side of the river, and as many of our officers attended as could be spared; Mr. Leslie is a member of the Methodist Mission established in the valley, and enjoys better reputation among the settlers than most of the other mission gentlemen. He is, they say, the only Missionary among them who pays any attention to his proper duties; this statement, if we may judge the tree by its fruit, is not erroneous. Most of these gentleman have turned their attention to farming, and think more about their crops than they do of the great cause which they have been sent out to advance; the number of Indian children to whom they give instruction does not exceed twenty, and the adult Indians living about the settlement, are entirely neglected.

On the 8th of September we bade adieu to the banks of the Willamette. A complete list of the names of the persons who now formed the party, will be found in the Appendix.

At first we had our share of drawbacks; a thousand things were now to be done, which had not been thought of before, nor could they have been foreseen. Many of the pack-saddles were found to be either too large or too small; the strength of a number of the horses had been overrated, and the packs which it had been intended they should carry, had in consequence to be reduced or exchanged for others which were lighter. Then there was a list to be taken of all the packs and the animals which belonged to the government, and those which did not. All this produced delay and confusion for a time, but, when finally all was right, and the expedition made a start, it moved on at a fine rate, and by 4 o'clock P. M. we reached Mr. Turner's place, where we encamped for the night.

Mr. Turner supports himself by supplying the Willamette settlement with beef semi-weekly, and he made us a present of a fine bullock. He is a native of New York, but has been thirteen years in Oregon; has an Indian woman to keep house for him, and seems perfectly contented. He has been to California several times, and in 1834 he formed one of a party of sixteen settlers, who set out to go there to purchase cattle, but they were attacked by the Indians during the night, near the base of the Shaste Mountains, and ten of his companions were massacred. Two of the party were killed immediately. Turner was seated by the fire when the savages rushed into the camp, he snatched up a brand and defended himself with it until his Indian woman brought him his rifle, with which he killed four. His surviving companions had now seized their fire-arms, and dealt such destruction among the Indians that they at last retreated, and allowed Turner and his five companions to make good their retreat to the settlement.

We were detained at Turner's place all the next day, on account of two of the horses having got astray. In the afternoon I took a stroll, and fell in with an encampment of Calipoya Indians. There were altogether five families of them, and each had its own fire and tent. They were miserably clad, and their habitations were swarming with vermin. The surrounding country was perfectly level, and produced luxuriant grasses and some trees.

On the 10th we left Mr. Turner's place, and directed our steps to the southward and eastward. We crossed during this day several small streams, which are tributary to the Willamette. The country continued level, but all the vegetation, except the trees, had been destroyed by fire, said to have been kindled by the Prairie Indians, for the purpose of procuring a certain species of root, which forms a principal part of their food. We spent the night on the banks of a creek, named Igneas.

At 9 o'clock the following day we resumed our march, and shortly after reached Guardepii Lake, which is not more than a mile in circumference. In the course of the afternoon we crossed Lumtumbuff River, which is a branch of the Willamette. It is a deep and turbid stream, but is fordable at certain points.

During the 13th it was very foggy, and we had much difficulty in finding the animals. Owing to this circumstance we advanced this day only two miles on our course. At this encampment we obtained observations, both on the dip and intensity needles. About dusk some Calipoya Indians paid us a visit; they proved to be acquaintances of the guide, and the meeting seemed to be one which afforded mutual pleasure to both parties. He represented them as being a perfectly harmless people, and there was nothing in their appearance to indicate the contrary. They were clothed in deer-skins, with fox-skin caps, or cast-off clothing of the whites. Their arms were bows and arrows; the latter were pointed with bone, and they carried them in a quiver made of seal-skin.

On the morning of the 14th we resumed our journey, and made about ten miles on our course. The soil now was composed of white sand, mixed with clay, and produced only prairie grass. I gave this day to one of the scientific gentlemen, Mr. Dana, a beautiful specimen of fresh-water *asticus*, which I captured in the stream, upon whose banks we encamped for the night.

On the 15th our route lay through a broken country, densely covered with pines, spruces, and oaks; some of the former were upwards of two hundred feet in height, and proportionally large in circumference. At 3.30 P. M. we reached the base of the Elk Mountains, which separate the valley of Willamette from that of Umpquoa. We estimated the greatest elevation of these mountains to be 1500 feet; they are clothed with trees and underbrush to their summit. We had a severe frost during the night, although the temperature during the day had been as high as 77° in the shade.

The Elk.

The Deer.

The Black-tailed Deer.

On the 16th we encamped on the Elk River. This river is so called because its banks abound in elk; it is about one-half of the size of the Willamette River, and has considerable current. We had scarcely pitched our tents, when some of the hunters succeeded in killing an elk and a deer. They were brought into camp, and divided among the different messes.

The following morning, Messrs. Emmons, Agate, and sergeant Stearns, with Boileau as a guide, left the camp for Fort Umpquoa, for the double object of examining the country and exchanging several of the pack-horses, which had nearly given out. This fort belongs to the Hudson's Bay Company, and is constructed after the manner of those of Nisqually and Vancouver. It is situated on the Umpquoa River, a fine stream, which empties into the ocean.

The Superintendent of the establishment, Mr. Gangriere, gave Mr. Emmons a very unfavorable account of the Indians who inhabited this region. He stated that he had long before heard of the intended journey, through the Indians, and that the news had passed on to all the tribes, who were collecting in large numbers, to oppose our passage. He also endeavored to dissuade Mr. Emmons from proceeding any further, by telling him that these Indians were a brave race, consequently in the event of an attack, our party must be destroyed, for he thought it was very small.

According to our hunters, the Umpquoa country abounds in beaver, deer, and bears. About dusk Mr. Emmons returned, accompanied by Mesdames Boileau and Gangriere, who wished to see the camp, and consult the doctor. He communicated to the party, what Mr. Gangriere had stated in relation to the Indians, and gave orders for increasing the number of sentries about the camp, to make more cartridges, and to put all the arms in the best fighting condition.

At an early hour on the 18th, we resumed our march. Mesdames Boileau and Grangriere accompanied us for a few miles, and then left, to return to Fort Umpquoa.

On the 19th we deviated from the direct road, in order to avoid any chance of an encounter with the Indians. This brought us to the north fork of the Umpquoa, which we forded without any accident, though, before making the attempt, it was reasonably feared that we might meet with many, from the fact that the current was very rapid, and the bottom extremely slippery. The rocks observed in this region, contain fossils, and occasionally exhibit seams of coal. During this day many friendly Indians were seen, who reported that the hostile tribes were preparing to dispute our passage. We passed one large party, composed entirely of women, who were out gathering roots. They were all passé, and extremely ugly. One old woman can only be described by Juvenal,—

> " Such wrinkles see,
> As in an Indian forest's solitude,
> Some old ape scrubs amidst her numerous brood."

During the 20th, our route lay through a succession of hills and valleys, intersected by numerous streams. None of the hills are more than four hundred feet in height, and all are susceptible of cultivation, the soil being apparently as good as that in the valleys. We saw, in the course of this day, several grisly bears, and the hunters fired many balls at them; but they did not succeed in killing any. At sunset we encamped on the south branch of the Umpquoa River. During the night our rest was much disturbed by the howling of wolves, which are very numerous in these parts.

The following day we crossed the Umpquoa River; it is not so broad nor so deep as the northern branch. We passed,

The Common Wolf.

The Dusky Wolf.

during this day's ride, a number of Indian graves; they were surrounded with poles, one end of which was stuck in the ground, to the other were suspended the goods of the deceased, such as mats, blankets, bows, and arrows. We also met several small parties of Umpquoa Indians, who declared themselves to be friendly to the whites, and were anxious to obtain powder and balls, but we refused to furnish them. We expected an attack during the night, from the hostile tribes, and had prepared to give them a warm reception; but none appeared.

On the 22d, at an early hour, we commenced to ascend the Umpquoa Mountains. The path was narrow and very steep, so much so, that several of the pack-horses stumbled and were considerably injured. At 11 A. M. we halted, for nearly half an hour, to rest the animals. At 4, having reached the summit of the ridge, we again rested for a few minutes, and then commenced descending, and by sunset we arrived at the valley beneath, where we spent the night. We found the greatest elevation of the mountain to be 1750 feet. During the 23d, we remained at the same encampment, in order to give the horses time to recover from the fatigue undergone, and to afford Mr. Peale an opportunity of finding his camera-lucida and drawings, which had dropped out of his carpet-bag, while crossing the mountains yesterday. At 3, he returned, and brought with him the camera-lucida; the other articles he was unable to find. We observed, in the neighborhood of this encampment, a considerable number of the Pinus Lambertiana Douglas.

On the 24th we resumed our route. The country looked much less inviting than it did on the other side of the mountain. Perhaps the contrast would not have been so striking, had there not been an almost entire destitution of vegetation, the fire having destroyed everything but the trees. The rocks are intersected with veins of quartz, and the soil is sandy and generally of a light-red color.

In the course of the day, the hunters discovered the fresh foot-prints of Indians, and in searching for the savages, they came upon three squaws, who had been left, when the others fled. It was clear that the savages were closely watching our movements, and only waited for a good opportunity to pounce upon us. At 4 P. M. we arrived, and encamped on the banks of Young's Creek, where we found a party of Klamet Indians ; they looked very innocent, and pretended to be glad to see us ; but the guide represented them as being the most rascally set in all Oregon—calling them horse-thieves, robbers, and murderers.

During the 25th and 26th, our road lay through an undulating country, interspersed with forests of the Pinus Lambertiana. I tasted the sugar produced by this singular tree, and found it to be slightly bitter. It is a powerful cathartic, yet I was told that the trappers used it as a substitute for sugar ; the Indian mode of collecting it is to burn a cavity in the tree, whence it exudes in large quantities. We passed, on the last of these days, Tootootutnas River, another beautiful stream, upwards of one hundred yards in width, and abounding in salmon and other fish. The land, a few hundred yards from its banks, rises into hills of considerable height, formed principally of granite sand.

Several Indians came about the camp and pretended to be friendly, but we placed no confidence in their professions, and sent them away before night came on. They had canoes with which they navigated the neighboring streams, but they were very rude, and dug out square at the extremes.

During both these days most of the gentlemen of the party

The Bison.

The Antelope.

and several of the sailors suffered excessively from attacks of the ague. In my own case, the chills were so violent, that it was impossible to travel while they lasted.

On the 27th, we reached one of those places where it was said the Indians never failed to make their attacks. We had one man in the party who had been twice assaulted at the same place. It was a steep rocky spot, close by the river Tootootutnas. As we passed on, many armed Indians were observed on the opposite side of the stream, and, occasionally, were heard to utter yells, which were absolutely infernal, but they did not attempt to oppose our progress. We were fully prepared for them, and, it was this, no doubt, which prevented their making an assault. Even the wives of the hunters were armed on the occasion.

We saw this day a great variety of game, among which was the antelope. It is said the Indians take this animal by exciting its curiosity; for this purpose, they conceal themselves behind a tree, or among the bushes, and making a rustling noise, the attention of the animal is soon attracted, when it is led to advance toward the place of concealment, until the fatal arrow pierces it. The animal strongly resembles the deer, and its flesh is very palatable. According to the hunters, they are found only in the prairies.

On the 29th, we crossed the boundary range which separates Oregon from Upper California. The greatest elevation of the range was found to be 2,000 feet. The ascent was steep and tedious, and every moment we expected to be attacked by hostile Indians. The hunter named Tibbats, was one of a large party which was nearly destroyed by the savages three years before. He flattered himself that he should now have an opportunity to take his revenge on them, but he was not gratified, as not an Indian was to be seen in passing the mountain, although they had evidently intended to attack us; fresh tracks were observable in every direction, and large trees felled across the path to prevent the party from advancing.

On arriving at the summit of the range, we obtained a view which more than repaid us for our trouble. The Shaste Mountains with their snowy peaks, were to be seen some fifty miles to the southward, swelling and soaring to the skies, while the Klamet Valley into which we descended, like that in which the poet built his Castle of Indolence, was

> "A lonely dale fast by the river side,
> And was, I ween, a lovely spot of ground."

This valley is watered by the Klamet River, and is bounded on all sides with hills of considerable elevation, rising one beyond the other, and covered with forests of oak, which added materially to the picturesque beauty of the scene.

During the 30th, we remained encamped to enable the sick to recover from the fatigue undergone in crossing the mountains. Near this camping-place was found an Indian hut constructed of bent twigs; it was small and extremely low. The temperature in the shade during the day was 100°, at night, it was 32°. No doubt these great and sudden changes in the atmosphere tended to aggravate the ague attacks from which we suffered during the journey.

On the 1st of October the sick were much better, and we pursued our way. At 10 A. M. we forded the Klamet River, where it was about seventy yards broad; it was between three and four feet deep, with a beautiful pebbly bottom. There were rapids both above and below the ford, and from the appearance of the banks, it is subject to overflow. After crossing the river, masses of volcanic rock were observable in all directions, and the soil was dry and barren. At sunset we pitched our tents on a spot of green grass, near the southern branch of the Klamet River, which is likewise a beautiful stream, and abounds in fish.

The Indians found here were well disposed and better looking than any we had seen before. They supplied us with some salmon which were of a whitish color, and greatly inferior in flavor to those taken in the Columbia. They were also willing to sell their bows and arrows, which were neatly made, and several were purchased for the Government.

October 2d, 9 A. M., we bade adieu to Klamet River, and directed our steps to the southward. The country was now more undulating, and apparently more fertile, than that we passed over the preceding day. We did not meet with any water till late in the day, in consequence of which, the poor animals suffered excessively from thirst. Large herds of antelopes and mountain-sheep were seen; the latter are of a grayish color, have long spreading horns, and are much larger animals than the ordinary sheep.

From the 3d and up to the 10th, we were engaged in crossing the Shaste Range. These mountains may be represented as being a succession of a range of high hills, separated from each other by narrow valleys, traversed by streams that are fed by the melting snows which cover the tops of the highest peaks. The path was serpentine and difficult, and several of the horses broke down before the summit of the last range could be gained. In the valleys the Pinus Lambertiana was seen flourishing in all its glory; several trees were measured, and found to be three hundred feet in height.

The day after we commenced to ascend these mountains, we fell in with the head waters of the Sacramento, which flow to the southward. At this point it was an insignificant stream, being not more than thirty feet broad and two feet deep.

The weather, with the exception of that of a single day, was cool, clear and bracing, and we all enjoyed much better health than while traversing the plains. Nor was there any want of game; indeed, some days our hunters killed more than it was possible for the company to consume. The scientific gentlemen made large collections in their respective departments.

We saw many Indians, and as we knew they were friendly; we permitted them to enter our camp. They are a large, fine-looking race, and of a sociable disposition. They do not compress their heads, and they allow their hair, which is fine and glossy, to hang down to their shoulders in natural ringlets. Their food consists of game, fish, and acorns, which they make into bread. Their huts are small, and devoid of comfort. They have bows and arrows, with which they shoot admirably. An ordinary sized button was set up as a mark thirty yards off, and they hit it three times out of five; they can also kill birds on the wing. The arrows are nearly three feet long, and feathered from six to ten inches. In shooting, the bow is held horizontally, braced by the thumb of the left hand, and drawn by the thumb and three fingers of the right hand; and to obviate the disadvantage of drawing to the breast, the chest is thrown backwards on discharging the arrow; they throw out the right leg, and stand on the left.

The few women we saw were much inferior in personal appearance to the men, which we attributed to hard work, for they seemed to be constantly employed, while the men did nothing but eat, drink, and amuse themselves. The artist of the party had much difficulty in taking their portraits, as they imagined that he was a medicine-man, and desired to practise some enchantment upon them.

The Ruffed Grouse.

The Pellican.

The Black Bear.

The Grisley Bear.

It was calculated that the width of the range we passed over was one hundred miles. We were allured from height to height by many splendid views of land and water, which open at every turn of the pass; still we felt quite relieved when we reached the Sacramento Valley on the other side of the mountain, and reflected that the remainder of our journey would be comparatively easy, and devoid of the anxiety caused by the constant anticipation of being assaulted by hostile tribes.

On reaching the Sacramento Valley, a material difference was observed in the character of the vegetation. Few pines or firs were now to be seen, while the oak, the sycamore, and the cotton-wood trees were abundant. Most of the plants were also unlike any we had been accustomed to see, and some were found which were not described in any of the botanical works.

On the 10th we fell in with several villages belonging to the Kinkla tribe of Indians; they consisted of a few rude huts constructed of poles—the whole surrounded by a brush-fence, which answered for a stockade. Most of the inhabitants were out gathering acrons and wild grapes. Their complexion was quite dark, but their features are more regular than those of the northern tribes. Some were seen who had the Roman nose and oval face. They wore their hair long, but had it tied in a bunch behind. Their ears were bored, and the upper part of each cheek had a triangular figure painted upon it with a blue-black substance. It was also observed that they tattooed their arms. They had nothing to cover their nakedness, except a piece of deer-skin thrown over their shoulders. Their weapons were bows and arrows, and a forked-spear which they use to kill fish.

Within half a mile of one of the villages our hunters killed two grisly bears. It is said this animal is very numerous in these parts, and not unfrequently enter the Indian villages, and carry off stray children. The soil of this portion of the valley is of an inferior quality, and bears but few trees or plants.

On the 12th we forded the Sacramento River, where it was between three and four feet deep and two hundred yards broad. It had been our intention to have disposed of the horses here, and proceed down the river in canoes, but these were not to be had, nor could we find suitable timber from which to make them ourselves. The soil now appeared more fertile, though we saw little vegetation, on account of the country having been run over by fire.

Game was very plentiful, and five bears were killed in the course of the afternoon.

During the 14th and 15th we traveled over a plain studded with a vast number of crater-shaped hills, which go by the name of Prairie Butes. It is generally believed that each of these has been a volcano. They can be seen at a great distance, as they have an elevation of from five hundred to eighteen hundred feet; the ground about them is strewed with a great quantity of bones of animals that resort here for protection during the season of the freshets, which flood the whole of the level country; a deposit of considerable thickness covered the surface. The rocks forming some of the butes were of a volcanic origin. A great number of wild fowl were seen on both of these days.

On the 17th we reached Feather River, which is a tributary to the Sacramento. As we were unable to find a place where it would be safe to ford it, we proceeded down its bank, and at sunset we encamped near its junction with the Sacramento River. It is a more rapid stream than the Sacramento, but its volume of water is considerably less. Its banks are from ten to fifteen feet high, and fringed with the sycamore and cotton-wood trees. It is navigable for boats.

The 18th brought us to Captain Sutter's place, or New Helvatia, where we found the "Vincennes'" launch, in which Messrs. Emmons, Dana, Agate, Dr. Whittle and myself embarked, and proceeded down to San Francisco. The rest of the party set out to reach San Francisco by land.

Captain Sutter* is a native of Switzerland, and has lived a most eventful life. He was a lieutenant in the Swiss Guards in the time of Charles X. Soon after the abdication of that monarch, he resigned his commission, and came over to the United States, and resided several years in St. Charles, Missouri.

We were most hospitably and kindly received by him; there was no ostentatious display, no pomp nor ceremony, but an easy and polite demeanor on the part of our host, that made us feel perfectly at home. He has been two years in California, and he informed us that he has obtained from the Government a conditional grant of ninety miles square in the Valley of the Sacramento. The location he has chosen for the erection of his dwelling and fort he has called New Helvatia. It is situated on the east bank of the Sacramento river, and about sixty miles from its mouth; his buildings are constructed of adobes, and cover a large extent of ground. He has commenced extensive operations in farming, and the extent of his stock amounts to two thousand sheep, three thousand cattle, and about one thousand horses.

As we approached the settlement, we passed the village of Indians who live on the farm and work it, with whose appear-

* It is well known that to his enterprise in erecting a mill, the first gold discovery in California was attributed.

ance I was much disappointed, in consequence of the filthiness of their looks; they are amply provided with the necessaries of life by Captain Sutter, but their natural inclination and habits are such as to prevent their advancement in civilized life.

Besides farming, Captain Sutter is engaged in trapping, and distilling a kind of liquor resembling Pisco, from the wild grape of the country.

On the 19th of October we arrived at San Francisco Bay, where we found the "Vincennes." The overland detachment arrived in the afternoon of the 24th.

The Valley of Sacramento is one hundred and seventy miles long and from twenty to sixty miles wide. Having heard much of its fruitfulness, we expected, on entering it, to see a perfect garden; but such was not the case. On the contrary, we saw but little good land; and as for the landscape, it was extremely uninteresting, being utterly devoid of either beauty or variety. The river is navigable for vessels of sixty tons burthen, as far as New Helvatia, and for boats and canoes, seventy miles farther. The banks are nowhere over twenty feet in height, and are lined with sycamore and cotton-wood trees; some of which are of large dimensions.

San Francisco Bay is an extensive body of water, studded with many islands, which look as fresh and verdant as nature can make them. It communicates with the ocean by a narrow passage, bounded on either side by rocky cliffs. The name of the principal town is Yerba-buena; it is located near the entrance, and contains about thirty buildings of one story high, constructed of adobes. The trade is limited to eight or ten vessels; these lay at their anchors until they retail out their cargoes, by which means part of the duties, which are very onerous on all landed articles, are saved.

Such was San Francisco at the time of our visit; since then the whole of California has undergone surprising changes, which cannot be better described than in the words of Mr. Walter Colton, author of "Deck and Port," and "Three Years in California."

"The Bay of San Francisco resembles a broad inland lake, communicating by a narrow channel with the ocean. This channel, as the tradition of the Aborigines runs, was opened by an earthquake, which a few centuries since convulsed the continent. The town is built on the south bend of the bay, near its communication with the sea. Its site is a succession of barren sand-hills, tumbled up into every variety of shape. No leveling process, on a scale of any magnitude, has been attempted. The buildings roll up and over these sand-ridges like a shoal of porpoises over the swell of a wave, only the fish has much the most order in the disposal of his head and tail. More incongruous combinations in architecture never danced in the dreams of men—brick warehouses, wooden shanties, sheet-iron huts, and shaking-tents, are blended in admirable confusion.

"But these grotesque habitations have as much uniformity and sobriety as the habits of those who occupy them. Hazards are made in commercial transactions, and projects of speculation that would throw Wall Street into spasms. I have seen merchants purchase cargoes without having even glanced into the invoice. The conditions of the sale were a hundred per cent. profits to the owner, and costs. In one cargo, when tumbled out, were found twenty thousand dollars in the single article of red cotton handkerchiefs! 'I'll get rid of these among the wild Indians,' said the purchaser, with a shrug of the shoulders.—'I've a water lot which I will sell,' cries another. 'Which way does it stretch?' inquire half-a-dozen.

'Right under the craft there,' is the reply. 'And what do you ask for it?' 'Fifteen thousand dollars.' 'I'll take it.' 'Then down with the dust.' So the water lot, which mortal eyes never yet beheld, changes its owners, without changing its fish.

"'I have two shares in a gold-mine,' cries another. 'Where are they?' inquire the crowd. 'Under the south branch of the Yuba River, which we have almost turned,' is the reply. 'And what will you take?' 'Fifteen thousand dollars.' 'I'll give ten.' 'Take it, stranger.' So the two shares of a *possibility* of gold, under a branch of the Yuba, where the water still rolls, rapid and deep, are sold for ten thousand dollars, paid down. Is there anything in the '*Arabian Nights*' that surpasses this?

"But glance at the large wooden building which looks as if the winds had shingled it, and the powers of the air pinned its clapboards in a storm. Enter, and you find a great hall filled with tables, and a motley group gathered around each. Some are laying down hundreds, and others thousands, on the turn of a card. Each has a bag of grain-gold in his hand, which he must double or lose, and is only anxious to reach the table where he can make the experiment. You would advise him at least to purchase a suit of clothes, or repair his old ones, before he loses his all; but what cares he for his outward garb, when piles of the yellow dust swell and glitter in his excited imagination? Down goes his bag of gold—and is lost! But does he look around for a rope, or pistol, that he may end his ruin? No: the river-bank where he gathered that gold has more; so he cheers his momentary despondency with a strong glass of brandy, and is off again for the mines. He found the gold by good fortune and has lost it by bad, and now considers himself about even with the world. Such is the moral effect of gold-hunting on a man whose principles are not as fixed and immovable as the rock. It begins in a lottery and ends in a lottery, where the blanks out-number the prizes ten to one.

"But you are hungry—want a breakfast—turn into a restaurant—call for ham, eggs, and coffee—then your bill. Six dollars! Your high boots, which have never seen a brush since you first put them on, have given out; you find a pair that can replace them; they are a tolerable fit; and now what is the price? Fifty dollars! Your beard has not felt a razor since you went to the mines; it must come off, and your frizzled hair be clipped. You find a barber; his dull shears hang in the knots of your hair, like a sheep-shearer's in a fleece matted with burrs. The razor he straps on the leg of his boot, and then hauls away, starting at every pull some new fountain of tears. You vow you will let the beard go, but then one side is partly off, and you try the agony again to get the other side something like it. And now what is the charge for this torture? Four dollars! Night is approaching, and you must have a place where you can sleep. To inquire for a bed would be as idle as to hunt a pearl in the jungle of a Greenland bear. You look around for the lee of some shanty or tent, and tumble down for the night; but a thousand fleas dispute the premises with you—the contest is hopeless; you tumble out as you tumble in, and spend the remainder of the night in finding a place not occupied by these aborigines of the soil.

"But you are not perhaps a gold-digger, as I had supposed. You are a supercargo, and have a valuable freight which you wish to land. You have warped your vessel in till her keel rakes, and yet you are several hundred yards off. Some lighter must be found that can skim these shallows—your own boats will not do. After waiting two or three weeks you get the use of a scow, called a lighter, for which you pay one hundred and fifty dollars a day.

"To-morrow you are going to commence unloading, and wake betimes; but find, that, during the night, every soul of your crew has escaped, and put out for the mines. You rush about on shore to find hands, and collect eight or ten loafers, who will assist you for fifteen dollars a-day each. Your cargo must be landed, and you close the bargain, though your fresh hands are already half-seas over. The scow is shoved from shore, brought along-side, loaded with goods, which are tumbled in as an Irishman dumps a load of dirt, and then with your oar and poles, push for the landing; but the tide has ebbed too soon; you are only half-way, and there your scow sticks fast in the midst of a great mud bottom, from which the last ripple of water has retreated. You cannot get forward, and you are now too late to get back; night is setting in, and the rain clouds are gathering fast—down comes a deluge, drenching your goods and filling your open scow. The returning tide will now be of no use—the scow wont float except under water, and that is a sort of floating which don't suit you; skin for skin—though in this case not dry—what will a man not give for his own life? So, out you jump, and by crawling and creeping, make your way through the mire to the landing, and bring up against a bin, where another sort of wallower gives you a grunt of welcome. Your loafers must be paid off in the morning and the scow recovered, or its loss will cost you half the profits of your voyage. But the storm last night has driven another brig into yours, and there they both are, like a bear and bull, that have gored and crushed each other. But 'misery loves company,' and you have it. The storm which swamped your scow and stove your brig last night, has been busy on shore. Piles of goods heaped up in every street, are in a condition which requires wreckers, as well as watchmen. But no one here is going to trouble himself about your misfortunes, nor much about his own. The reverses of to-day are to be more than repaired by the successes of to-morrow. These are only the broken pick-axes and spades by which the great mine is to be reached. What is the loss of a few thousands to one who is so soon to possess millions? Only a coon back in his hole, while the buffalo remains within rifle shot—only a periwinkle lost, while the whale is beneath the harpoon—only a farthing candle consumed, while the dowered bride, blushing in beauty and bliss, is kneeling at the nuptial altar. But let that pass.

"But you are not alone in your destitution and dirt. There are hundreds around you who were quite as daintily reared, and who are doing here what they dodged at home. Do you see that youth in red flannel shirt and coarse brogans, rolling a wheel-barrow? He was a clerk in a counting-house in New York, and came here to shovel up gold, as you scoop up sand. He has been to the mines, gathered no gold, and returned, but now makes his ten dollars a-day by rolling that wheel-barrow; it costs him six, however, to live, and the other four he loses at *monte*.

"See you that young man with a long whip in his hand, cracking it over an ox-team? He was one of the most learned geologists, for his age, in the United States, and came out here to apply his science to the discovery of gold deposits; but, somehow, his diving-rods always dipped wrong, and now, he has taken about which there is no mistake, so at least think his cattle. He would accumulate a fortune, did he not lose it as fast as made in some phrenzied speculation. But look yonder—do you see that young gentleman with a string of fish, which he offers for sale? He was one of the best Greek and Latin scholars of his class in Yale College, and, subsequently, one of the most promising Members of our Bar. But he exchanged his Blackstone for a pick, and, instead of picking fees out of his clients' pockets, he came here to pick gold out of the mines; but, the deuce was it, for whenever his pick struck close upon a deposit, it was no longer there; so he exchanged his pick for a hook and line, and now angles for pike, pickerel, and perch, and can describe each fish by some apt line from Catulus. He would do well at his new piscatory profession but for the gilded hook of the gambler. He laughs at the trout for darting at a fictitious fly, and then chases a bait himself equally fanciful and false.

"But look again—do you see that pulperia, with its gathered groups of soldiers and sailors, poets and politicians, merchants and mendicants, doctors and draymen, clerks and cobblers, trappers and tinkers? That little man who stands behind the bar, and deals to each his dram of fire, was once a preacher, and deemed almost a prophet, as he depicted the pangs of that worm which dieth not, but now he has exchanged that worm for another, but preserved his consistency, for his worm, too, distilleth delirium and death. And that thick-set man who stands in the midst of the crowd, with ruby countenance and reveling eye, whose repartee sets the whole pulperia in a roar, and who is now watching the liquor in his glass to see if it stirreth itself aright, once lectured in the west on the temptations of those who tarry late at the wine; but now his teetotalism covers all liquors as goodly gifts graciously bestowed. But one brief year, and some dame quickly may describe his pale exit, as that of his delirious prototype. 'I saw him fumble with the sheets, and play with flowers, and smile upon his fingers' ends.'

"And, yet, with all these drawbacks, with all these gambling-tables, grog-shops, shanties, shavers, and fleas, San Francisco is swelling into a town of the highest commercial importance. She commands the trade of the great valleys, through which the Sacramento and San Joaquin, with their numerous tributaries, roll. She gathers to her bosom the product and manufactures of the United States, of England, China, the shores and islands of the Pacific. But now let us glance at California as she was a few years since, as she is now, and as she is fast becoming.

"Three years ago, the white population of California could not have exceeded ten thousand souls. She has now a population of two hundred thousand, and a resistless tide of emigration rolling in, through the heart of Mexico, over the Isthmus of Panama, around Cape Horn, and over the steeps of the Rocky Mountains. Then the great staple of the country was confined to wild cattle; now it is found in exhaustless mines of quicksilver and gold. Then, the shipping which frequented her waters, was confined to a few *drogers*, that waddled along her coast in quest of hides and tallow; now, the richest *argosies* of the commercial world are bound to her ports.

"Three years ago, the dwellings of her citizens were reared under the hands of Indians, from sun-baked adobes of mud and straw; now, a thousand hammers are ringing on rafter and roof, over walls of iron and brick. Then, the plough which furrowed her fields, was the crotch of a tree, which a stone or root might shiver; now, the shares of the New England farmer glitter in her soil. Then, the wheels of her carts were cut from the butts of trees, with a hole in the centre, for the rude axle; now, the iron-bound wheel of the finished mechanic, rolls over her hills and valleys. Then, only the canoe of the Indian disturbed the sleeping surface of her waters; now, a fleet of steamers plough her ample rivers and bays. Then, not a school-house, public teacher, magazine, or newspaper, could be found in the whole territory; now, they are met with in most of the larger towns. Then, the tastes and passions of an idle throng rang on the guitar and the fandango; now, the calculations of the busy multitudes turn to the cultured field and productive mine. Then, California was a dependency of Mexico, and subject to revolutions, with the success of every daring military chieftain; now, she is an independent State, with an enlightened constitution, which guarantees equal rights and privileges to all. Then, she was in arms against our flag; now, she unrolls it on the breeze, with the star of her own being and pride glowing in the constellation which blazes on its folds.

"Three years ago, and San Francisco contained three hundred souls; now she has a population of twenty-seven thousand.* Then, a building-lot within her limits cost fifteen dollars; now, the same lot cannot be purchased at a less sum than fifteen thousand. Then, her commerce was confined to a few Indian blankets, and Mexican reboses and beads; now, from two to three hundred merchantmen are unloading their costly cargoes on her quay. Then, the famished whaler could hardly find a temporary relief in her markets; now, she has phrenzied the world with her wealth. Then, Benicia was a pasture, covered with lowing herds; now, she is a commercial mart, threatening to rival her sister nearer the sea. Then, Stockton and Sacramento City were covered with wild oats, where the elk and deer gamboled at will; now, they are laced with streets and walled with warehouses, through which the great tide of commerce rolls off into a hundred mountain glens. Then, the banks of the Sacramento and San Joaquin

* According to tho last accounts, it has increased to 45,000.

were cheered only by the curling smoke of the Indian's hut; now, they throw on the eye, at every bend, the cheerful aspect of some new hamlet or town. Then, the silence of the Sierra Nevada was broken only by the voice of its streams; now, every cavern and cliff is echoing under the blows of the sturdy miner. The wild horse, startled in his glen, leaves on the hill the clatter of his hoofs, while the huge bear, roused from his patrimonial jungle, grimly retires to some new mountain-fastness.

"But I must drop this contrast of the past with the present, and glance at a few facts which affect the future. The gold deposits which have hitherto been discovered, are confined. mainly, to the banks and beds of perpetual streams, or the bottoms of ravines, through which roll the waters of the transient freshet. These deposits are the natural results of the law of gravitation; the treasures which they contain must have been washed from the slopes of the surrounding hills. The elevations, like spendthrifts, seem to have parted entirely with their golden inheritance, except what may linger still in the quartz. And these gold-containing quartz will be found to have their confined localities; they will crown the insular peaks of a mountain-ridge, or fret the verge of some extinguished volcano; they have never been found in a continuous range, except in the dreams of enchantment; you might as well look for a wall of diamonds or a solid bank of pearls. Nature has played off many a prodigal caprice in California, but a mountain of gold is not one of them. The alluvial gold, will, at no distant day, be measurably exhausted, and the miners be driven into the mountains. Here, the work can be successfully prosecuted only by companies, with heavy capitals. All the uncertainties which are connected with mining operations, will gather around these enterprises. Wealth will reward the labors of the few, whose success was mainly the result of good fortune, while disappointment will attend the efforts of the many, equally skillful and persevering. These wide inequalities in the proceeds of the miner's labor, have exhibited themselves, wherever a gold deposit has been hunted or found in California. The past is the reliable prophecy of the future.

"Not one in ten of the thousands who have gone, or may go to California to hunt for gold, will return with a fortune; still the great tide for emigration will set there, till her valleys and mountain-glens teem with a hardy enterprising population. As the gold deposits diminish, or become more difficult of access, the quicksilver mines will call forth their unflagging energies. This metal slumbers in her mountain-spurs in massive richness; the process is simple which converts it into that form, through which the mechanic arts subserve the thousand purposes of science and social refinement, while the medical profession, through its strange abuse, keep up a Carnival in the Court of Death; but for this they who mine the ore are not responsible—they will find their reward in the wealth which will follow their labors. It will be in their power to silence the hammers in those mines which have hitherto monopolized the markets of the world.

But the enterprise and wealth of California are not confined to her mines. Her ample forests of oak, redwood and pine, only wait the requisite machinery to convert them into elegant residences and strong-ribbed ships. Her exhaustless quarries of granite and marble will yet pillar the domes of metropolitan splendor and pride. The hammer and drill will be relinquished by multitudes for the plough and sickle. Her arable land, stretching through her spacious valleys, and along the broad banks of her rivers, will wave with the golden har-

The Swan.

vest; the rain-cloud may not visit her in the summer months, but the mountain-stream will he induced to throw its showers over her thirsty plains.

"Such was California a few years since—such is she now, and such will she become even before they who now rush to her shores, find their footsteps within the shadows of the pale realm."

CHAPTER XXII.

GENERAL OBSERVATIONS ON CALIFORNIA.

California was discovered by the Spaniards about 1534, and towards the close of the succeeding century, the Jesuits established themselves in it to convert the natives. The efforts of the missionaries have nominally converted about half the natives to Christianity, but the number of the native inhabitants are rapidly decreasing, and they do not number at present more than fourteen thousand. Though divided into many tribes, they are understood to belong to the same family, speaking the same language, and having similar manners and customs.

The stature of these people varies with their habits. Those who subsist chiefly on fish, and inhabit the sea-coast, are seldom more than five feet and six inches in height, with slender forms, while those who occupy the great valleys in the interior are tall and robust. Their complexion is a shade or two darker than that of the Indians in Oregon and about the Columbia; their noses are broad and flat; the hair is black, coarse, and straight, and their lips are thick, like the negro. The forehead is low and contracted; eyebrows and beard scanty. They have the habit common to all American Indians of extracting the beard and hair of other parts of the body. During the summer months the men seldom conceal their nakedness; but the females always have a rush or a skin-covering around the waist. The women are also fond of tattooing, and ornament their arms and breasts with it. Their habitations are formed of pliable poles, with their butts inserted into the ground and tied together at the top. These are interwoven with brush and thatched with bulrushes; the interior of these wigwams is usually very filthy, and contain no furniture, except a few wooden bowls, a small netting-sack in which to put their fruit and seeds, another in the form of a bag to sling on the shoulders, for the purpose of carrying their infants when traveling, one or two fishing-nets, and a sea-shell for dipping water to drink.

Among some of the tribes, parentage and other relations of consanguinity are no obstacles to matrimony. A man often marries a whole family, the mother and daughters, and it is said that in such cases no jealousies ever appear among these families of wives. They seem to consider their offspring as the property of all, and the husband as their common protector.

It is known that those tribes which have not embraced Christianity do nevertheless believe in the control of good and evil spirits, to whom they occasionally offer prayers; and as a proof of their having some idea of a future state, they invariably deposit bows and arrrows, and cooking utensils in the graves of their dead.

The part of Upper California inhabited by foreign settlers, is a tract extending five hundred miles along the shore of the Pacific, and bounded inland at an average distance of forty miles from the coast by a range of hills. The most southern portion of this region is torrid and parched, but as we proceed north, the climate becomes more favorable, though the country is subject to long and severe droughts, which occasion great distress. There are many streams in this part of California, which carry off the water in torrents to the ocean, during the rainy season, and cause the valleys which they water, to afford good pasturage for the cattle which are found there in large numbers. There are but two tracts of country capable of supporting a large population—one west of Mount San Barnardino, and the other surrounding the Bay of San Francisco and the lower part of the Sacramento. To the east of the California Mountains are the vast sandy plains, of which but little is known ; nor have any attempts been made to explore the more northern portion of this section.

The valleys of San Juan and that of Sacramento, are capable of producing great crops of wheat, rye, oats, Indian corn, potatoes, &c., with all the fruits and vegetables of the temperate, and many of the tropical climates. The cultivation of the grape increases yearly, and the vineyards about the Missions yield most abundantly as finely-flavored fruit as there is to be found in any part of the world.

All this portion of California is well adapted to the rearing of cattle and sheep; they can find plenty of nutritious food the whole year round, and they require no watching. The mutton is of very fine flavor, and the usual price for a sheep is from one dollar to one dollar and a half.

The Sacramento, and other rivers of California abound in salmon, and might be made a source of considerable profit. Many more valuable species are taken in these waters.

The white and mixed population of this section is estimated at five thousand. They are robust and tall, and pride themselves on their horsemanship ; they early become expert and fearless riders, and they have been known to ride upwards of two hundred miles in one day. Descended from the old Spaniards, they are found to have all their vices and scarcely any of their virtues ; they are cowardly, ignorant, lazy, and addicted to gambling and drinking ; very few of them are able to read or write, and know nothing of science or literature, nothing of government but its brutal force, nothing of religion but ceremonies of the national ritual. Their amusements are music, cock-fighting, bear-baiting, and horse-racing. Weddings generally last for three or four days, and usually end in some quarrel. The "cuchillo" is always worn, and is resorted to in all their affrays. The females are very fond of dress, and their propensity for gambling is as great as that of the male portion of the community.

CHAPTER XXIII.

CONQUEST OF CALIFORNIA BY THE UNITED STATES.

The Commander-in-Chief of the Pacific Squadron, Commodore Sloat, received reliable information, at Mazatlan, on the 7th of June, 1846, that the Mexican troops, six or seven thousand in number, had invaded the territory of the United States, and attacked General Taylor. He was told, that the American Squadron, under Commodore Conner, was blockading the eastern coast, and he immediately sailed for Monterey, where he found the "Cyane" and "Levant." After an examination of the defences of the town, and completing his arrangements for capturing it, he sent Captain Mervine, on the 7th of July, to the governor of the town to demand its surrender, and on his declining to comply with the summons, it was taken by a detachment of two hundred and fifty seamen and marines from the vessels. Masters of the town, they speedily raised the American flag from the Custom-house, amid the cheers from the troops and bystanders, and a national salute from the squadron. A proclamation from the Commodore was then posted up, stating the existence of hostilities between Mexico and the United States, and his intention to take possession of all California. It also announced that, although the Commander-in-Chief came in arms, he came as a friend, and all the peaceable inhabitants of the country would be confirmed in the rights they then enjoyed, and have in addition the superior advantages afforded to the people

Capture of Monterey by an American Squadron.

by the constitution and laws of the United States, under which they might reasonably hope to advance and improve rapidly, both in commerce and agriculture. Such of the inhabitants as were disposed to live peaceably under the government of the United States, were to be allowed time to dispose of their property, and to leave the country, if they chose, without any restriction, or to remain in it, in the observance of strict neutrality. The civil functionaries were desired to retain their offices, and preserve tranquillity; and the people and clergy were assured of their being unmolested in their property, rights and possessions. Under the orders of the Commodore, Captain Montgomery, with seventy sailors and marines of the United States sloop-of-war "Portsmouth," landed at the settlement of Yerba Buena, in the Bay of San Francisco, and took possession of that place. On the 11th of July, Captain Montgomery informed the Commodore that the American flag was flying at Yerba Buena, at Sutter's Fort, at Bodega, and at Sonoura; and added, that the protection of persons and property, which the American flag promised to the land and the people, was hailed with joy by the people, some of whom had enrolled themselves into a new company, under the auspices of the American officers, styled "The Volunteer Guards of Yerba Buena." On the day on which he sent this communication to the Commodore, a British vessel of twenty-six guns, the "Juno," arrived at San Francisco, and anchored. Captain Montgomery brought all his crew from the shore to the ship, with a view of defending his position, in case the English commander should think proper to interfere. The "Volunteer Guards of Yerba Buena" took upon themselves the task of defending the flag of the United States, assuring the commander that it should wave while a single man of their body lived to defend it. Don Francisco Sancher, the military commander of the district, promptly complied with the requisition of Captain Montgomery, that he should come in and deliver up the arms and public property in his possession. He assured the American commander that he had no public property, but told where several guns were buried. Lieut. Missroon, of the "Portsmouth," went to the Mission of Dolores, but found only a quantity of public documents, which were taken possession of and deposited in the Custom-house.

On the 13th of July, at their own request, Commodore Sloat furnished a flag to the foreigners of the Pueblo of San Jose, a place about seventy miles distant from the coast, and about eighty miles from Monterey. He had just completed the organization of a company of thirty-five dragoons, made up of volunteers from the ships and citizens, to reconnoitre the country, and keep open the land-communication between the different places held by the Americans. Purser Fauntleroy was appointed to command this body, and Mr. McLane was appointed first-lieutenant. On the 17th, Mr. Fauntleroy reconnoitered as far as the Mission of St. John's, intending to capture that place and recover ten brass field-pieces, said to have been buried there by the Mexicans some time previously. On his arrival there, he found the gallant Captain Fremont already in possession, and the two returned together to Monterey, the head-quarters of the Commodore.

Captain Fremont had left Washington in 1845, to make a third expedition, for scientific purposes, to the regions west of the Rocky Mountains, and his arrangements for the journey contemplated only its legitimate objects. He took no officer or soldier with him; and the whole company which he led, consisted of only sixty-two men, engaged by himself as security against the Indians, and for assistants in the duties of his mission. He approached the settlements in California, about the beginning of the year 1846; and, as he was aware of the difficulties existing between the United States and Mexico, he determined to be very circumspect in his conduct. He left his men on the frontiers, while he advanced alone a hundred miles to Monterey, where he visited the principal officers of the Government, in company with the United States Consul and Navy Agent, Mr. Larkin. He informed them of his expedition, and its purposes, and Governor Castro gave him permission to pass the winter in the Valley of San Joaquin, where was feed for his horses and game for his men. Captain Fremont then returned to his men, and led them leisurely to the place designated, but he had hardly reached it, before he received orders from the Governor to leave the country. He was even threatened with forcible ejection, if he disobeyed the command. After the permission given him in person by Castro, Captain Fremont determined not to obey these uncourteous messages, and the Governor made great preparations to carry his threats into execution. Of these he was informed by Mr. Larkin, whom he answered by a letter, stating, that if Governor Castro brought against him an armed force, he should try to defend himself, though not one of his men had ever been a soldier. He, moreover, informed the Consul that he had hoisted the American flag, and he should keep it flying as the only protection he had to look to. On the 7th of March, and the three following days, he employed himself in fortifying his position, by erecting a breastwork of logs and brush. The position of the Americans was on a high hill, whence they could see with their telescopes the preparations of the Governor, in his camp at the Mission of St. John's. Mr. Larkin now received another letter from Captain Fremont, and at the earnest request of the Alcade, it was immediately translated into Spanish, and sent to the

Governor. Here follows a portion of the letter:—"I am making myself as strong as possible, in the intention that, if we are unjustly attacked, we will fight to extremity, and refuse quarter, trusting to our country to avenge our death. No one has reached our camp; and from the heights we are able to see troops mustering at St. John's, and preparing cannon. I thank you for your kindness and good wishes, and would write more at length, as to my intentions, did I not fear my letter would be intercepted. We have in no-wise done wrong to the people, or the authorities of the country, and if we are hemmed in and assaulted here, we will die, every man of us, under the flag of our country."

Castro continued his preparations for an attack against our countrymen, but he took special care not to crowd them too closely.

Not wishing, however, to be the cause of embroiling his nation in difficulties, Captain Fremont determined to abandon his mission, and return to the United States, rather than continue it against the opposition of the Mexican authorities. Accordingly, on the 10th of March, he left his encampment, and retired towards Oregon, followed some distance by the forces commanded by the Governor, which amounted to four hundred men. But the valiant General always avoided coming to an action, and on the same day returned to Monterey, bringing with him some old clothes and two or three pack-saddles, all thrown away as useless, when our people struck their tents. These were paraded as trophies, and the Governor published a placard, in which he announced, that a band of highwaymen, under Captain Fremont, of the United States army, had come into his department, but that he had chased them out with two hundred patriots, and if they dared to show themselves again about Monterey, he would march out to meet them, and destroy them to a man. About the middle of May, Captain Fremont arrived at the great Hamath Lake, in the Oregon Territory. He intended to return to the United States, by the Columbia and Missouri, through the northern pass in the Rocky Mountains; but he found his pro gress stopped by bands of hostile Indians, who had been stirred up against him, particularly the Hamath tribe, who killed and wounded several of his followers, in a night attack. Two days after, he had another fight with the same Indians, and destroyed one or two of their villages. It was in this engagement that Fremont saved Carson's life, as an Indian was about killing him. Captain Fremont now discovered that if he persevered in his route, he would have to fight almost every step of his way, besides marching over mountains on which the snow was still falling, and though he and his men were suffering from fatigue and famine, he remained for some days deliberating upon the proper course to pursue.

From various sources he received information that Governor Castro was assembling troops, with the avowed object of attacking his party and all the American settlers, because, he alleged, the Captain had come for the purpose of inciting the settlers to revolt.

With these facts before him, he at length determined upon the proper course to pursue, which was to turn back and act the offensive. On the 11th of June, he struck the first blow. At day-light on that day he surprised an officer and fourteen men on the way to the Mexican camp, with two hundred horses for Castro's army. The horses were retained, and the officer and the men released. At early dawn on the 15th, the military rendzevous and intended head-quarters was surprised by the Americans, who captured there nine pieces of brass cannon, two hundred and fifty muskets, and other arms and ammunition, a general, a colonel, and many other officers. The gallant captain left a party of fourteen men here as a garrison, and repaired to the Rio de los Americanos, to obtain aid from the American settlers. While there an express arrived from Sonoma, with information of the approach of a large force under General Castro. He therefore immediately set out, with a force of ninety horsemen, armed with rifles, and traveled day and night. He reached Sonoma, after marching eighty miles, at two o'clock on the morning of the 25th of June. On the same morning, a squadron of seventy dragoons, the vanguard of Castro's force, crossed the bay, and were attacked and defeated by a party of twenty Americans, with the loss of only two men killed. Two of Captain Fremont's men were taken by the Mexicans, and cut to pieces alive with knives. The Americans retaliated this cruel and cowardly act, by instantly shooting three of the enemy whom they had captured. Having cleared the north side of the bay of San Francisco of the Mexicans, Captain Fremont called the Americans together at Sonoma, addressed them upon the dangers of their situation, and recommended, as their only means of safety, a declaration of independence and war upon Castro and his troops. The independence was declared, and the war followed. A few days afterwards, they heard of the taking of Monterey by the American Squadron, and the existence of the war. The Star-spangled Banner was promptly substituted for that of the Californian revolutionist. The valiant Castro fled south at the head of nearly five hundred men, well armed; and Captain Fremont, leaving some fifty men in garrisons, pursued him with a hundred and sixty riflemen. It was at this stage of his proceedings that he met Purser Fauntleroy, and received Commodore Sloat's request that he would repair to Monterey. They arrived there on the

19th of July. Soon after Commodore Sloat resigned the command of the naval forces to Commodore Stockton, and sailed for home to recruit his health, which had been enfeebled by long and arduous services. This gallant and meritorious officer was highly applauded for his course by the government, having observed the line of conduct prescribed by his instructions, "with such intelligence and fidelity, that no complaint has ever been made of any anauthorized aggression on his part."

Commodore Stockton commenced his part of the conquest by organizing the "California Battalion of Mounted Riflemen," appointing their officers, and receiving them into the service of the United States. Captain Fremont was appointed Major, and lieutenant Gillespie, Captain of the battalion. Major Fremont sailed with his battalion, in the United States ship "Cyane," for San Diego, in the hope of getting in advance of General Castro, and cutting off his retreat. He arrived at San Diego on the 29th of July, but the Californians had driven off all the horses, and consequently he was unable to move until the 8th of August, when he resumed his pursuit. Commodore Stockton meanwhile had sailed to San Pedro, where he landed three hundred and sixty of the sailors belonging to his ship, the frigate "Congress." With this sailor-army he commenced his march towards the camp of Meza, a strongly-fortified position held by General Castro, three miles from the City of the Angels, and the capital of the Californians. On the approach of our gallant tars within sight of the Mexican camp, the General shamefully abandoned it and fled. His men followed his example, and ran away in all directions. Major Fremont joined the Commodore on the 13th of August, with eighty mounted riflemen, and the united forces entered the City of the Angels, and took possession of the Government-house. On the 16th, Major Fremont again set off in pursuit of Castro, but it was soon found that the valiant Governor had made good his escape towards the city of Mexico. Most of his officers, however, were captured, and brought to the City of the Angels, where Commodore Stockton had been busy in establishing a civil government.

The Commodore directed Major Fremont to increase his force and post it in garrisons in the different places :—Fifty were to be stationed in the City of the Angels under Captain Gillespie, fifty at Monterey, fifty at San Francisco, and twenty-five at Santa Barbara. He embarked for San Francisco to recruit, making, in the meanwhile, a temporary disposition of his forces. He took but forty men with him, and nine of these he left at Santa Barbara, in charge of Lieutenant Talbot. During his absence, on the 23d of September, a Californian army invested the City of the Angels, and by their superior numbers caused Captain Gillespie to surrender that place. He returned with his thirty riflemen to San Pedro, and from there sailed for Monterey. The Californian Chief, Manual Gaspar, then led two hundred of his men against Santa Barbara, but Lieut. Talbot and his nine men defended themselves with heroic courage. He held the town until he was completely besieged, and then refusing to surrender, fought his way through the enemy to the mountains of the vicinity, where he remained eight days, suffering from cold and hunger. A detachment of forty men advanced to take him, but was driven back. They then offered to permit him to retire, if he would pledge himself and his men to neutrality during the war, but he sent word to the Mexican Chief that he preferred to fight. At length, finding that neither force or persuasion would cause him to leave his position, they set fire to the grass and brush around him and burned him out. Still determined not to surrender, he commenced a march of five hundred miles to Monterey a-foot, where his arrival was hailed with the utmost joy by all the Americans. The brave fellows were welcomed by their companions as from the grave; for the enemy had reported that they had all been slain.

Major Fremont had made an effort to go from San Francisco to the relief of Captain Gillespie, but he was forced back to Monterey by bad weather. A few days after the arrival of Lieutenant Talbot, a party of fifty-seven Americans, under Captains Burrows and Thompson, were attacked by the Californians, eighty in number. Captain Burrows and three Americans were slain. Major Fremont marched to their assistance, and the whole party arrived at San Fernando on the 11th of January, 1847.

While these events were passing in California, General Kearney was on his way from the United States, with a force intended to conquer that country. On the 6th of October, he met Carson, with fifteen men, coming as an express from the City of the Angels, with an account of the conquest of that country by Commodore Stockton and Major Fremont. In consequence of this intelligence, the General sent back the greater part of his troops. On the 5th of December, he met Captain Gillespie coming with a small party of volunteers, to give him information of the state of the country. Captain Gillespie informed him that there was an armed party of Californians, with a number of extra horses, encamped at San Pasquel, three leagues distant. General Kearney immediately set out to meet them, in the double hope of gaining a victory and a remount for his poor soldiers, who had completely worn out their horses in the march from Santa Fe. The Californians were numerous, and a desperate fight ensued, which at one time well nigh proved fatal to the Americans, their line becoming scattered by the sorry condition of the animals on which some of them were mounted. Captain Johnson made a furious charge upon the enemy with the advance guard. He fell almost in the very commencement of the fight, but the courage of our countrymen did not flag, and the enemy was eventually forced to retreat. Captain Moore led off rapidly in pursuit, but the mules of the dragoons could not keep up with his horses, and the enemy seeing the break in the line, renewed the action, and charged with the lance, in the use of which they are very expert. They fought well, and the American loss was heavy. General Kearney himself was wounded in two places, Captain Gillespie and Lieutenant Warner each in three, and Captain Gibson and eleven others were also wounded, having from two to ten marks of lances on their bodies. Captain Johnson, Captain Moore, Lieutenant Hammond, two sergeants, two corporals, eleven privates, and a man attached to the topographical department, were slain. The severe wounds of the actors in this fight caused the march of the army to be delayed, and it did not reach San Diego until the 12th of December.

When Commodore Stockton heard of the outbreak of the Californians, he dispatched the frigate "Savannah" to relieve Captain Gillespie, but she arrived too late. Three hundred and twenty of her crew landed and marched towards the City of the Angels, but the Californians met them, well appointed with fine horses and artillery, and though the sailors fought heroically, they were eventually compelled to retire before such an overwhelming superiority of numbers. They lost eleven in killed and wounded. Commodore Stockton came down himself to San Pedro in the "Congress," and made another march upon the City of the Angels with a detachment of sailors, who now took some of the ship's cannons with them, dragged by hand with ropes. At the Rancho Sepulrida, they encountered the enemy, who were decoyed by Commodore Stockton into a favourable position, and then fired upon with the guns which had been concealed from their view. More than a hundred were killed, one hundred and fifty wounded, a hundred taken prisoners, and the whole force of the Californians put to flight. Mounted on horses, while the sailors were on foot, the enemy had, hitherto, the advantage of choosing his own time, place, and distance of attack, but the means of transportation were placed by this splendid victory in the hands of the sailors, and as soon as they could be mounted, a series of skirmishes were commenced, in which they displayed the utmost courage and activity.

Commodore Stockton found General Kearney at San Diego. This meeting was opportune; and the two commanders immediately proceeded to fix upon a plan for bringing the war to a speedy termination. On the 29th of December, their forces composed of sixty dismounted dragoons, fifty California Volunteers, and four hundred sailors and marines, started on the march from San Diego to the City of the Angels. At the Rio San Gabriel they found the enemy in a strong position, with six hundred mounted men and four field pieces, prepared to dispute the passage of the river. The battle was fought on the 8th of January, 1847. The Americans waded through the water under a galling fire, dragging their guns after them. They reserved their own fire until they reached the opposite side of the river; here they repelled a charge of the enemy, and then charged up the bank; and after fighting about one hour became masters of the field. The enemy made another stand on the plains of Mera, in the hope of saving the capital;

but they were again driven from the field, and on the 10th the American army entered the capital in triumph. They had lost one private killed, and thirteen of their number wounded in the two fights. The enemy carried off their dead and wounded, so that the extent of their loss is unknown, but both General Kearney and Commodore Stockton estimate it at between seventy and eighty. The insurgents fled and surrendered to Major Fremont, who met them as he was approaching the capital.

Major Fremont joined the forces of Kearney and Stockton at the City of the Angels on the 15th of January, and it was here the misunderstanding arose between General Kearney and himself, which for so long a time excited public attention. In January, 1847, Commodore Shubrick arrived at Monterey, and assumed the command of the naval forces on that station. Soon after this Lieutenant-Colonel Cooke joined General Kearney at San Diego with the Mormon battalion, which enabled the General to provide against any reinforcements from the Mexican province of Senoura to the Californians, by stationing it as a guard and garrison at the Mission of San Luis Rego. Captain Tompkins arrived in the country in February, with his company of U. S. Artillery, and was stationed at Monterey, and the arrival of Colonel Stevenson, with his regiment of New York Volunteers, formed such a force as was considered sufficient to overawe all disaffection and opposition.

In July, three companies of the New York regiment were stationed at La Paz, in Lower California, under Lieutenant-Colonel Burton. They numbered about one hundred men, with two pieces of artillery. The United States sloop-of-war "Dale" cruised for some time in the vicinity, and afforded protection to the garrison in La Paz, but Commodore Shu-

brick ordered the "Dale" to Guaymas. This emboldened the enemy, who collected all their disposable force and marched against the little garrison. The battle was begun on the morning of the 16th, at two o'clock; a loud roll of musketry, followed by shouts, gave the sleeping soldiers the first notice of the enemy's presence. The Americans stood to their posts amid a shower of bullets, although the night was so dark that they were unable to see the foe, except by the flashing of the musketry. They brought their artillery to bear in the direction of the enemy's position, and a few discharges was followed by a complete silence. At day-light the enemy was seen to be posted on a hill near by, waiting until the women and children had been removed from the town to renew the attack. The garrison availed themselves of the pause to fortify the roofs of their quarters with bales of cotton. The enemy gained possession of the bushes surrounding the camp, and kept up a heavy fire from eight o'clock until night. All the stratagems of the garrison failed to induce them to come nearer, yet Colonel Burton lost only one man.

In the afternoon the enemy entered the town, and destroyed the houses of all who had been favorable to the Americans. On the 20th they dragged a piece of artillery on the most commanding site in the town. A hot fire then commenced on both sides, which resulted in the defeat of the Mexicans. They had six of their number killed and forty-four wounded, while the loss of Colonel Burton was only three men. After this repulse the enemy distributed themselves in the neighborhood, to cut off supplies from the Americans.

Meanwhile a force of nearly four hundred of the insurgents marched upon San Jose, where Lieutenant Heywood of the navy was stationed with twenty men and one nine-pounder. He was besieged for thirty days, but he refused to surrender, despite of thirst and famine. On the night of the second day, a grand assault was made. The leader of the Californians, Mejares, led forty men against the front of the post, while more than a hundred men, with scaling-ladders, came upon the rear. The nine-pounder opened upon them, killed Mejares and three of his soldiers, and drove the remainder back in great disorder. A firing was kept up until morning, when two American whalers entered the harbor, the crews of which landed, and with this assistance Lieutenant Heywood soon put the enemy to flight. In the month of October, the frigate "Congress" and the sloop-of-war "Portsmouth" captured the town of Guaymas, which was garrisoned by eight hundred efficient men.

The country now became quiet, and by the terms of the treaty of peace between the two governments, the boundary line was made to run along the southern line of New Mexico to its westward termination, thence northwardly along the western line of New Mexico until it intersects the first branch of the river Gila, thence down the middle of said branch and of the said river until it empties into the Rio Colorado, following the division-line between Upper and Lower California to the ocean. Agreeably to this treaty the American forces abandoned the posts they held in Lower California.

The discovery of Gold in the waters of the Sacramento and other streams, as also among the rocks and in the mountains, has drawn to the country thousands of emigrants from the United States and other parts of the globe, and it bids fair to become at an early day one of the most populous of the territories of the United States.

CHAPTER XXIV.

FROM SAN FRANCISCO TO SINGAPORE, EAST INDIES.

On the 25th of October I received orders to join the brig "Oregon;" this vessel was purchased by Captain Wilkes after the loss of the "Peacock" for the sum of 9,000 dollars. She was built in Baltimore, is of 170 tons burthen, was originally named "Thomas Perkins," came out to the Sandwich Islands with an assorted cargo, and when purchased was lying at Astoria taking in a quantity of salmon. In a day or two after having been purchased, she was stripped, and her masts lifted and made several feet shorter, after which she proceeded up to Vancouver, where she underwent some further alterations and repairs. After these changes were made, Captain Hudson repaired on board and took command, and on the 21st of September, she got under-way, in company with the "Porpoise," and dropped down to Fort George, (Astoria,) where she laid until the 12th of October, when she sailed for San Francisco. Captain Hudson then gave up the command, and repaired to the "Vincennes," and Lieutenant Overton Carr was ordered in his stead.

October 31st. At 3.30 P. M. we got under-way in company with the "Vincennes" and the "Porpoise," and proceeded to sea. The wind being a-head, we were compelled to beat, which afforded us a fine opportunity of seeing the Bay. In one of the stretches we stood on until our jib-boom almost touched the cliff on which the Precidio is situated. This was built by the Spaniards, and while they retained possession of the country was strongly fortified and well garrisoned.

About 7 P. M., the flood-tide begun to make, and we were compelled to let-go the anchor. During the night the weather was thick and disagreeable, and a heavy swell set in from the westward.

On the morning of November 1st, we again tripped our anchor. At 11 discovered the "Vincennes" under sail on our starboard quarter, but soon lost sight of her from the density of the fog. Nor did we see anything of her until about 1 o'clock, when we observed both her and the "Porpoise" lying at anchor. We wore ship, and bore down for them, and when close a-board spoke with the "Vincennes." We then hove-to, and continued to remain so until about half-past 4, when both vessels proceeded to sea, ourselves following in their wake. In communicating with the "Vincennes," we learned that she experienced a very uncomfortable night. Having anchored right over the bar, she felt the swell much more than either the "Porpoise" or ourselves. She rolled almost gunwales under, and several seas broke on board, one of which swept away a portion of her bulwarks, and killed one of the crew. It is understood that we are bound to the Sandwich Islands.

On the 6th, the "Vincennes" and "Porpoise" parted company with us.

On the 8th, we passed over the position of Cooper's Island, as given upon Arrowsmith's Chart, but saw no indications of land. At noon our latitude was 25° 45′ 55″ north, longitude 132° 16′ 15″ west.

At 11 A. M. on the 19th, we reached Honolulu, where we found the remainder of the squadron.

Our principal object in returning to Honolulu was, to fill

up with provisions and water. This being accomplished, we again spread our sails, and on the 22d of January we reached Singapore, where we found the United States frigate "Constellation," Commodore Kearney, and the sloop-of-war "Boston," Captain Long, forming the East India Squadron. We communicated with both vessels, and received some late newspapers from them.

The Island of Singapore is twenty-seven miles long, and from five to fifteen miles wide. It is separated from the peninsula of Malacca by the Strait of Singapore, formerly followed by navigators, instead of the one which is now universally used. We were informed that the interior of the island is infested with tigers, and that it is a common thing for the inhabitants to be destroyed by them within a few miles of the town. Owing to these attacks, the Government has been induced to offer a premium of fifty dollars for every tiger that should be killed, and parties have been organized, which frequently go out to hunt these ferocious animals.

The situation of the town* is low, for which reason it does not appear to advantage from the anchorage. It covers a great extent of ground, and many of the buildings are spacious, and built in the European style. The Governor's dwelling is situated on the summit of a knoll which overlooks the city and harbor. In the rear of the European buildings are the locations of the Malay and Chinese quarters. The houses of the former are built on posts rising four or five feet above the ground. The object of this is to keep the houses dry during the rainy seasons, and to prevent reptiles and other noxious animals from entering them.

As for the inhabitants, a more motley crowd in color and

The town bears the same name as the island.

costume cannot well be conceived. The language of nearly every Asiatic nation throws its peculiar accents on the ear.

The trades, like most of the eastern cities, are carried on in the streets. Some of the streets are exclusively inhabited by castes who work at the same trade. In one may be seen the workmen in brass and copper, which department of trade generally embraces the manufacture of cooking-pans, lamps, and drinking vessels, and similar articles of domestic use ; for all these things are made of copper and brass, and hammered out to the proper size and shape by manual labor. In another street, you see the palankeen builders, house-joiners, cabinet-makers, shoemakers, tailors, blacksmiths, and so on. The money-changers take up their position at the corner of the streets, with their little tables before them ready to transact business at a moment's notice. These men act sometimes in the capacity of pawnbrokers, by lending small sums of money upon the gold and silver ornaments which all here possess in a greater or less degree. The opium vender has also his little table in the public street, with his box and scales upon it, and tempting samples of the "dreamy drug."

This fearful species of intoxication is more generally practised among the people of British India, than has been commonly supposed. The Mohammedans are particularly addicted to its use, and much of the apathy and indifference observable in the native character, may be attributed to this universal evil, which would seem to be daily gaining ground among them. Few can be surprised that the Emperor of China is so anxious to prevent the importation of opium* into his do-

* The engrossing taste of all ranks and degrees in China, for opium, a drug whose importation has of late years exceeded the aggregate value of every other English import combined, deserves some particular notice, especially in connection with the revenues of British India, of which it forms an important item. The use of this pernicious narcotic has become as extensive as the increasing demand for it was rapid from the first.—*Chinese Repository*.

minions by the English. Well might this monarch regard that potent drug as a curse to a nation, which has already begun to suffer from its dangerous seduction, and which shows for it a decided taste.

A single glance of these opium dealers will convince you that they are their own best customers. Their soiled and disorderly dress, the palsied hand and pale cheek, the sunken eye and vacant stare of each of these wretched men, show you that they are not themselves.

The Chinese Bazaar is filled with goods manufactured in that industrious country. Here you may purchase beautiful Canton shawls, for fifteen or twenty dollars, rich silks and satins, carved ivory-work in chessmen, backgammon boxes, card-cases, grass-cloth handkerchiefs, vases, chimney-piece ornaments, tea-pots, and the familiar little tea-cups and saucers so highly esteemed by the ladies. There are also found here camphor-wood trunks, so useful to preserve clothing, books, and furs, from the white ants, which are so destructive to this sort of property.

But in trading with the Chinese, it is necessary to be careful. They call all Europeans "foreign devils," and consider them a fair game. But the greatest cheats among them are those who come off to the ships to sell their goods, as these not only ask the highest prices, but invariably give you a bad article.

The Chinese are very numerous in Singapore, and all seem to be industrious. They dress after the manner of their country; and we saw some whose *queus* almost touched the ground. It is said that they return home as soon as they have acquired something like a competency, though they run the risk of being punished by the Emperor, for having left China. They have a popular saying, "If he, who attains to honors or wealth, never returns to his native place, he is like a finely-dressed person walking in the dark—it is all thrown away."

The extent to which they carried gaming, after the regular business hours were over, could not fail to attract our attention. Gaming was going on in all their shops and houses, and their whole soul seemed to be staked with their money. They use cards and dice; but their games are different from our own. The stake in general was a small copper coin, not larger than a dime. It was also observed, that they are passionately fond of theatrical entertainments. These take place under a temporary shed, which is only large enough to accommodate the performers. The interior is decorated with silk hangings, and illuminated with many colored lamps. The stage is furnished with a table and chairs, but without scenical decorations to assist the story, as in our theatres. The actors are magnificently dressed in silk and gold cloth, adorned with jewels. The females are represented by young men. I cannot say much for the acting, or music; the former appeared stiff, the latter a perfect jargon.

One day I visited their principal Josh-house, or temple. It is a very singular-looking edifice; the roof is surmounted with dragons, and a thousand of other whimsical devices. The columns supporting the front are likewise very curiously sculptured. It has no windows; and the main entrance, instead of being in the centre of the building, is near one of the corners. Its interior may be described as a square court, surrounded by a portico filled with niches, containing the wooden images to which adoration is paid. The space in the centre of the court is paved and furnished with seats, which are occupied by the worshipers. All the idols are representations of the human form in its most bulky aspect; they seemed to have quite as much circumference as height. One of them was a female figure, dressed in silks, and painted, with much tinsel and gilding about the head. In front of each idol were altars, on which were Josh-sticks burning, colored wax-candles, flowers, dried fruits, and sugar plums wrapped up in colored paper. At the time I entered, the priesthood, five in number, were assembled, worshiping, chanting, striking gongs, and frequently prostrating themselves before their wooden-deities. This mummery lasted nearly half an hour, and the priests appeared to go through it with devotion. They were all young men, had the crown of their heads shaved, and wore long yellow robes. As soon as the mummery had ceased, they left the temple, retired to their private apartments, and divested themselves of their official robes; and the gods were left to themselves, with the Josh-sticks burning on the altars.

On another day I set out to visit the Mohammedan Mosque, but I found the entrance of this guarded by two or three stupid-looking fellows, who would not allow me admittance, although I offered to take off my shoes before entering. It is a neat, handsome building externally, but only the upper portion of it can be seen when viewed from the street, as it stands at the further end of a long court, surrounded by a high stone wall. Its mineret is kept white-washed, and forms a beautiful and a conspicuous object in the landscape.

The majority of the Mohammedans at Singapore are Malays and their descendants, and it is universally conceded by travelers that they constitute the most worthless part of the population, being excessively lazy, treacherous, quarrelsome, and addicted to the use of opium.

The color of their skin is several shades darker than that of the Chinese, and they usually wear moustaches and beard. Their dress consists of a white turban, a shirt with very ample sleeves, a colored embroidered vest, fitting tight to the body, loose trowsers made of white cotton cloth, and yellow or red slippers. To beautify themselves, they chew the betal-nut, which causes their teeth to become as black as ebony. They make good soldiers, or sepoys, and many of them are employed to act in that capacity by the British East India Government. The women, who are not so much exposed to the rays of the sun, are less tawny than the men; their countenance is comely, their hair black and fine; they have a delicate hand, brilliant eyes, and a graceful figure.

There are many Parsees residing in Singapore, and some of the best shops are kept by them; they prefer trading in English and French goods, which they have consigned to them, or purchase at the auctions. Some of them have acquired large fortunes, and live in a princely style. They are a handsome race, and there is an easy grace about all their movements. The ladies pass their lives in great seclusion from the world, for they are supposed to lose caste if they appear in public.

The Persic language is celebrated for its strength, beauty, and melody, and they write it from the right to the left.

The Parsees* do not tolerate polygamy, unless the first wife prove barren, nor do their laws allow concubinage. They cannot eat or drink out of the same vessel with one of a different religion, nor are they fond even of using the cup of another, for fear of partaking of his sins. Their religion, however, admits of proselytism. They have no fasts, and reject everything of the nature of penance. God, they say, delights in the happiness of his creatures; and they hold it meritorious to enjoy the best of everything they can obtain.

* The Hindoos say the Persees are outcasts of Persia; but this they indignantly deny, though it is supposed many of them were driven out in the eighth century.

Birds and beasts of prey, the dog and the hare, are forbidden as food. Their faith inculcates general benevolence, to be honest in bargains, to be kind to one's cattle, and faithful to masters; to give the priests their due, physicians their fees, and those last are enjoined to try their sanitory experiments on infidels before practising on Parsees. They never willingly throw filth either into fire or water. This reverence for the elements prevents them from being sailors, as in a long voyage they might be forced to defile the sea.

When a relation is dying, they recite over him prescribed prayers, and have a dog at hand to drive away the evil spirits that flock around the bed; after death the body is dressed in old but clean clothes, and conveyed on an iron frame to the tomb on the shoulders of the bearers, who are tied together with a piece of tape, in order to deter the demons, which are supposed to be hovering near, from molesting the corpse. It is well known that they neither burn nor bury their dead. They have circular towers called *dockmehs*, in which are constructed inclined planes, and on these they expose the bodies, courting the fowls of the air to feed upon them. They even draw augeries regarding the happiness or misery of the deceased, according as the left eye or the right eye is first picked out by the vultures.

There are several pleasant rides about Singapore The surrounding country is interspersed with groves and gardens, and the roads are good, and free from dust, for almost every day in the year the island is visited by one or two refreshing showers. The vehicle most used is the palankeen, which is capable of containing two persons; it is drawn by a single horse, and the driver, who is usually a Malay, runs by the side of a carriage; the charge for a whole day is a dollar, and it is customary to give something to the driver.

There are good markets in Singapore for the sale of butcher's meat, fish, fruits, and vegetables. Everything in the shape of food is very cheap, and our mess bill was as small here as at any place we visited in the course of our long cruise.

Some idea may be formed of the commerce of Singapore, when it is stated, that, for the last two or three years, it has been valued at $25,000,000. It is a free port; there are no duties on imports or exports, and every vessel is allowed to come and go when it pleases. There are many articles shipped here which are the products of other places; among these are opium, nutmegs, cloves, coffee, sugar, teas, and a variety of shells. Business is conducted upon a sure basis; payment must be made at the delivery of the goods. Accounts are kept in dollars and cents, and almost every thing is sold by weight.

On the 25th of February we sailed for St. Helena, where we arrived after a pleasant passage of thirteen days.

CHAPTER XXV.

FROM ST. HELENA TO THE UNITED STATES.

THE appearance which St. Helena presents, when viewed from the ocean, is anything but inviting; nearly the whole of its coast is steep and perpendicular like a wall, dotted here and there with miserably stunted trees.

The island was discovered by the Portuguese on the 21st of May, in the year 1502, and was called by them St. Helena, from the fact that the same day was the anniversary of the Empress Helena, a Saint in the Roman Catholic calendar.

In a valley, where they found a productive soil and abundance of excellent water, the discoverers planted a small colony; they also stocked the valley with goats, horses, cattle, and many other animals useful to man, which soon multiplied and spread over the whole island.

About the year 1651, the English East India Company took possession of the island, it having been abandoned some time before by the Dutch, who took it from the Portuguese in the early part of the 17th century. The English introduced into the island, as the Portuguese had done before them, horses, sheep, grains and fruits. Tempting inducements were held out to emigrants, and many were induced to settle in its rich and romantic valleys.

In 1815, the island became the involuntary residence of Napoleon, a circumstance which has shed over it undying interest, and rendered its name in every part of the civilized globe as familiar as a household word.

The island remained in the hands of the East India Company until 1836, when it was transferred to the British Government.

The climate is salubrious. One old voyager who describes it, informs us that the sick men who had been carried on shore in hammocks, and utterly unable to walk, were cured and made perfect in a week's time, and were soon able to "leap and dance" as well as their companions. All of which wonderful effects were attributed the wholesomeness of the air, and the fresh trade-winds constantly sweeping over the island, and driving away all distempers.

The population is estimated at five thousand, and consists of whites, negroes, mulattoes, and Chinese. The negroes were brought to the island by the East India Company from Madagascar, and were treated as slaves until the year 1823; they and their descendants now form the largest portion of the population.

Vessels going to and from the East Indies usually touch at the island to replenish their stock of water and procure fresh provisions.

Jamestown, the capital, is the largest town that the island can boast of, and is a free port. It is situated in a valley, or rather a gorge between two lofty hills, both of which terminate abruptly, and form the eastern and western boundaries of the town, as also a small bay in which the vessels anchor that visit the place. The harbor is defended by fortifications, which cover the shore from the water-line to the highest peaks. A ladder, of nearly a perpendicular height, is built up the side of the western mountain, called Ladder Hill. It is said to have five hundred steps in it, and is a conspicuous object from the anchorage.

The landing is convenient for visitors and trade; it is furnished with a stone stairs and a crane for loading and unloading boats. From the landing a good road leads toward the town at the mouth of the valley, which is protected from an attack by sea by a ditch and a high massive wall, bristling with guns.

There is but one entrance into the town, and that is closed at nightfall. There are also sentinels stationed here at all hours. Just beyond the gateway is the grand parade, around which stand the church, the principal hotel of the place, and the building occupied by Napoleon on his first landing.

The houses are from one to two stories in height, and have their walls painted white or yellow. Some of them are also furnished with verandahs.

The market is good, but meats and eggs are excessively dear. The price for beef is 20 cents per lb.; mutton, 18 cents; eggs, 50 cents per dozen.

Of course, before leaving the island, we rode out to Longwood, and the tomb. Our conveyance was a covered carriage, drawn by a pair of horses, and just large enough to accommodate two persons comfortably.

The road we pursued, and there is no other leading to the tomb from the town, is cut on the side of the eastern hill, which gradually rises to an elevation of upwards of a thousand feet. This afforded us several fine views of Jamestown—We could see all the houses, the gardens, the soldiers' hospital, the barracks, the church, the botanic garden, and the grand parade.

After leaving the town we did not fall in with a solitary tree until we reached the head of the valley. Here the soil is capable of cultivation, and we passed many a garden in which were to be seen, besides a great variety of vegetables, trelisses of vines, from which depended clusters of the tempting and delicious fruit, peach, almond and date trees, and patches of flowers, among which the rose and pink were conspicuous. We likewise observed on our right and left, but some miles in the distance, a succession of hills in wood, looking verdant, cool and beautiful.

The next object which attracted our attention was the "Briars," a little hamlet, composed of some half-dozen cottages, one of which was the residence of the ex-Emperor, until Longwood could be prepared for his reception. It is a small, quaint building, with a high, steep roof, gable ends, and a verandah. The grounds attached to it are also of limited extent, and surrounded by a common stone-wall. Indeed, there is scarcely a New England farmer whose abode is not superior to it in every respect. Yet I was informed by the inhabitants that Napoleon préferred the place to better houses in the town, where he would be annoyed by the curiosity of the populace.

The road beyond the "Briars" is winding, and presents a great variety of landscape. In one place it sweeps by thick hedges, inclosing fields in which sheep, cattle, and horses are feeding; in another, it passes through dark masses of fir and pine; in another, it runs down into a deep ravine; and in another again, it traverses a plain overshadowed with trees and sprinkled with cottages, looking so neat and prim that one cannot help envying their owners, and wish that he could share with them the delights which such charming abodes must afford.

Not many yards distant from these sylvan residences, lies a dell, shut in by hills, covered with grass and brambles. At the foot of the most lofty hill stands a lonely cottage, surrounded by trees—a little beyond the solitary dwelling, among some weeping willows, and two or three melancholy cypress, is the Tomb. The spot is private property, belonging to the widow lady, Mrs. Talbot, who occupies the cottage, and who furnishes visitors with refreshments. There is a poetic effusion in the "Visitors' Book," alluding to the circumstance last mentioned:—

"There you will find an excellent cheer,
Bread and cheese, and ale and beer;
And while Mrs. T. gives bread and butter,
Its my intention never to cut her."

One end of the iron railing round the Tomb is open for the purpose of admitting visitors. The grave remains uncovered, or just as the French left it when they exhumed the body.

"Napoleon 's gone! the Island Tomb
No more his corpse contains;
A prince and noble ship have come,
And taken his remains."

What remained of the original willows planted by the hand of Madame Bertrand around the Tomb, were carried away by Prince Joinville, as well as the slabs that closed the recess in which the coffin was placed. The Tomb is carried only a few feet above the ground, and is utterly devoid of ornament; nor does it bear any date, name, or inscription. The location is a very appropriate one, but the tomb itself excites our disgust and indignation, for the inference is, that the enemies of Napoleon sought to gratify their animosity after his death, by insulting his remains, than which nothing can be more despicable and unmanly. The slabs taken away by Prince Joinville formed a part of the kitchen-hearth of the house at Longwood!

Mrs. Talbot resided at the cottage while the Emperor was living, and she informed us that the site of the grave was chosen by himself. She also pointed out to us the spring near the cottage, which supplied him with water up to the day of his death.

One pleasant afternoon while walking through the grounds, Napoleon observed the spring, admired its beautiful pebbly bottom, dipped up some of the water with his hand, and drank it, found it to be delightfully cool, refreshing, and delicious; he requested that while he lived he might be allowed to obtain all his water from the same spring, and the favor was granted.

Mrs. Talbot hinted to us, as she had done before about the refreshments, that it was customary for visitors to purchase some of the water by way of paying her for seeing the Tomb, and we were not slow in taking the hint. Each of us filled a quart bottle with the precious liquid, for which she received several dollars. We had also to satisfy the demands of the garrulous old sergeant who exhibits the Tomb, so that altogether it was expensive sight-seeing.

The old fellow's account, rattled off as it was by him, amused me much, and I took care to write it down on the spot. The following is a correct copy of the original:—
"Misters, how d'ye do? Fine day to see sights, gentlemen. Well, misters, here's the railing round the ground, and there's the paling round the tomb, eight feet deep, six feet long, and three feet wide. Napoleon was buried in three coffins, one in another—his head was here—his feet was there; he was dressed in a green coat, white breeches, and jack-boots—beautifully polished, with his cocked hat between his legs, and his heart in a silver pot at his feet. All the island came to the funeral, and the soldiers fired a royal salute. These are not the willers that have been taken away, but I have got some slips from the real tree in charge of my good woman—will you

come and look at them, misters? They are the best that can be had, mister. That's a fine one; yes, indeed, h'ill grow —stick him in this bottle; its worth two shillings, any man's money, but you may have it for one. Hum! thank you, mister, and God bless you, and all like you. This is the spring, and that's the water; here's a mug to taste; oh! it is cool, just as Napoleon used to drink it, when he came here afore he was buried, to play with Madame Bertrand's children, and read there where the willers used to stand what are gone now, the present time. Here's the Visitors' Book, what they write their names in—here, this way, in the sentry-box—here's the ink, and there's the pen; please to write your name, all you gentlemen—A-hem!—it is full of poetry in all kinds of lingoes. See, misters, for yourself. I once could read a little, but now I am very old—A-hem!—Misters, when you got your names in the book—a-hem!—please give a trifle for showing; this way, sir. Thank ye, sir—you are fine gentlemen—good day."

From the Tomb we proceeded to Longwood, which we reached in less than half an hour. The road is good, and occasionally offers pieces of landscape, which are singularly wild and romantic. On our way we passed "Hut's Gate," which for some time was the residence of General Bertrand. At this retired spot Napoleon passed many a pleasant hour in the society of his faithful friend and family. It is stated that he was very fond of the General's children, and frequently joined them in their sports.

On reaching the gate at Longwood we were required to pay an admission fee of fifty cents for each person. A retired army officer has obtained a lease of the place from the government, and by his order the entrance fee is demanded before the gate is opened.

Longwood is a long narrow field, interspersed with clumps of firs and gumwood trees. The house in which the ex-Emperor spent the last years of his strange and varied life, the stables, the fences, everything is sadly neglected, and, ere another quarter of a century passes away, nothing will be left of the scene but a pile of ruins. The house is built of wood, and was once painted green. It has a small trellised porch before the main entrance, is ascended by one or two wooden steps, almost entirely overgrown with moss and grass, and the sides of the building are covered with names, initials, dates, and lines of poetry. Viewed externally, it appears an extensive pile, but many of the buildings now seen on the spot were not there during the life of Napoleon; they were brought from the surrounding country, where they had served, for the soldiers stationed there to watch the Emperor and prevent his escape. He was allowed to walk and ride at almost any hour he pleased, but he could not stir without being seen from some of the numerous observation-towers erected on the neighboring hills. About a mile from Longwood was a large encampment of soldiers. At dusk they mounted guard, and the place was surrounded by sentinels.

We looked into the rooms; they are small and badly lighted—the wood-work much decayed—the walls scribbled over, and the floors covered with dust and filth. The room in which the Emperor breathed his last is occupied by a huge winnowing machine, and was strewed with chaff and straw. The apartment in which he laid in state after his death, is now used as a stable. The library serves as a hen-house, and we found it filled with chickens and turkeys. His bed-room, like all the rest, is sadly dilapidated, and the window which lighted it is boarded up. Taken altogether, it is a pile of universal ruin, doomed, as I have before observed, at no distant time to entirely disappear.

There are no traces remaining of the gardens, but the little-fish pond is still in tolerable preservation. It is asserted that before the Emperor's own earthly career was closed, all the fishes sickened and died, and that the incident deeply affected him, for he sought amusement in attending them himself, and watching their gambolings. When the last little favorite was gone, he exclaimed, "Yes, everything I love, everything that belongs to me is immediately struck. Heaven and mankind unite to afflict me."

Not many paces distant from the crumbling and deserted building we have been describing, may be seen the new residence built for the use of Napoleon. It is constructed of yellow sand-stone, one story in height, and stands on the declivity of a gently sloping hill. The house is much larger and more convenient than the old one; but he took a strong dislike to it, and would never occupy it. The grounds are rather pretty, and the whole is surrounded with a neat stone-wall, surmounted by an iron-railing. It was the sight of these walls and iron-rails that gave the Emperor such disgust for the new residence; for, he said they would constantly remind him he was a prisoner-of-war. We found the building occupied by Lieutenant Smith, of the Artillery, who had charge of the Magnetic Observatory.

It may be interesting to add to this description the following particulars. Napoleon and his suite arrived at St. Helena on the 15th of October, 1815, under charge of Admiral Cockburn. It is stated the island was first suggested as a suitable place of confinement for the fallen Emperor by the Duke of Wellington, who had been there himself, and was forcibly impressed with its natural strength.

Immediately the royal captive was delivered over to Sir Hudson Lowe, who was made responsible for his security. This officer received all his orders relative to the treatment of Napoleon from the ministry, and was not allowed to exercise any discretion in the execution of them.

On the 5th of May, 1821, the great man departed this life; his body was subjected to a post mortem examination, and it was discovered that he died of cancer of the stomach.

He expired amidst a tempest of wind and rain.

> 'Dark was the night, and wild the storm,
> And loud the torrents roar;
> And loud the sea was heard to dash
> Against the distant shore."

Many trees were laid prostrate by the storm, and among the rest his favorite willow, beneath whose shade he often sat reading, or wrapt up in meditation.

On the 9th of May, he was buried with military honors. It was his dying wish to repose in France. After a lapse of nearly twenty years his request was complied with; England then gave her consent to his removal, and the frigate "Belle Poule," under the command of Prince Joinville, was dispatched to St. Helena by the French Government to fulfill the mission. Among the men that accompanied the Prince, were four who were devoted friends of the Emperor, and lived with him in his captivity—Marchand, Gourgaud, Las Casses, and Bertrand.

After the coffin was disinterred, it was conveyed to a tent prepared for its reception. There it was opened, and the mortal remains of Napoleon were found unchanged. He seemed asleep, so perfect were all his features. His old friends beheld him there just as they had placed him some twenty years before; and it is almost impossible for language to describe their emotion. They kissed the coffin again and again, and streams of tears flowed down their cheeks.

Amid the roar of guns and other martial honors the body was embarked, and on the 18th of October, 1840, the "Belle Poule" weighed her anchors, and sailed for France.

On the arrival of the frigate at Brest, the body was conveyed to Paris, and there reinterred beneath the Tomb of the Invalides.

From St. Helena we proceeded to Rio Janiero. Here we remained several days, during which we replenished our stock of water and provisions. Leaving Rio Janeiro, we shaped our course for New York, where we arrived on the 3d of July, after having been absent from home and friends three years and eleven months.

APPENDIX.

COMMERCIAL REGULATIONS, MADE BY THE PRINCIPAL CHIEFS OF THE SAMOA GROUP OF ISLANDS, AFTER FULL CONSIDERATION IN COUNCIL, ON THE 5TH DAY OF NOVEMBER, 1839.—PRINTED AT SAMOA GROUP OF ISLANDS, 1840.

ARTICLE 1st. All Consuls duly appointed, and received in Samoa, shall be protected, both in their persons and property, and all foreigners obtaining the consent of the government, and conforming to the laws, shall receive the protection of the government.

ARTICLE 2d. All foreign vessels shall be received into the ports and harbors of Samoa, for the purpose of obtaining supplies, and for commerce; and with their officers and crews, so long as they comply with these regulations, and behave themselves peaceably. shall secure the protection of the Government.

ARTICLE 3d. The fullest protection snall be given to all foreign ships and vessels which may be wrecked; and any property saved, shall be taken possession of by the Consul of the country to which the vessel belongs, who will allow a salvage, or portion of the property so saved, to those who may aid in saving, and protecting the same, and no embezzlement will be permitted under any circumstances whatever. The effects of all persons deceased, shall be given up to the Consul of the nation to which they may have belonged.

Article 4th. Any person guilty of the crime of murder, upon any foreigner, shall be given up without delay to the Commander of any public vessel of the nation, to which the deceased may have belonged, upon his demanding the same.

Article 5th. Every vessel shall pay a Port-charge of five dollars, for anchorage and water, before she will be allowed to receive refreshments on board; and shall pay for pilotage in and out, the sum of seven dollars before she leaves the harbor; and pilots shall be appointed, subject to the approval of the Consuls.

Article 6th. No work shall be done on shore, nor shall any natives be employed on board vessels on the Sabbath day, under a penalty of ten dollars, unless under circumstances of absolute necessity.

Article 7th. All trading in spirituous liquors, or landing the same, is strictly forbidden. Any person offending, shall pay a fine of twenty-five dollars, and the vessel to which he belongs shall receive no more refreshments. Any spirituous liquors found on shore shall be seized and destroyed.

Article 8th. All deserters from vessels will be apprehended, and a reward paid, of five dollars, to the person who apprehends him; and three dollars to the Chief of the district in which he may be apprehended, shall be paid on his delivery to the proper officer of the vessel. No Master shall refuse to receive such deserter, under a penalty of twenty-five dollars. Deserters taken after the vessel has sailed, shall be delivered up to the Consul, to be dealt with as he may think fit. Any person who entices another to desert, or in any way assists him, shall be subject to a penalty of five dollars, or one month's hard labor on the public roads.

Article 9th. No Master shall land a passenger without permission of the Government under a penalty of twenty-five dollars, and no individual shall be permitted to land or reside on the Samoa Group of Islands, without the special permission of the Government. Any one so landing, shall be compelled to leave by the first opportunity.

Article 10th. If a sick person be left on shore from any vessel, for the recovery of his health, he shall be placed under charge of the Consul, who shall be responsible for his sick expenses, and will send him away by the first opportunity after his recovery.

Article 11th. Any seaman remaining on shore after 9 o'clock at night, shall be made a prisoner until the next morning, when he shall be sent on board, and shall pay a penalty of five dollars.

Article 12th. All fines to be paid in specie, or its equivalent, or be commuted by the Government, at the rate of one month's hard labor on the public roads for five dollars.

Article 13th. Should the Master of any vessel refuse to comply with any of these regulations, a statement of the case shall be furnished to the nation, or the Consul of the nation to which he belongs, and redress sought from thence.

Article 14th. All Magistrates, or Chiefs of districts, where vessels or boats may visit, shall enforce the rules and regulations relative to the landing of foreigners and apprehension of deserters, or pay such fine as the Malo shall impose.

Article 15th. For carrying into effect the foregoing rules and regulations, the Chiefs and *tula fale* of the respective districts, shall meet and elect one of their number to act as Magistrate or Judge, to execute the laws.

Article 16th. These regulations shall be printed, promulgated, and a copy furnished to the master of each vessel visiting these Islands.

Similar regulations were adopted by the Fejee Chiefs, omitting the 6th, 9th, 10th, 12th, and 15th Articles, and signed by the following chiefs:—

Their	Their
Ro × TANOA,	Ro × MATANABABA,
Ro × TUIDREKETI	Ro × VEIBALIYAKI,
PHILIPS × COKANAUTO,	Ro × LIGALEVU,
Ro × NAVUNIVALU,	Ro × KALAI,
Ro × KOROITIUSAVAU,	Ro × VAKACOKAI.
Ro × QUARANIGIO,	Marks.
Marks.	

Done in Council by the principal Kings and Chiefs of the Fejee Group, this 10th day of June, 1840. The foregoing Rules and Regulations having been signed by the Kings and Chiefs in my presence, and submitted to me, I consider them just and proper, and shall forward to the American Government a copy of the same for the information of all masters of vessels visiting the Fejee Group of Islands.

(Signed) CHARLES WILKES,
Commanding U. States
Exploring Expedition.

U. S. ship "Vincennes,"
Harbor of Ban, June 10th, 1840.

In presence of

WM. L. HUDSON, commanding U. S. ship "Peacock,"
Commander RINGGOLD, commanding U. S. brig "Porpoise,"
R. R. WALDRON, U. S. Navy,
B. VANDERFORD, Pilot.

Names of the persons composing the Expedition to Alta California:—

Lieutenant EMMONS,
Passed Midshipman ELD,
Passed Midshipman COLVOCORESSES,
Assistant-Surgeon WHITTLE,
J. R. PEALE, Naturalist,
J. D. DANA, Geologist,
W. R. RICH, Botanist,
A. J. AGATE, Artist,
J. D. BRACKENRIDGE, Assistant-Botanist,
Sergeant STEARNS,
Corporal HUGHES,
Privates SMITH and MARSH,
DOUGHTY, SUTTON, MERZER, and WALTHAM, Seamen,
BAPTIST GUARDIPI, Guide,
TIBBATS, BLACK, WOOD, WARFIELD, OLAN, and INASS, Hunters,
Mr. WALKER and family, emigrating to California,
Mr. BARROWS, wife and child, do. do.
Mr. NICHOLS,
Mrs. WARFIELD and child.

The whole party numbered thirty-nine, with seventy-six animals, thirty-two of which were Government property.